To John and Suzanne,
With very best wishes,
Richard Wallace
10/23/07

Mizzou Today

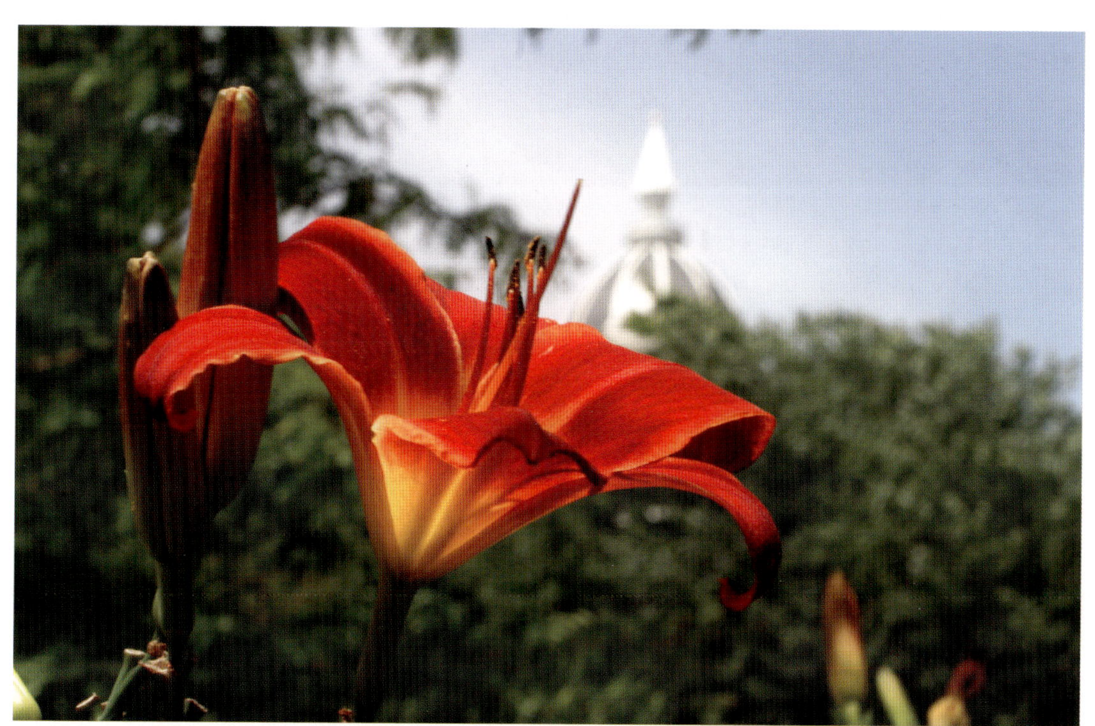

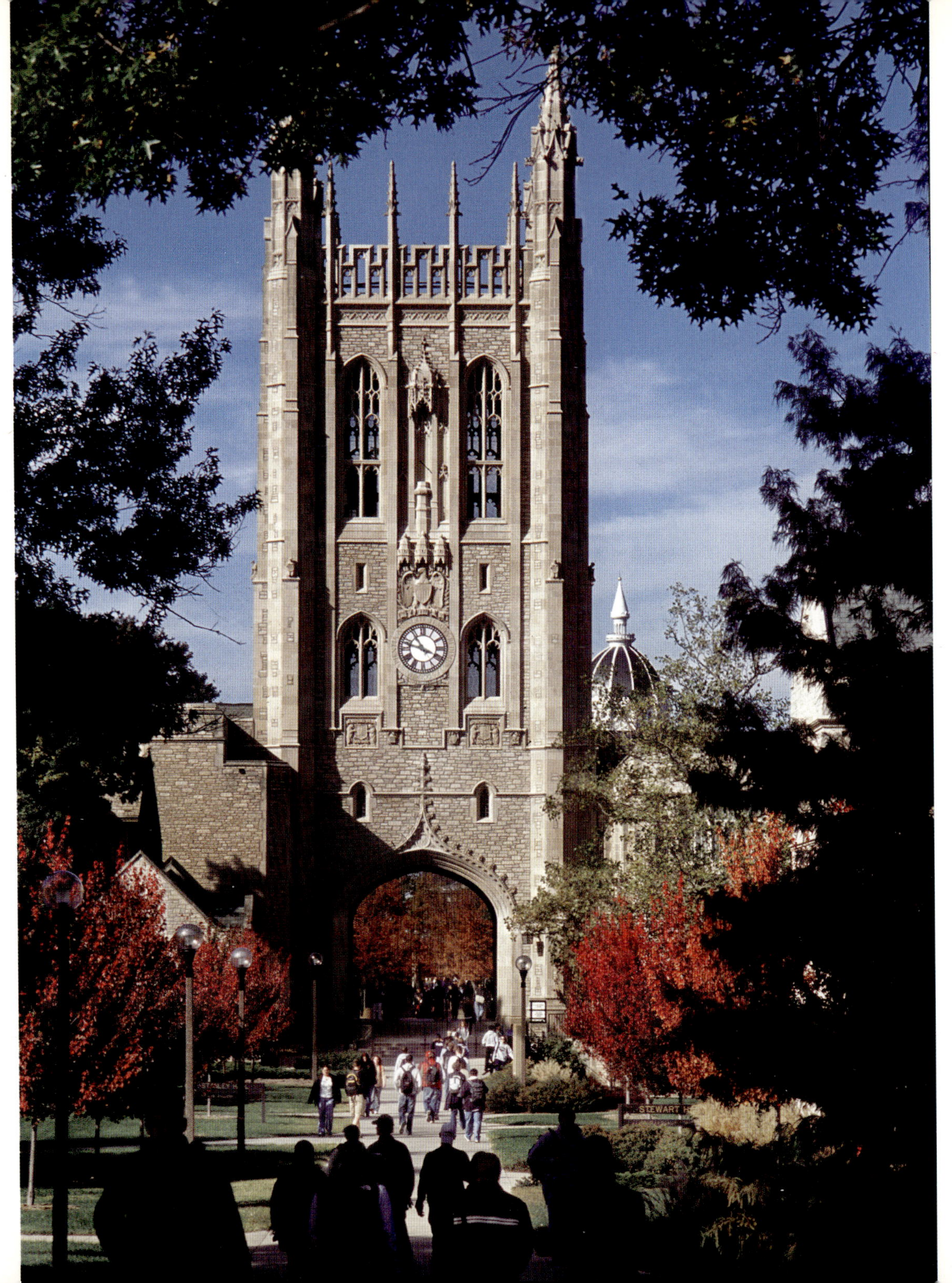
STEWART

Photographs by Rob Hill

Mizzou Today

Text by Richard L. Wallace

Edited by Karen Flandermeyer Worley

University of Missouri Press Columbia and London

University of Missouri Press, Columbia, Missouri 65201
Printed and bound in China

5 4 3 2 1   11 10 09 08 07

Library of Congress Cataloging-in-Publication Data

Hill, Rob, 1954-
Mizzou today / photographs by Rob Hill ; text by Richard L. Wallace ; edited by Karen Flandermeyer Worley.
p. cm.
Summary: "The University of Missouri's rich record of accomplishment and service to Missouri, the nation, and the world is captured in this collection of photographs of campus landmarks, people, events, and Tiger spirit. Includes a history of the campus and timelines of key milestones and achievements"—Provided by publisher.
ISBN 978-0-8262-1776-9 (alk. paper)
1. University of Missouri—Pictorial works. 2. University of Missouri—History. I. Wallace, Richard L., 1936- II. Worley, Karen Flandermeyer. III. Title.
LD3473.H55 2007
378.778′29—dc22
2007011430

∞™ This paper meets the requirements of the American National Standard for Permanence of Paper for Printed Library Materials, Z39.48, 1984.

Design and composition: Jennifer Cropp
Printing and binding: Regent Publishing Services Limited
Typefaces: Minion, Eplica, and LTZapfino

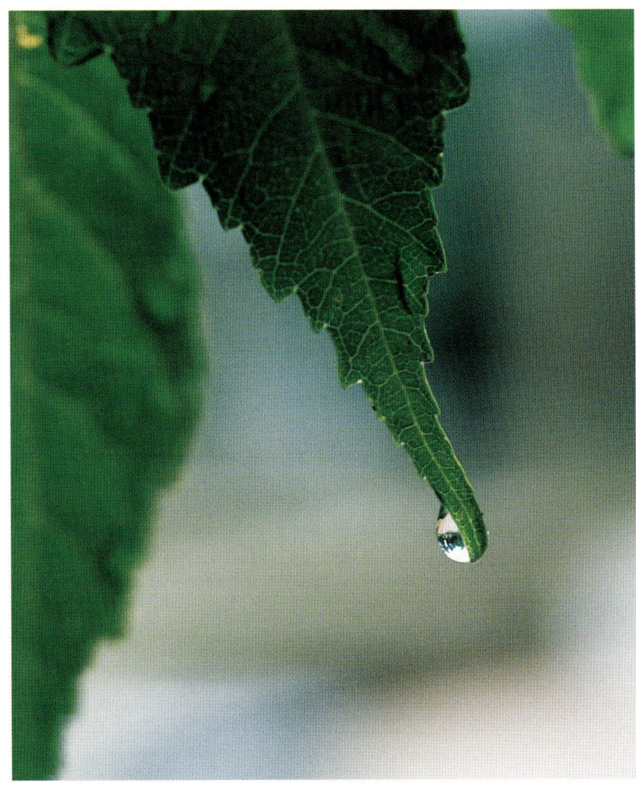

p. i: A daylily near the Reynolds Alumni Center basks in the warm summer sun.
p. ii: Students head to class through the tower of Memorial Union. The Jesse Hall dome is visible beyond.
p. iv: Near Ellis Library, a drop of water clings to an Amur maple leaf during a summer morning rain.
p. v: A sign of spring, a rosy dogwood blossom catches the sunlight on the south lawn of Jesse Hall.
p. vi: Professor John Faaborg extracts a songbird from a mist net in order to record data for a forest ecosystem study in the Missouri Ozarks; the setting sun highlights faculty office windows in Cornell Hall.
p. viii: On Francis Quadrangle, the Columns and Jesse Hall form the physical and emotional center of the campus.
p. ix: A migrating monarch butterfly finds a zinnia along Francis Quadrangle's Circle Drive.
p. x: In a quiet moment, Nicki Marder uses her laptop to check her e-mail on a warm November day; a fall disk game on Francis Quadrangle just got better with a hug from a friend.

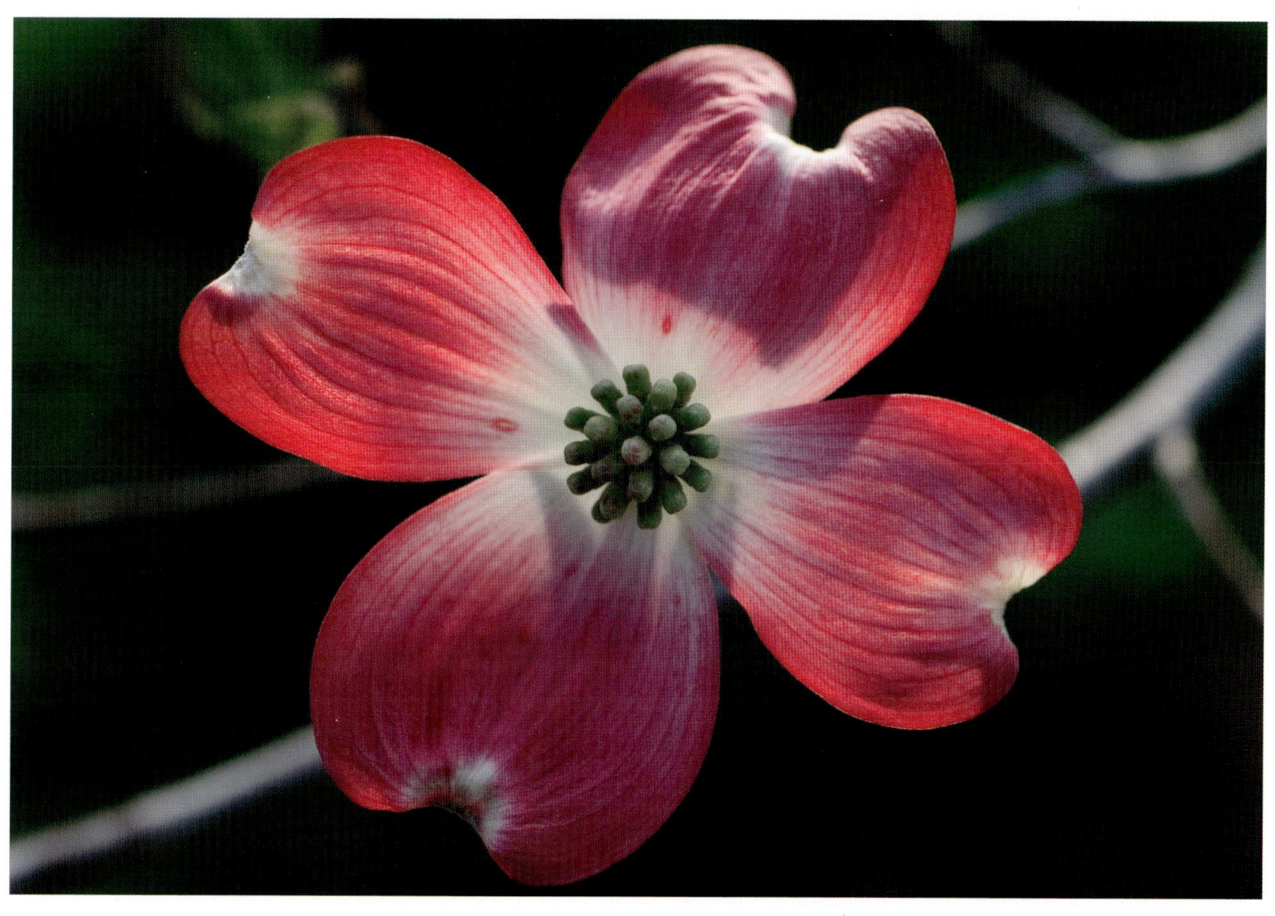

To members of the Mizzou family everywhere.

Your passion for Mizzou fuels our work.

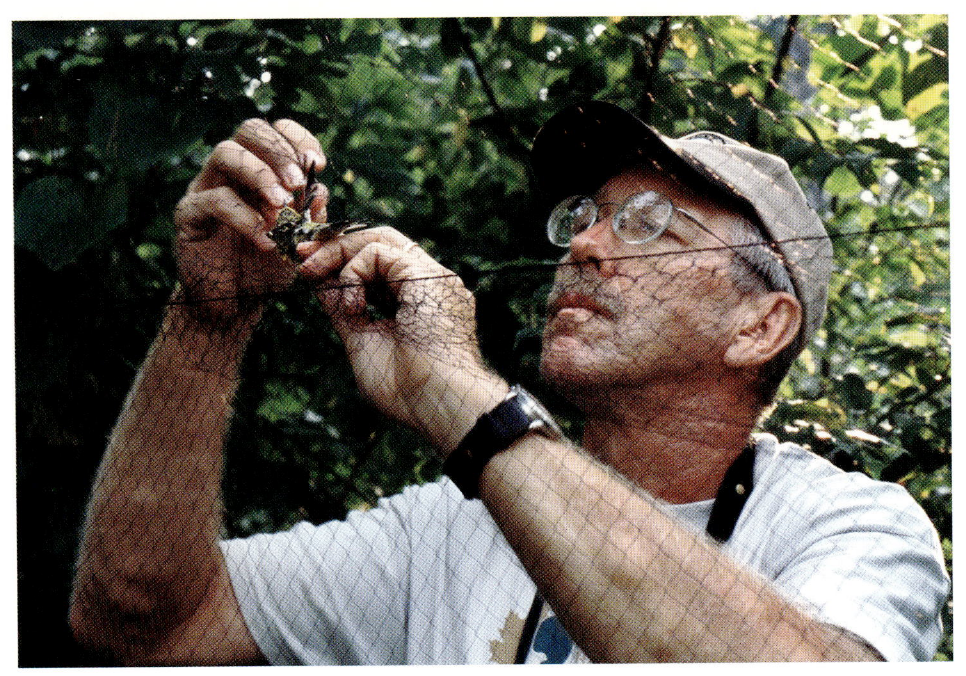

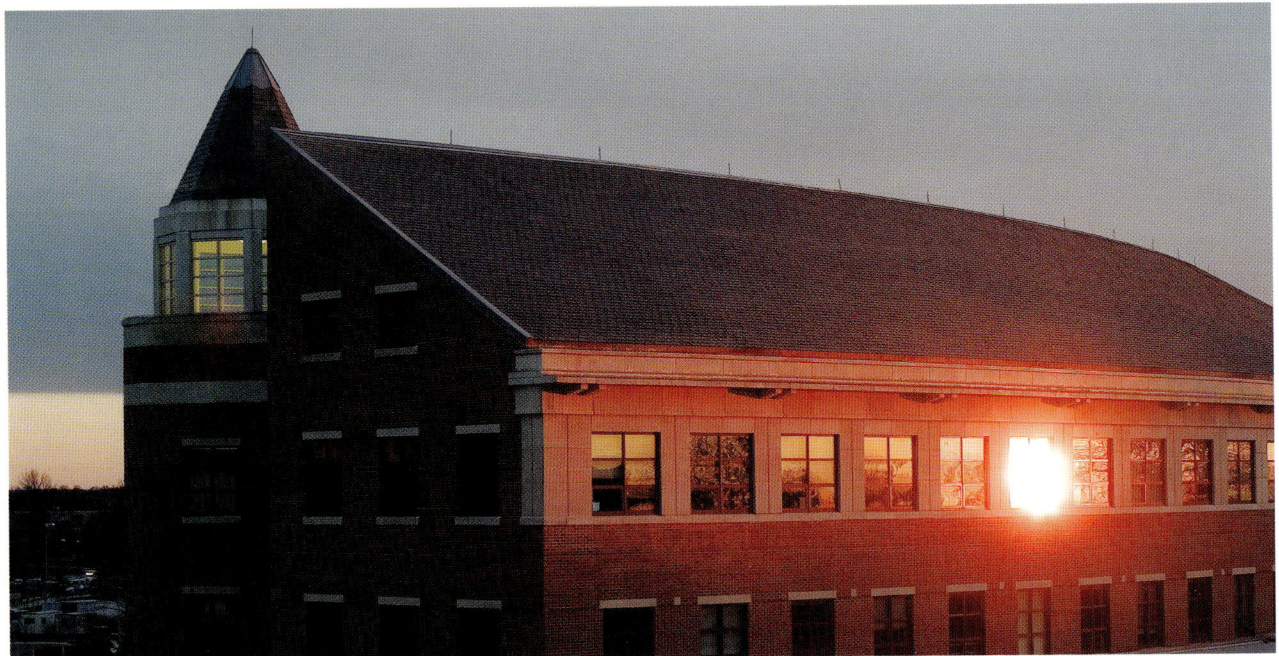

Acknowlegments

We are grateful to many for advice and information. Vicki Dennison, Beverly Jarrett, Chris Koukola, Jane Lago, and Charles E. Reineke provided editorial and other assistance. Many others provided information and assisted with checking facts and dates. We are indebted to Kris Anstine, Noor Azizan-Gardner, Christian Basi, Jo Behymer, Nicholas Benner, Pamela Benoit, Chris Blose, William M. Crist, James S. Coleman, Gary Cox, Kenneth D. Dean, Rebecca Dieckmann, Susan M. Dunkin, Eric Gater, Cheri Ghan, Kate Gray, Beth Hammock, Kathryn A. Healy, Suzette T. Heiman, Thomas Howard, Jacquelyn K. Jones, Stephen R. Jorgensen, Ann Korschgen, Carrie Lanham, Linda L'Hote, Todd McCubbin, Randall J. Mertens, Linda Metz, Frankie D. Minor, Chad Moller, Eric Morrison, Pat Morton, Michael J. O'Brien, Osmund Overby, Sona Pai, Rose T. Porter, Laura Roloff, Tim Rooney, Cathy Scroggs, Roberta Settergren, Scott Shader, Philip J. Shocklee, Gary L. Smith, James E. Thompson, David Trinklein, Bruce J. Walker, Susan Wampler, Robert O. Weagley, Barton Wechsler, John Wedman, Candace A. Whittet, and Marvin E. Wright. Any remaining errors or oversights are our own.

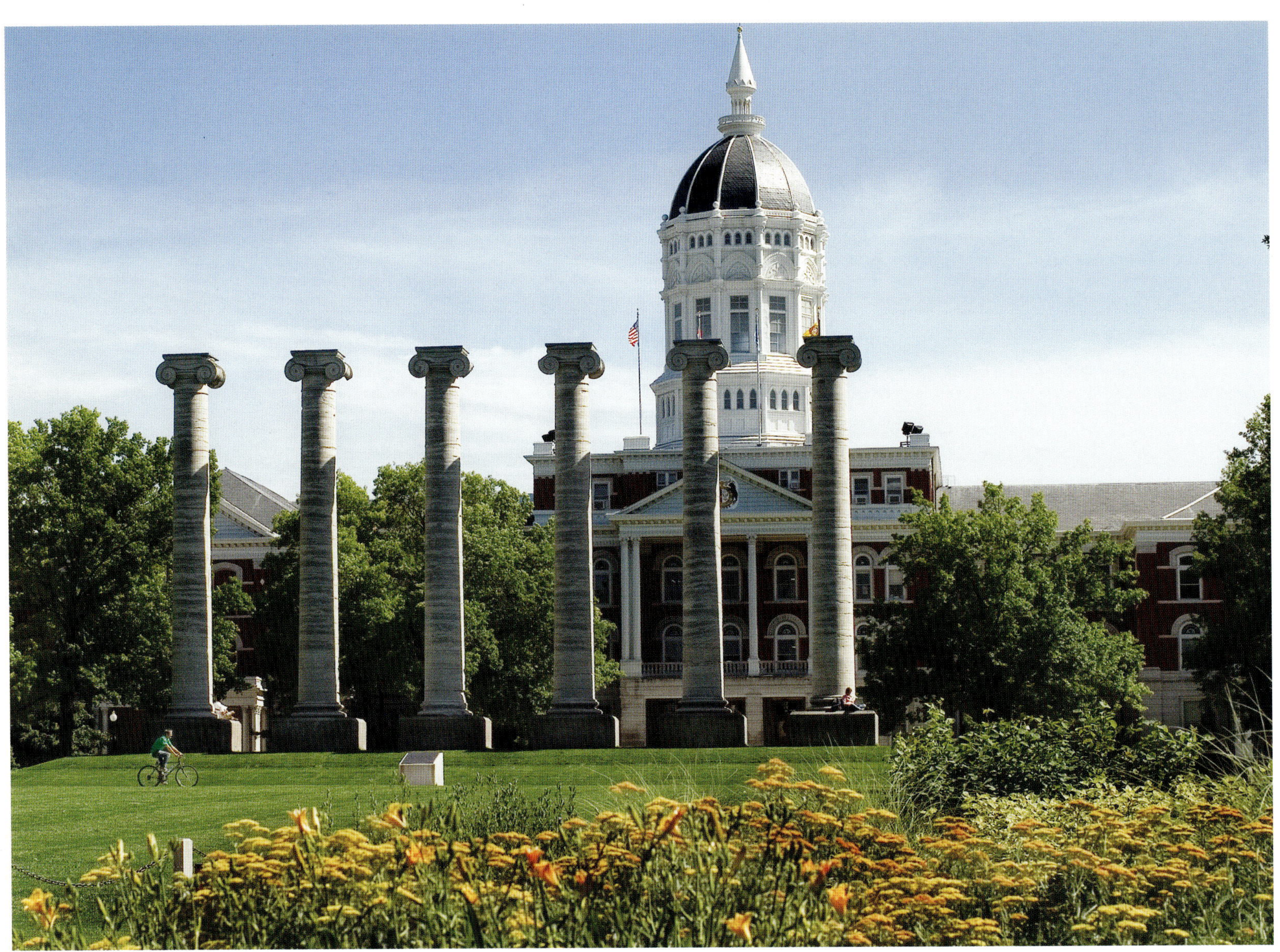

Mizzou Today

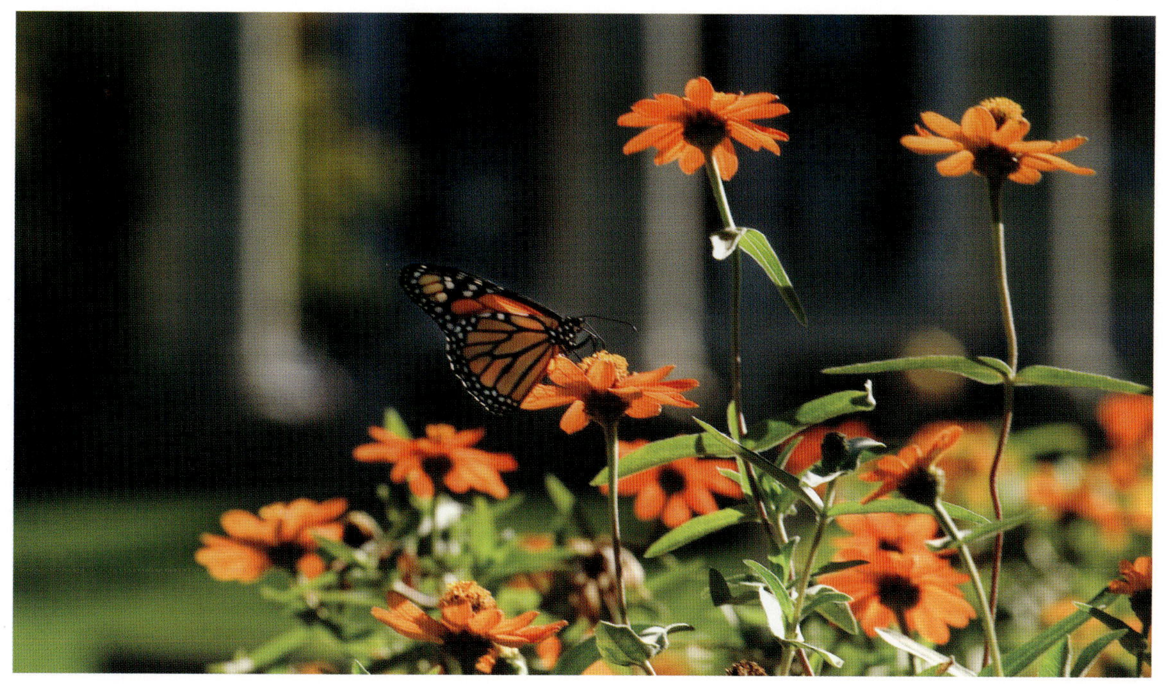

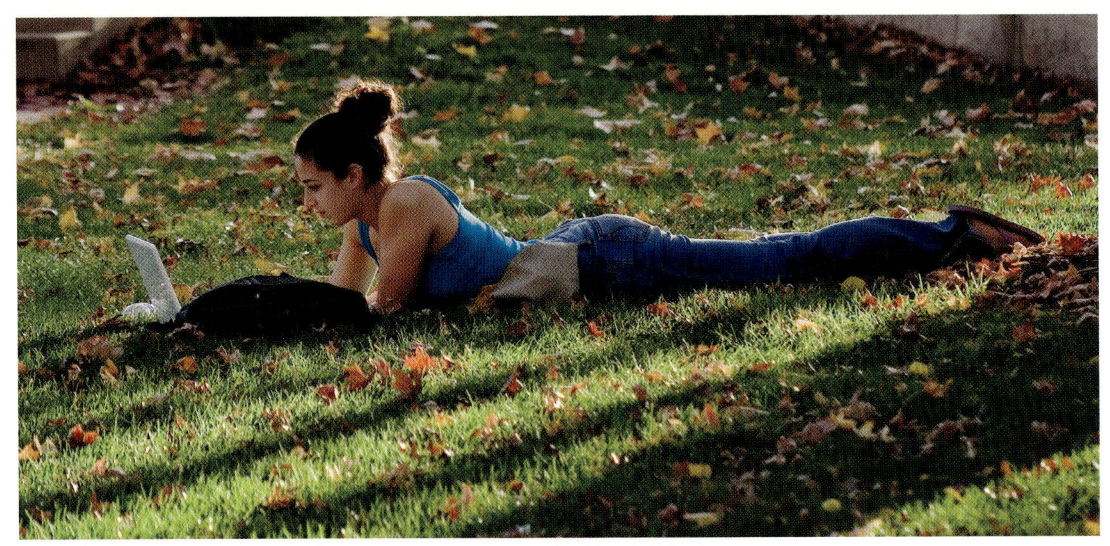

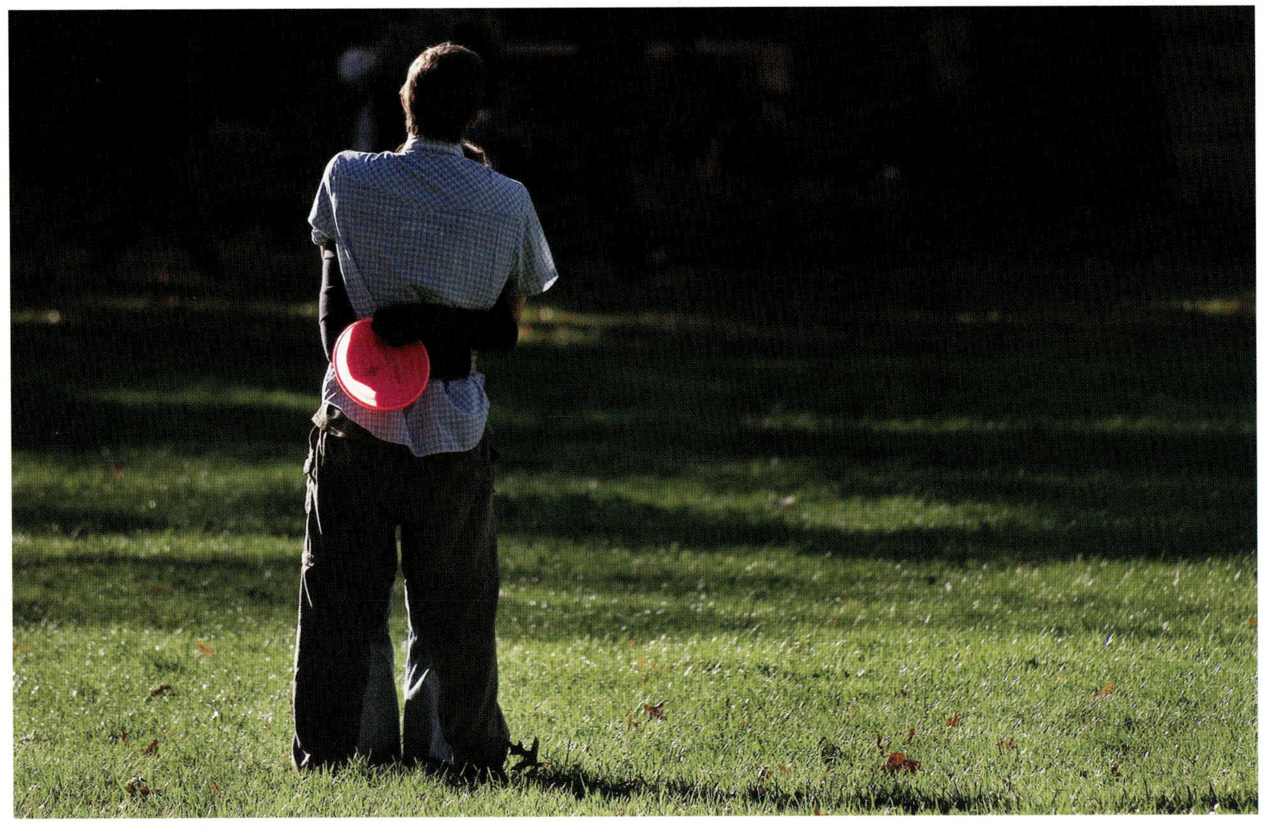

Mizzou Past and Present

The University of Missouri was founded in 1839 by visionary citizens whose dreams would develop into a global institution of renown. Since that time, Missouri's flagship university has established a rich and long history of accomplishment and service to Missouri, the nation, and the world.

Today the University of Missouri–Columbia offers comprehensive programs of instruction at all levels, involving research and creativity as well as outreach and extension. Frequently called MU or Mizzou, the University serves the state as a whole and plays a vital role in the sustenance and growth of the Missouri economy.

A Botanical Garden

Mizzou today is a wondrous place. Its grand architecture includes old and new structures located in a botanical garden covering 296 meticulously landscaped acres, with plants and trees carefully labeled for the benefit of visitors and the campus community.

The placement of new buildings, gardens, paths, and walkways is guided by a campus master planning process that was initiated in the 1980s by then Chancellor Barbara S. Uehling. This process has made the campus a beautiful place to study, learn, live, and work. This striking aspect of Mizzou today is portrayed vividly in the spectacular photographs that are the heart of this volume. A monument dedicated to Chancellor Uehling is located on Ninth Street facing Lowry Mall, which itself was a street prior to the development of the master plan.

Spirit Enriched by Memories and Shared Traditions

Mizzou is much more than its campus and programs. With its never-ending flow of students, faculty, and staff, Mizzou is also a spirit, perhaps captured best in Thomas Jefferson as he gazes from a bench across Francis Quadrangle toward Jesse Hall. Jefferson's presence, on his bench and through his original tombstone, both located on the lawn of the Chancellor's Residence, underscores in a dramatic way that the University of Missouri was founded in the image of Jefferson's University of Virginia. Even more important, MU embodies the strength of Jefferson's ideals, which so effectively helped shape the character and the boundaries of our nation.

It is fitting that the ideals embraced at Mizzou today—Respect, Responsibility, Discovery, and Excellence—are displayed on a plaque located on Francis Quadrangle immediately in front of the six Columns that remain from old Academic Hall. These Columns still reach to the sky a few feet from the Jefferson monuments, standing boldly as a reminder of our founders' great aspirations, which we continue to pursue today.

The Columns are a reminder of another important connection between Mizzou's past and present. They would not be there today if the good folks of Columbia had not stood in defiance of an order by the president of the Board of Curators to tear them down after the 1892 fire that destroyed Academic Hall. Indeed, the mules were there to do the job, and it was a band of local citizens, many of them alumni, who circled the Columns and saved them from destruction.

This local pride and support for the University date to its founding. In 1839, Boone County citizens convinced the legislature to locate the University of Missouri in Columbia. They did so by contributing substantial money and working through the political challenges in the state legislature. More than once since 1839, Mizzou has been threatened with the loss of critical programs or with being moved to alternative sites in Missouri; time and time again, the citizens of Columbia and Boone County have stood tall in defense of their University.

This powerful support of Mizzou by local citizens also characterizes the day-to-day working relationship between the University and the community. The two work in harmony and mutual respect based on the recognition that the University is a vital part of Columbia and that the community is a vital part of the University. This magnificent town-gown relationship is not always found in university cities.

Mizzou has a rich history of traditions and shared memories—the Hink, the Shack, Coke dates, Homecoming, silence under Memorial Tower, long hours at the library, jobs to pay the bills, friendships that last a lifetime, and romances that blossom into marriages and families. Generations of families proud to be Mizzou graduates have known the excitement of coming to Mizzou from high schools scattered across the state and from countries around the world. They have shared good times on the campus, in residence halls, and in Greektown.

Although there are many reasons for the strong loyalty of MU alumni, a major factor was the return of thousands of veterans to Mizzou classrooms at the end of World War II. Supported by the GI bill and a university that responded to this sudden surge in enrollment with temporary living quarters (the last of which was demolished in 1983) and other changes that made a high-quality education possible, these students were older, mature, focused, and eager to get on with lives that had been interrupted by service to their country under the most difficult of circumstances.

These veteran students had little patience with many of the old freshman rituals and traditions, such as beanies and freshman hazing, but they were grateful for the opportunity provided to them and made the most of it. Many of these alumni are now in leadership positions in diverse careers, and they share an undying, fierce loyalty to MU that has helped spark that same loyalty in the generations of students that have followed. They are also generous with their time, talent, and resources in support of MU.

And there are new and better traditions than beanies and hazing! At Tiger Walk the day before classes start in August, freshmen run south through the Columns and are served Tiger Stripe ice cream by faculty and staff in front of Jesse Hall. At Tiger Prowl in May, seniors walk back north through the Columns as they symbolically leave the campus to meet their next challenges. The Honors Convocation, in which honors graduates accompanied by their faculty mentors are recognized and honorary degrees are awarded, takes place during May's commencement weekend in the splendor of a spring morning on Francis Quadrangle.

Today's graduates share a treasure with the many thousands who have gone before. They leave the campus, but they never leave Mizzou. And Mizzou never leaves them. They are a part of the rich fabric of education, culture, and friendships woven here in the heart of the nation—part of the extended Mizzou family that reaches back to 1839 and around the globe in the twenty-first century.

Students and Award-Winning Educational Programs

Above all, Mizzou, both past and present, is about students learning, teaching, growing, and maturing. The University's founding purpose was to serve the citizens of Missouri with educational programs. When MU became a land-grant institution in 1870 under the federal Morrill Act of 1862, the responsibility for teaching the arts and sciences was expanded to include a broad range of practical educational programs responsive to the everyday needs of all Missourians.

Today, Mizzou has an all-time peak enrollment of more than twenty-eight thousand students from every county in Missouri, every state in the nation, and more than one hundred countries. Mizzou students are bright, focused, and hardworking.

Mizzou recognizes that a diverse student body and faculty are essential for a major public research university to prepare its students for a global society, and the campus has made substantial progress in creating that diversity. African American students now constitute 6 percent of undergraduate enrollment, and the number of Hispanic students is growing rapidly. The Graduate School has also made excellent progress in diversity, particularly with underrepresented, international, and female students.

MU recognizes that much remains to be done in regard to diversity. MU did not admit women until 1867 and did not build the first women's residence hall until 1903, thirteen years after the first men's residence hall opened. The campus still works to overcome a history that denied admission to black students until 1950 and did not appoint the first black faculty member until 1969. Dr. Arvarh Strickland is now a distinguished professor emeritus of history. The Board of Curators voted in April 2007 to name the General Classroom Building in Strickland's honor. The campus continues to give high priority to increasing minority student enrollment and to increasing the numbers of minority and women faculty members and administrators.

In addition to their study and class time, most MU students work part- or full-time jobs in order to help pay for their education. At any one time, as many as 60 percent of Mizzou students have jobs either on campus or in restaurants, stores, and offices scattered across the city. Just as most Mizzou students through the years have had to adjust to a regimen of study and work, so it is with their counterparts today.

The highest priority for faculty, staff, and administrators is to ensure the best educational experience possible for these talented students. The result has been educational opportunities that are among the finest in the nation—and Mizzou has the student achievements, national recognition, and awards to prove it.

Mizzou students have won many major national awards. Recent examples of such recognition include four graduate students who received fellowships funded at $30,000 per year by the U.S. Congress; a School of Accountancy student who made the highest score of the fifty thousand students taking the Certified Public Accounting examination; a senior music student who won the 2006 National Young Artist Composition Competition and received a $3,000 award; a nursing student who has received two grants to support his research in microcirculation; a recent graduate of the Harry S Truman School of Public Affairs who is completing a prestigious Presidential Management Fellowship in the U.S. Department of Homeland Security; and a recent alumna who was chosen by the *Chronicle of Higher Education* as one of its "Rising Stars in the Academy"—an honor bestowed on only five doctoral students in the nation.

Mizzou's educational programs also have garnered many national awards. The general education program required of all undergraduates was the product of a decade of work by the faculty, and it earned the most esteemed recognition in all of higher education in 1997. The Theodore M. Hesburgh Award, which is bestowed on only one public or private institution each year, was presented to Mizzou at a ceremony in Washington, D.C., attended by representatives of virtually all the major public and private universities in the nation.

Mizzou's writing-intensive program, Writing Across the Curriculum, also received national recognition. All MU undergraduates enroll in at least one course that integrates effective writing with course content.

In 1997, the National Science Foundation (NSF) recognized Mizzou for offering one of the ten best programs in the nation for involving undergraduates in research. Today, many Mizzou undergraduates not only participate in the research of a faculty member but, under the supervision of faculty mentors, also conduct their own original research for publication and presentation at professional meetings. Many of these students consider their involvement in the discovery of new knowledge as one of the most exciting and life-shaping aspects of their time on campus.

In the 1990s, Mizzou pioneered "living-learning" environments for residence hall students. At the beginning, the program focused on freshmen, and this aspect of the program continues today. An incoming freshman has the opportunity to live in a residence hall with fifteen to twenty-five other freshmen with similar academic interests—perhaps journalism, business, agriculture, or engineering. These clusters of students also enroll in at least three classes together and often have the same academic adviser, who keeps hours in the residence hall.

Experience has shown that those who participate in these Freshman Interest Groups (FIGs) do better academically, make more rapid and more positive adjustments as they move from high school to the larger and more challenging university setting, and are more likely to graduate. This approach has worked so well that it has been extended to undergraduates at all levels in several innovative ways.

One of the most important indicators of the success of an undergraduate program is the percentage of entering freshmen who graduate within six years, which is the standard by which programs are compared across the nation. Within the past ten years, this percentage for Mizzou has increased dramatically, and it is still on the rise. From 55 percent ten years ago, this measurement is now approaching 70 percent, which far exceeds the national average. One of Mizzou's top priorities is to continue to strengthen the undergraduate program and further increase the percentage of students completing their degrees.

The achievements of Mizzou graduates mirror the caliber of their experiences during their time as students. In a recent study of the undergraduate institutions of Fortune 500 CEOs, Mizzou ranked eighth among all universities in the nation—both public and private. In the world of business, MU graduates include Glen Barton Jr., retired CEO of Caterpillar Inc.; Alan "Ace" Greenberg, chairman of Bear Stearns Companies Inc.; Harry M. Cornell Jr., chairman emeritus of Leggett & Platt Inc.; Richard Kinder, CEO of Kinder Morgan Inc.; William S. Thompson Jr., CEO and managing director of PIMCO; and Sam Walton, founder of Wal-Mart.

Mizzou alumni play exciting, visible roles in entertainment and the performing arts, among them Chris Cooper, Jann Carl, Brad Pitt, and Sheryl Crow. MU graduates Caroline Worra and Ryan MacPherson are international opera stars and members of the New York City Opera.

The more than seventeen thousand graduates of the School of Journalism are publishers, editors, reporters, photographers, designers, account executives, producers, and other leaders at thousands of media outlets, communication agencies, and major businesses in the United States and more than thirty countries around the world. Among the journalism graduates in leadership roles are Lisa Myers, NBC News senior investigative correspondent; Russ Mitchell, CBS News anchor; Jim Lehrer, host of PBS's *NewsHour;* and Ken Paulson, editor of *USA Today.*

In the world of politics and government, Mizzou alumni are also well represented and include Ann Covington, the first woman chief justice of the Missouri Supreme Court; Tim Kaine, governor of Virginia; Duk Kyu Kim, congressman in the Korean National Assembly; Dale Klein, chairman of the U.S. Nuclear Regulatory Commission; Ted Kulongoski, governor of Oregon; and Claire McCaskill, U.S. senator.

Other notables include Jeffrey Bonner, president and CEO of the Saint Louis Zoo; Teresa Carpenter, author, Pulitzer Prize winner, and former senior editor of the *Village Voice;* James Fergason, inventor of the modern liquid crystal display; Linda Godwin, NASA astronaut; and Mort Walker, creator of Beetle Bailey.

While the University takes great pride in the achievements of these extraordinary alumni, it is perhaps most important to the state that Mizzou graduates, at all levels and from a multitude of disciplines, are a substantial part of the flow of new talent that fills critically important jobs in Missouri's businesses, schools, governments, and professions year after year. These graduates are broadly educated to meet their responsibilities as citizens and to expand the horizons of their personal lives, and they are also well trained in their chosen fields and professions.

While many fill leadership positions in Missouri, others quietly go about doing superb jobs that are collectively of great importance to the intellectual, social, and economic health of the state. There are thousands of MU grads in the state's K–12 classrooms, in accounting jobs, in health care, and serving as lawyers, financial advisers, artists, and musicians. The list goes on and on.

The University's role is all the more significant because Mizzou offers many programs that are unique among the state's public institutions, and many others that are of exceptional strength. Based on the scholarly productivity of the faculty, the *Chronicle of Higher Education* recently included these MU programs among the top ten in the nation in their respective areas: animal science, horticulture, nutrition, nuclear engineering, communication, fisheries science and management, forestry, counseling psychology, and educational psychology. Other MU programs generally ranked among the top five or ten in the nation include journalism (best in the world!), family and community medicine, law dispute resolution, creative writing, oral studies, exercise physiology, and nanoscience.

An important area of unique strength is health care. Through the University's medical, nursing, and health professions programs, Mizzou plays a critical role in providing health care to Missourians in all parts of the state. More Missouri physicians received their training from MU than from any other university, and many of the twenty-three hundred physician alumni in Missouri serve rural areas. University of Missouri Health Care serves patients from every county in the state and provides more than $43 million of medical care each year to patients who lack health insurance and cannot afford to pay. School of Medicine faculty physicians who provide this care also conduct lifesaving research in treating such conditions as cancer, diabetes, heart disease, and arthritis.

Indeed, Mizzou is a leading contributor to medical research that vastly improves the diagnosis and treatment provided to patients in Missouri and around the globe. The Sinclair School of Nursing is a strong partner with the School of Medicine and researchers in other disciplines across the campus in this regard. Among schools of nursing nationwide, MU's ranks eighteenth in National Institutes of Health (NIH) grant support for the work conducted by its faculty and students. Each year, the school adds to the workforce about one hundred and fifty graduates with bachelor of science in nursing degrees. With their degrees and training, these nurses fill important leadership positions in Missouri health care institutions.

The School of Health Professions also plays a significant role in providing high-quality health care to the citizens of Missouri and elsewhere. Eighty-six percent of its approximately 140 graduates each year take jobs in their specialties within Missouri; more than 3,800 of the school's graduates are now spread nearly equally between the state's metropolitan and rural areas.

Three other professional schools play important roles in providing top-quality research and service. The College of Veterinary Medicine trains most of Missouri's practicing veterinarians and is an outstanding contributor to Mizzou's strength in comparative medicine, focusing on the commonalities in treatment of animal and human diseases. Graduates of the School of Law have the highest pass rate on the Missouri bar exam of any school in the state, public or private. The Harry S Truman School of

Public Affairs prepares its graduates for leadership roles in public service, and many serve as Missouri legislators, state agency heads, city managers, federal officials, and other public leaders.

Nationally Competitive, Cutting-Edge Research

Mizzou is one of the nation's premier research universities, with scientific discovery and achievements in the arts and humanities serving as the cornerstones of its mission, values, and educational programs. This focus on integrating research, scholarship, and student education continues to receive national recognition. At Mizzou, it is not a question of research *or* instruction but, rather, of achieving an effective integration of the two.

The result is a distinguished history of faculty and student achievements in research and creativity. These include the development of a grafting technique that helped save the threatened French wine industry in the 1870s; the development in the 1940s of the antibiotic aureomycin from a Sanborn Field soil sample; the production of a rust-resistant wheat variety in the early 1950s that became a worldwide food source; and, more recently, medical research findings that have led to both the first automatic and completely implanted heart defibrillator and the first home dialysis for kidney patients.

Contributions outside the biological and physical sciences have been equally impressive. In 1914, Missouri School of Journalism founder Walter Williams wrote the Journalist's Creed, which continues to provide the ethical standards for the world's practicing journalists. In 1946, a Mizzou educator laid the groundwork for the Dick and Jane book series, which taught generations of grade-school children how to read. In 1978, the first issue of the *Missouri Review* was published. The journal is now recognized as one of the nation's premier university literary publications. (For a more comprehensive, though by no means exhaustive, record of MU research and creative achievements see p. 139.)

In 1908, Mizzou became one of only seven public universities in the nation to achieve membership in the prestigious Association of American Universities (AAU). Today, this association represents the nation's top public and private research universities. At present, there are sixty-two AAU member institutions, and thirty-four of those are public. Together, they are a major force in expanding the frontiers of human knowledge and enriching the lives of people around the globe. Based in Washington, AAU is a major voice in shaping federal research policy and funding.

Over the past ten years, Mizzou's scientific and scholarly activities have grown rapidly in scope and magnitude. Today, news regarding research accomplishments at Mizzou routinely appears in major media outlets around the globe. For example, recent findings of geneticist Randall Prather, an MU professor of reproductive biology, have made international headlines. Funded by a $10 million grant from the National Science Foundation, Prather has created transgenic swine with organs that lack the gene responsible for triggering organ rejection in humans—a breakthrough that has brought the "xenotransplantation" of animal organs into humans a step closer to reality. With nearly a hundred thousand people in the United States alone on waiting lists for organ transplants, Prather's research has enormous implications for improving human health.

In 2004, Robert Benfer, professor emeritus of anthropology, led an excavation team, including eleven Mizzou students, to a site near Buena Vista, Peru. There the team unearthed the Temple of the Fox, a thirty-three-foot-tall stepped pyramid that is a thousand years older than anything of its kind previously unearthed. News of Benfer's discovery appeared in most major national newspapers around the world and also in the *National Geographic* and *Smithsonian* magazines. Support for the project was provided by the National Geographic Society.

The work of both Prather and Benfer was included in *Discover* magazine's list of the top one hundred science stories of 2006. Nebraska was the only other Big 12 university to make the list, and Mizzou was one of only fifteen institutions with more than one project on the list.

Another widely reported discovery involves the creation of custom knee implants using a patient's own biological tissue. James Cook, an associate professor of small animal and orthopedic surgery, uses both tissue from pigs and the cells from a patient's own injured knee to regenerate damaged meniscus cartilage. Developed using canine models, the procedure has proved so successful in restoring dogs' mobility—while minimizing the threat of arthritis developing in the damaged joint—that the FDA has approved the technique for testing in humans.

Other findings, too, have focused the national spotlight on MU. One group of scientists from the College of Agriculture, Food, and Natural Resources has taken the lead in developing the first integrated map of the maize genome. Other researchers have identified the family of genes responsible for establishing and maintaining pregnancy in livestock species and have unraveled the mystery of how a plant determines whether or not a particular pollen is suitable for fertilization.

Scholars from the College of Arts and Science, meanwhile, have solved the problem known as Kato's Conjecture, one of the thorniest puzzles in higher mathematics. They have also helped resolve a decades-old argument about the origins of the ancient Olmec people and guided MU creative writing students to some of the nation's top literary awards.

Education and mathematics faculty are garnering accolades for revitalizing math instruction in our nation's middle schools. One MU physicist recently gained national attention for his ideas about using tiny carbon nanotubes for volatile fuel storage, while another has captured the imagination of millions by charting the "speed" with which gravity propagates through space.

An MU engineering professor was recently awarded a contract of $10 million by the U.S. Department of Defense to further the development of next-generation weapons systems; another has founded an interdisciplinary center for geospatial intelligence to make better use of satellite and remote sensing data. Both programs promise to make our nation stronger and more secure.

Discovering new ways to combat chronic illness—and to address associated quality-of-life issues—is also a major priority at MU. During the early 1980s, for example, Gary Ehrhardt, a senior research scientist at the MU Research Reactor Center, collaborated with Delbert Day, an engineer and ceramics specialist at the University of Missouri–Rolla, to investigate how medical science might assist patients with inoperable liver cancer. Their ingenious solution involved injecting millions of tiny radioactive glass beads into arteries feeding the liver. After reaching the cancerous organ, the radiation-emitting beads became lodged in the tumor, attacking the malignant tissue while leaving healthy cells unharmed. The product developed from Ehrhardt and Day's discovery, TheraSphere, was licensed in 1988. It is not a cure, but it has helped thousands of desperately ill patients live longer, with less pain.

Another group of MU scientists from the Department of Biomedical Sciences, the School of Medicine's Department of Medical Pharmacology and Physiology, and the Dalton Cardiovascular Research Center is at the forefront of the fight against a more common, but no less deadly, malady—heart disease. Led by Harold Laughlin, a professor of biomedical sciences, and supported by major grants from the National Institutes of Health, MU faculty have produced significant findings detailing how physical inactivity contributes to the onset and severity of coronary artery disease, the nation's number-one killer of both men and women.

Tom Thomas, a professor of nutritional sciences in the College of Human Environmental Sciences, and other MU scholars are using NIH support to explore the physiological relationship between fitness and lifestyle. NIH has also funded studies by gerontology researchers in the Sinclair School of Nursing to improve the health and well-being of elders. In the School of Social Work, NIH funding is helping scholars better understand how contemporary communications technology might improve the accessibility and effectiveness of hospice care for cancer patients.

Other achievements include those of MU's School of Law, which, in addition to training some of the nation's best litigators, is a world leader in developing approaches for the resolution of disputes outside the courtroom. Additionally, scholars at MU's School of Information Sciences and Learning Technologies have become leaders in developing programs to take full advantage of today's vast information resources. Faculty and graduate student researchers at the Harry S Truman School of Public Affairs are using these and other tools to make major contributions to the theory and practice of governance.

These scientists and scholars, along with hundreds of their peers, have made MU a powerful engine for discovery. And their successes have the added benefit of making the University a magnet for similar talent and federal research funds.

"A major research university like the University of Missouri has to cultivate within it some of the best minds in the nation. In doing that, we also then attract some of the best minds from around the world," said MU Chancellor Brady Deaton. Deaton's remark came during the announcement that Fred Hawthorne, a member of the National Academy of Sciences and a leader in the international fight against cancer, was leaving UCLA after forty years to join an interdisciplinary team focused on nanomedicine at Mizzou. Hawthorne, who works with fellow nanomedicine pioneer Kattesh Katti at MU's Research Reactor, said he was attracted to Mizzou by the breadth and depth of its interdisciplinary research, its emphasis on student instruction, and its facilities.

Recruiting researchers of Hawthorne's stature reinforces MU's commitment to the twin goals that define the University's mission: working toward tangible, long-lasting improvements in the lives of Missourians and others around the world, and using this scientific and scholarly search for solutions to bolster the quality and relevance of student learning.

MU's research programs provide another substantial benefit to Missouri. Because of the quality of Missouri's flagship university, MU faculty and students are in a unique position to compete successfully for federal and other outside funding to support research and creative programs. Of Mizzou's total research expenditures of nearly $175 million in fiscal year 2006, federal grants provided $139 million, or 79 percent.

Indeed, Mizzou is the only public university in Missouri that is a major player in obtaining federal support for research. During fiscal year 2005, for example, Mizzou was awarded $19 million from perhaps the most rigorous and competitive of all federal funding sources, the National Science Foundation. This figure is almost double what the NSF awarded the remainder of Missouri's public colleges and universities combined.

In the life sciences, an area of research that has assumed increasing importance in recent years, Mizzou is again a leader. In fiscal year 2006, NSF reported that MU ranked eleventh among the nation's universities in overall life sciences funding and fourth in funding for plant genome research.

Mizzou also compares favorably to its peers within the AAU in terms of research funding. According to the most recent data from NSF, Mizzou's research and development expenditures exceeded those at institutions such as Carnegie Mellon, Princeton, the University of Kansas, and the University of California at Santa Barbara. Even more significant, Mizzou's rate of growth in federal funding for these expenditures has exceeded that of all other public AAU institutions for the past ten years. Mizzou's faculty and students stand tall in the highly competitive peer-review process that determines the distribution of most federal research dollars.

MU's research programs drive economic growth in Missouri. Mizzou brings dollars to Missouri that would otherwise flow to other states. This funding supports critically important research programs that are closely integrated with instruction; it also results in new money being spent in the state. This spending, in turn, creates a "multiplier effect" on the state and local economies. An analysis by MU economists found that the University's research and development spending annually generates close to $440 million in economic activity and supports close to nine thousand jobs for Missouri citizens.

Mizzou's research produces state economic development in other important ways as well. Between 2001 and 2006, Mizzou filed for 220 patents and was awarded 65. Mizzou's patent holdings generated nearly $22 million in licensing fees to support research and other programs, and a dozen new start-up companies were created based on the commercialization of Mizzou technology.

And more start-ups are on the horizon. The University is building a Life Science Business Incubator near the Research Reactor and a major research park, Discovery Ridge, located in southeast Columbia. Both of these facilities will speed the commercialization of Mizzou technology, increase patent fee revenues to support more research, and further stimulate the Missouri economy.

Land-Grant Responsibility, Outreach, and Extension

Another significant, long-standing way in which Mizzou improves the Missouri economy and the quality of life for Missourians is through MU Extension. Thousands of Missourians, past and present, know Mizzou principally through their interactions with statewide Extension programs.

This important "outreach" aspect of the University's mission is the result of Mizzou's designation as the state's land-grant university under the federal Morrill Act of 1862. This act provided grants of public lands to universities whose missions included a focus on making practical education and solutions to everyday problems broadly available to a state's population. As a result of this legislation, the University began to offer agricultural, engineering, and other applied programs and, in 1888, established the Agricultural Experiment Station, which now has research centers located strategically in all the major agricultural regions of the state.

Also in support of the University's agricultural outreach, Extension agents were located in every county of the state. The research centers have been a rich source of new knowledge to fuel the efficiency and competitiveness of Missouri agriculture, and the county Extension agents have been there to help farmers apply this new knowledge to their operations. This combination has been the principal reason that Missouri agriculture has been and remains competitive in domestic and international markets for farm products.

The county agents and MU Extension were initially focused on agriculture, which was appropriate at a time when a high percentage of Missouri's economy was driven by agriculture. Through the years, the role of MU Extension and the county agent has been extended to include other aspects of life in both rural and urban Missouri, including programs for youth and the elderly, community economic development, family health, and nutrition. One in ten Missouri children benefits from 4-H. A highly successful Youth Futures Program focuses on helping young people from economically disadvantaged communities prepare for college.

About one million Missourians, almost a fifth of the state's population, annually use MU Extension programs to make informed decisions. This includes one hundred thousand teachers, health care professionals, lawyers, firefighters, and police officers. The Extension program in business development serves more than twenty thousand clients throughout the state, and it is estimated that this support helps create more than $130 million in sales and sustains more than fifteen hundred jobs.

Through MU Extension, the University touches the lives of far more Missourians annually than is possible through its on-campus programs. This statewide "campus" is a vital part of Mizzou's land-grant responsibility to take needed educational programs, technical know-how, and solutions to important problems to the four corners of the state.

Division I Intercollegiate Athletics

Building on an early and rich tradition of athletic success and the winning records of legendary coaches such as Sparky Stalcup, Don Faurot, Dan Devine, Norm Stewart, John "Hi" Simmons, and Tom Botts, Mizzou is a leading player in virtually all major intercollegiate sports. There is excitement, color, music, and fast action as the Tigers take the field and the court. Tiger fans are loyal and take great pride in all aspects of the University. M-I-Z-Z-O-U! resonates with all.

And it resonates with no one more than former Curator William "Bill" Cocos, who has traveled from St. Louis to Columbia for every home football game since 1948. From 1972 through 2006, Cocos has attended 396 of 397 home and away games, and on occasion he has had to make the trip with a cane, crutches, or a walker—but Bill is not to be denied his Tigers!

Alumni and friends in Missouri and around the world follow the Tigers with great interest and pride. During 2007, the wrestling team ranked number three in the country, and Ben

Askren won MU's second wrestling national championship. In 2006, football got off to a 6–0 start for the first time since 1973, and the team played in the Sun Bowl; new head basketball coach Mike Anderson and his team got off to a 9–0 start; and overall Mizzou finished fourth in the Big 12 All-Sport standings. All of this was achieved by student athletes who have for several years ranked academically at or near the top in the Big 12.

Athletic success is not new for the Tigers. Mizzou has won national team championships in both baseball (1954) and track (1965). Between 1925 and 2005, MU athletes won fifteen national championships in men's track and three national championships in women's track.

Mizzou has been a member of five athletic conferences over the years, starting with the Missouri Valley Conference in 1907 and including the Big 6, Big 7, Big 8, and now the Big 12. The Tigers have an outstanding record of conference championships, including twelve in football, fifteen in men's basketball, twenty-two in men's track and field and cross-country, sixteen in baseball, five in women's basketball, two in women's cross-country, and three in softball.

State-of-the-Art Facilities

Another great strength of the Mizzou campus for all students, as well as for faculty and staff, is its facilities. For example, *Sports Illustrated* recently ranked Mizzou's new Student Recreation Complex as the best on any university campus in the nation.

Many of Mizzou's classrooms, laboratories, and other facilities are state of the art and are located in new or recently renovated structures. These include Cornell Hall, home of the College of Business, which was made possible by private funding in excess of $10 million.

Students, faculty, and staff in the College of Education work in a fully renovated and expanded Townsend Hall, whose facilities provide support for innovative educational programs. Students and faculty in the School of Natural Resources are served by a beautiful new building made possible by a lead gift from the Anheuser-Busch Foundation.

Students often fill to capacity a spacious, comfortable Information Commons, located in renovated space on the first floor of Ellis Library and made possible by a gift from the James B. Nutter family. Within the area, students have access to computers and the Internet, and coffee and other refreshments are permitted. The latter are available in a coffee shop located in the Ellis atrium. Major renovations and additions have been completed over the past ten years for several other buildings used for physics, chemistry, and engineering.

Dedicated in 2004, the Christopher S. Bond Life Sciences Center provides advanced research and teaching facilities for the many faculty and students on campus who are studying and doing research related to the life sciences. This $70 million structure was funded by approximately equal federal and state support; private support funded major equipment, the lobby, the auditorium, and artwork. This facility is critically important to Mizzou's focus on the life sciences, and it is shared by faculty and students from five MU colleges and schools that have major programs in the life sciences.

The residence halls on campus are being replaced or renovated as part of a fifteen-year plan to provide modern, attractive on-campus living space. These halls are being constructed in groups that include dining halls, study facilities, classrooms, and meeting spaces; they are replacing residence halls that are more than forty years old. Residence hall fees paid by students are financing those projects.

Mizzou students and supporters from across the state enjoy watching the Tigers in high-tech athletic facilities. Starting in the late 1990s, Faurot Field and Memorial Stadium were given face-lifts, and suites were added in 2000. Thanks to a gift of $25 million from Bill and Nancy Laurie, the basketball Tigers, both men and women, play their games in Mizzou Arena, one of the best in the nation. The state of Missouri provided $35 million for the arena, and several other private donors gave significant amounts.

Made possible by generous gifts from other donors, the Mizzou Sports Park also includes a new track and soccer stadium, a new baseball stadium, a new indoor football practice facility named for Dan Devine, a new tennis facility, and extensive facilities on the southwest corner of Stadium and Providence for training, studying, eating, and sports medicine for all of Mizzou's sports.

Funding Sources and Private Fund-Raising

Funding sources for Mizzou programs have changed dramatically. Forty years ago, state appropriations provided more than forty-five cents of every dollar in MU's budget. Today, the state provides less than fifteen cents out of every dollar in MU's budget. In 1966, state appropriations were nearly five times higher than revenue from tuition and fees. Today, tuition and fee revenue exceeds state appropriations. For comparative purposes, the hospitals and clinics budget is included in these calculations.

In addition to tuition and fees, outside support for the University's research and creativity, much of it federal, has also grown rapidly and is now a major part of Mizzou's budget. Research programs are supported heavily by nonstate sources, with huge benefits flowing to Missouri.

Another rapidly growing source of support is the University's development effort. Mizzou has long had a development program to generate private, corporate, and foundation gifts. The Jefferson Club, which recognizes major donors to the University, was founded in 1969. Since 1999, membership has doubled and now exceeds five thousand households.

In 1989, with leadership from then Chancellor Haskell Monroe and former alumni and development director Bus Entsminger, Mizzou received a gift of $9 million from the Reynolds Foundation to construct and maintain the Reynolds Alumni Center. At the time, this gift was the largest ever received by the University, and it was the precursor to an even larger gift from the foundation. This facility, which was dedicated with Donald W. Reynolds (BJ '27) present for the ceremony, is a preferred site for campus and community events. It also provides office space for alumni, development, and publications staff and is home to the University Club.

Mizzou's first capital campaign targeted $150 million, and MU reached this goal in conjunction with the University's sesquicentennial in 1989. In 2000, the University began a five-year

$600 million fund-raising campaign, For All We Call Mizzou. The campaign reached its initial goal several months ahead of schedule in 2005. On the recommendation of the National Campaign Steering Committee, the goal was increased to $1 billion by 2008. Mizzou is one of only seven public universities in the nation now engaged in a campaign of this magnitude.

The National Campaign Steering Committee has been critically important in the success of Mizzou's development effort. This group is composed of about fifty alumni and friends from Missouri and from across the country who have been a valuable source of ideas and generous gifts. Larry McMullen (BA '53, JD '59) of Kansas City and William S. Thompson Jr. (BS CiE '68), of Irvine, California, have cochaired the committee from the outset. They were joined in 2006 by Cynthia Brinkley (BJ '91) of St. Louis as a third chair.

The For All We Call Mizzou campaign has generated extraordinary support for students, faculty, programs, and facilities. More than 650 student scholarships and fellowships have been created through endowments totaling $175 million, and the campaign has generated support for seventy-two fully and partially endowed faculty positions that will help Mizzou keep pace with international competition for the very best faculty minds. These endowments total $64 million and have attracted outstanding faculty talent across the campus. Of the more than $794 million raised by April 30, 2007, about 50 percent supports endowments with the rest designated for immediate needs.

To date, the University has received more than eighty-four gifts of $1 million or more. (For information about gifts of $5 million or more, see p. 145.)

Mizzou Alumni Association

The foundation for an effective development program is provided by proud alumni and an active alumni association. An alumni association helps keep graduates focused on their alma mater as they locate across Missouri and the nation and around the world. An active alumni association is also the source of vibrant political, student, faculty, and program support, and Mizzou has one of the best.

Established in 1853, the University of Missouri Alumni Association celebrated its sesquicentennial with an elaborate dinner and ceremony held in the Reynolds Alumni Center. With almost thirty-seven thousand dues-paying members and more than a hundred and thirty local chapters, the Mizzou Alumni Association extends the spirit of Mizzou around the globe. Through these chapters and its national award-winning magazine, MIZZOU, the association keeps alumni in touch with the campus and provides a broad variety of services and opportunities, including organized travel for sporting events and tours around the world. In 2005–2006, the association sponsored more than a thousand events worldwide with more than 103,000 alumni and friends in attendance.

The association has not only kept traditions from the past alive (including Homecoming, sponsoring the nation's first in 1911) but has also added marvelous new traditions such as Tiger Walk and Tiger Prowl. Beautiful touches have been added to Mizzou's botanical garden campus. From a re-created "Shack" table (close to the location of the original establishment), Beetle

Bailey gazes at the campus; on Tiger Plaza, a magnificent Bengal tiger stands guard over a cascading fountain at the south end of Carnahan Quadrangle.

The association also provides substantial support and recognition through the annual Faculty–Alumni Awards, established in 1967. More than 300 faculty and 460 alumni have been recognized at one of the best-attended annual dinner events on the campus. Through the Richard Wallace Faculty Development Incentive Grants program, the association has provided support for research and creativity to more than eighty professors since 1989. In 2006, the association awarded $225,000 in student scholarship support.

Missouri's Flagship AAU University

In a 1998 address entitled "The Future of Flagship Universities," Robert M. Berdahl, then chancellor of the University of California, Berkeley, and currently the president of the AAU, told an audience at Texas A&M that "it was always clear that the one or two institutions that were the original land-grant or public universities in the states were the flagships—the leaders—even though they may not have been referred to as such. They became the centers for research and graduate education, and they developed an array of professional schools that added to their size, scope, and preeminence."

Toward the end of his address, Berdahl pointed out that the flagship universities in the United States "have accomplished a great deal and are the envy of the world. We have created institutions that are superior to the revered institutions of Europe, and we have provided a model of excellence that is being emulated everywhere."

It takes decades to build flagship programs that are nationally competitive, particularly in the search for research support, and they are expensive both to build and to maintain. They must have the best academic minds; they must engage in cutting-edge research; they must have the latest in equipment and support; they must have students who are bright, well prepared, and highly motivated; they must have clearly defined but broad missions that reach out to serve the state as a whole. They are also fragile; the quality that has been built by decades of public investment, dedication, and hard work must be nourished and protected.

The Great Seal of the State of Missouri is displayed on the north portico of Jesse Hall, just beneath the dome. It bears the motto *Salus Populi Suprema Lex Esto,* or "Let the welfare of the people be the supreme law." No doubt our founders were thinking about serving all those generations to come when they established Missouri's great flagship university. They can take pride in the fact that the motto is as true today as it was at the beginning.

— *For the Black and Gold* —

Richard L. Wallace, Chancellor Emeritus

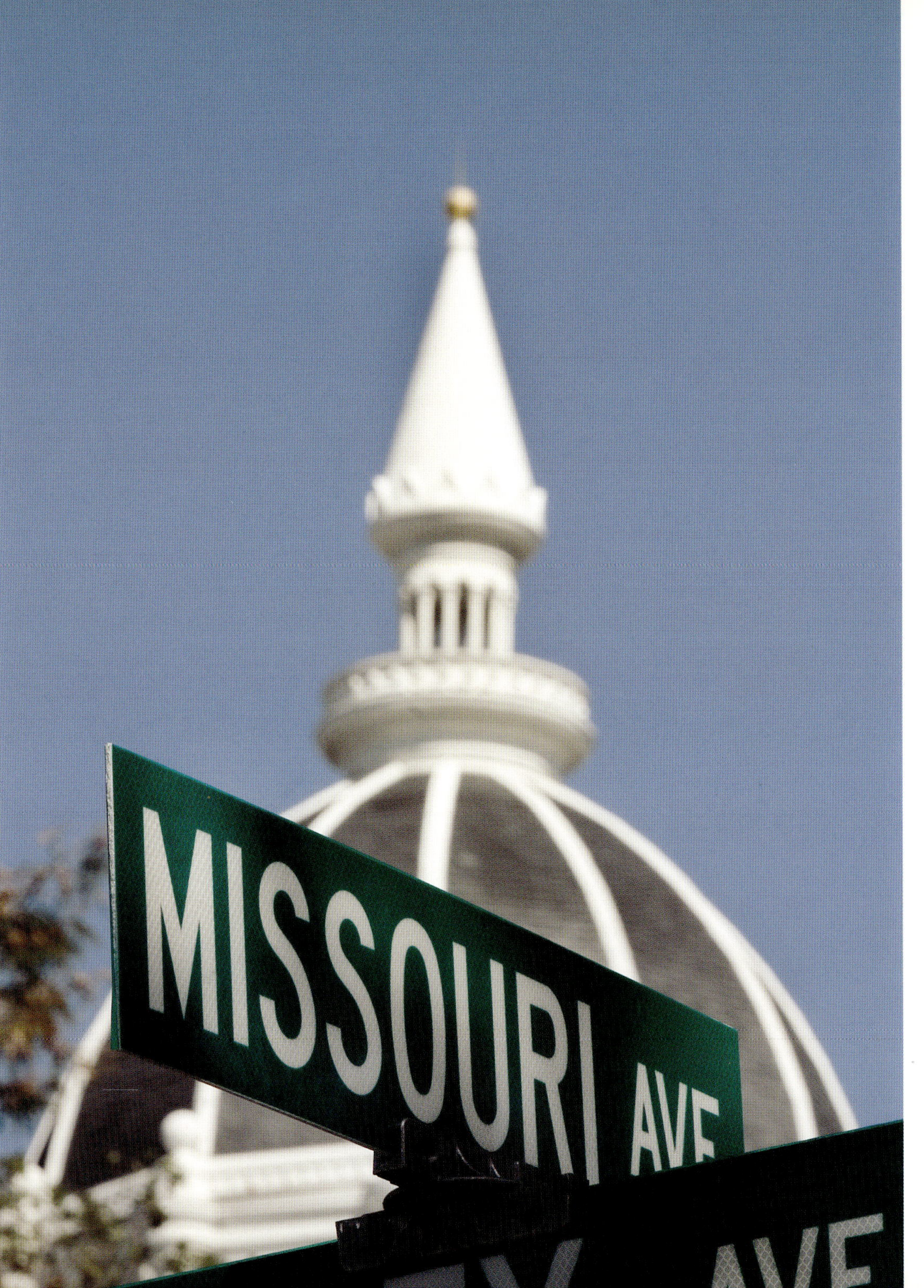

A street sign and the Jesse Hall dome leave no doubt that this is Mizzou.

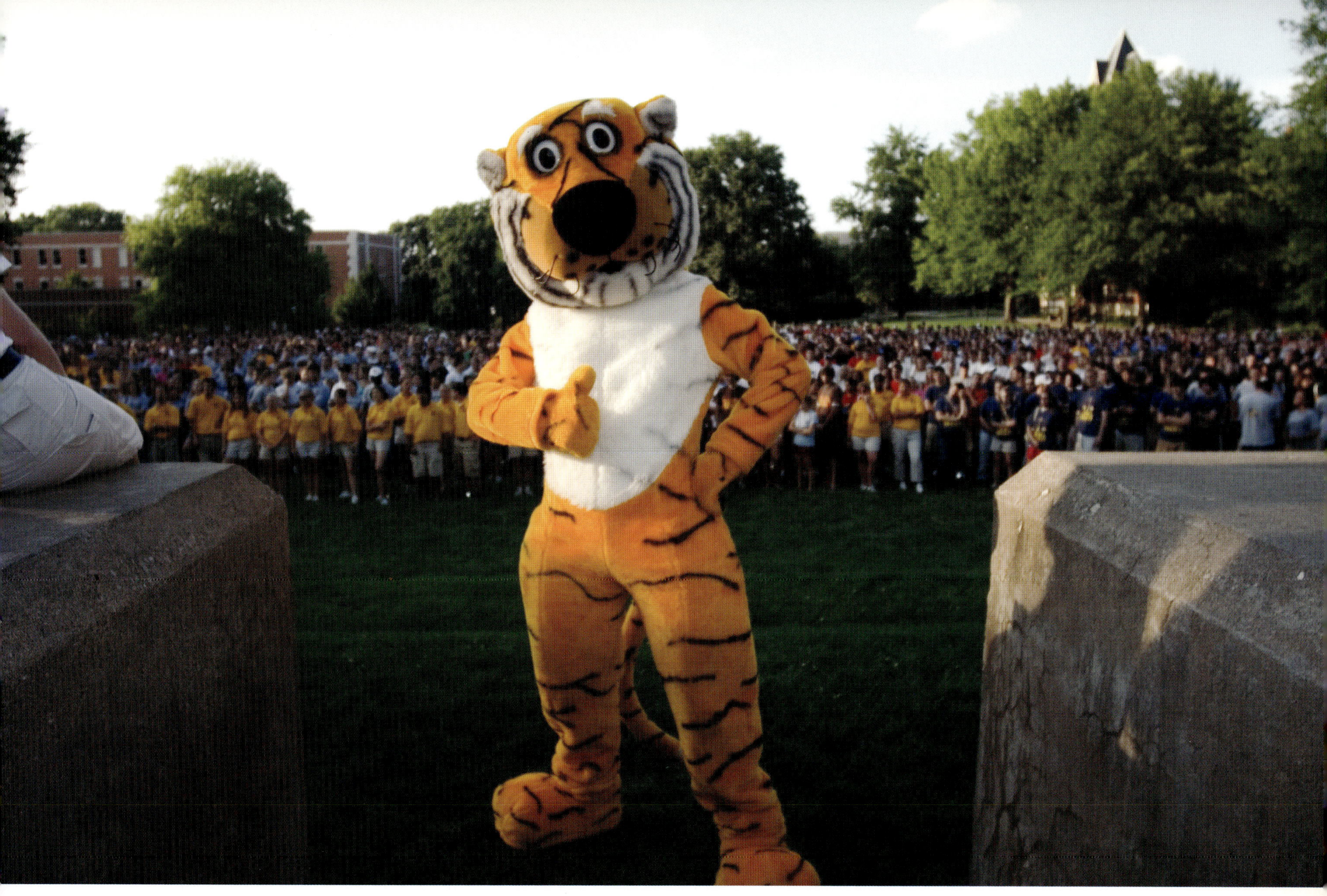

At the base of the Columns, Truman the Tiger signals thumbs-up as about four thousand freshmen wait to participate in Tiger Walk on Francis Quadrangle.

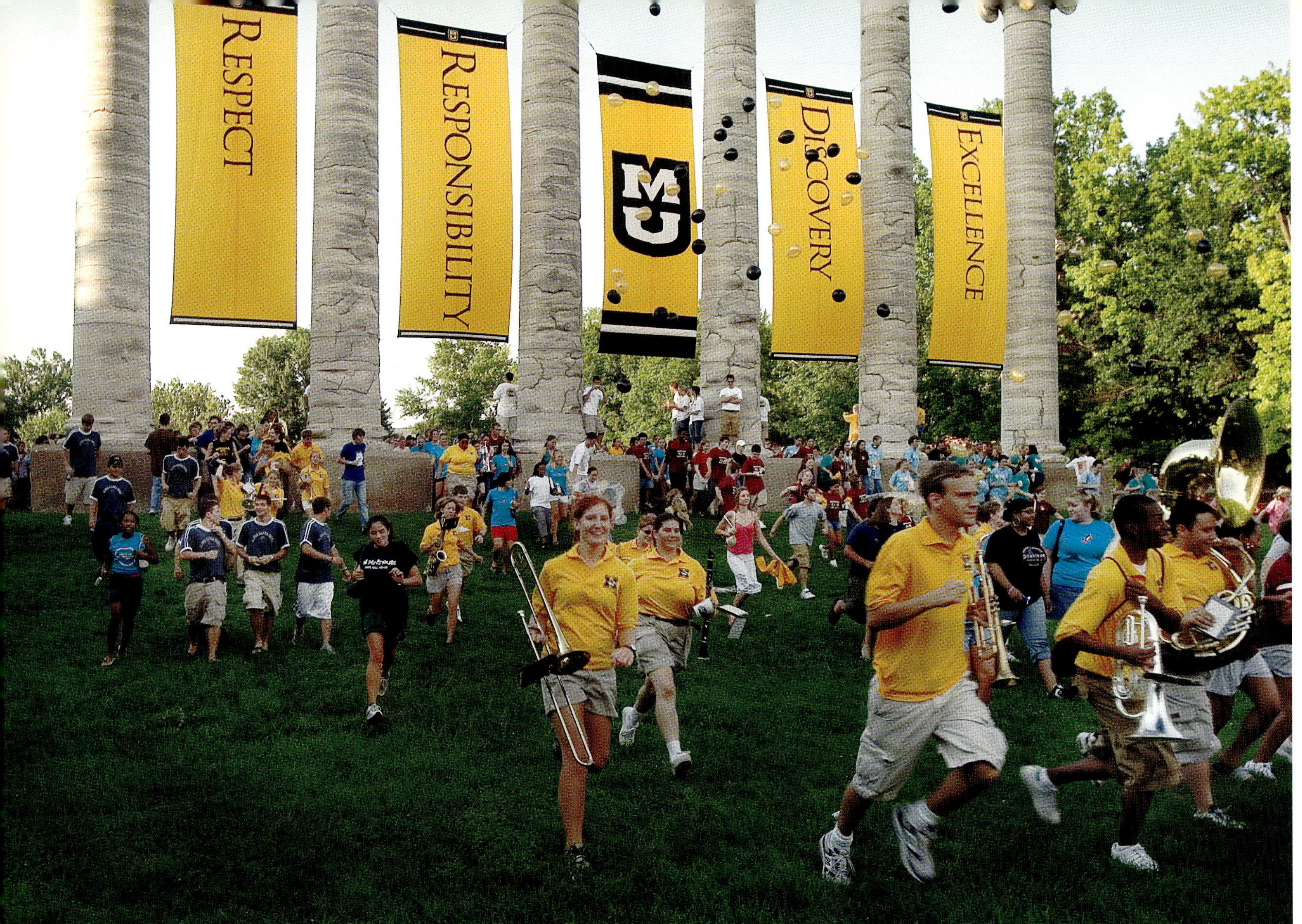

New students don't walk, they run through the Columns toward Jesse Hall to signify their entrance into the University. The annual event is sponsored by the Mizzou Alumni Association.

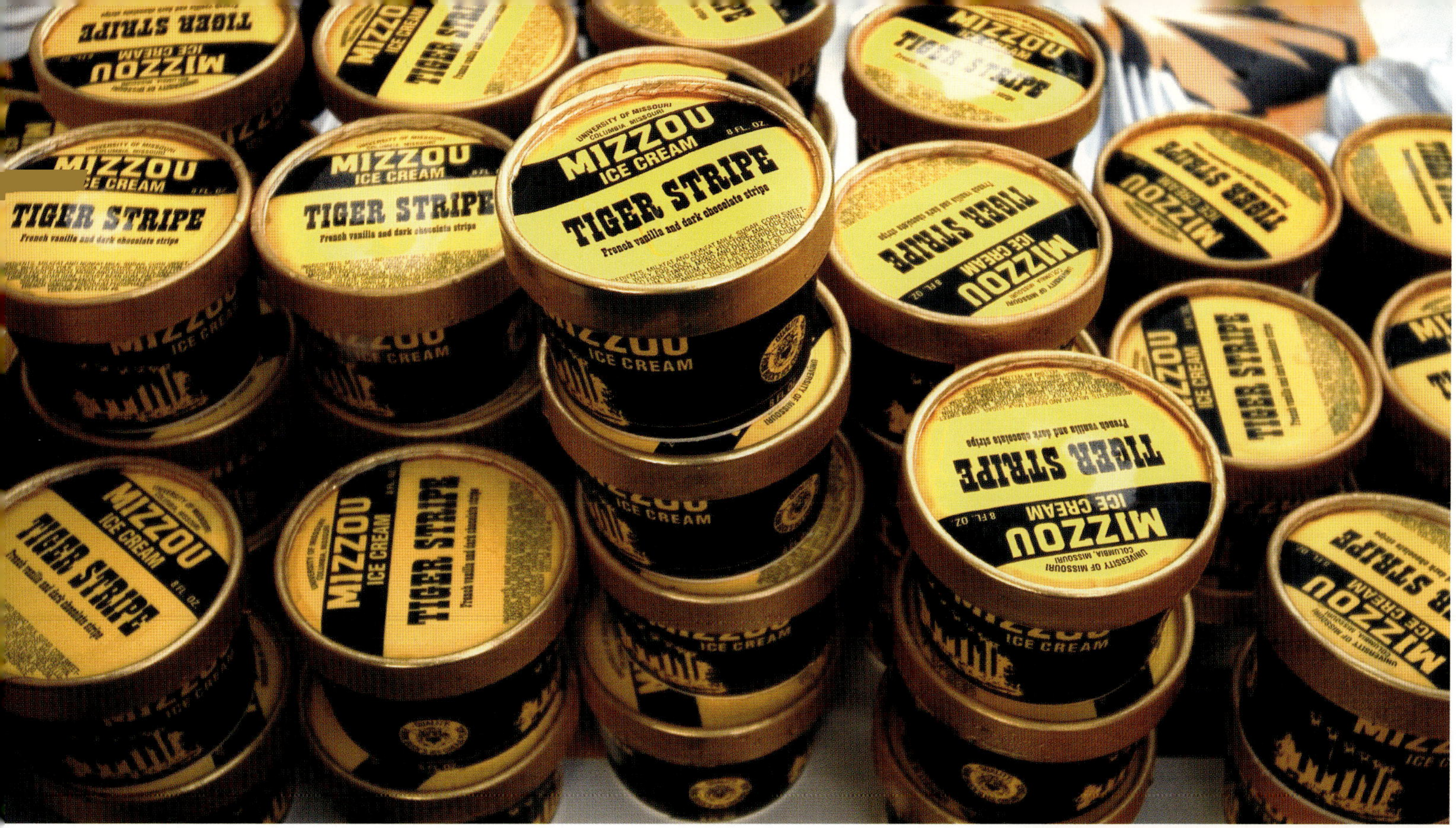

Single-serving containers of Tiger Stripe ice cream await hot and hungry students. Robert Marshall, professor emeritus of food science and nutrition in the College of Agriculture, Food, and Natural Resources, is responsible for creating the unique flavor, a rich combination of French vanilla and dark chocolate ripple.

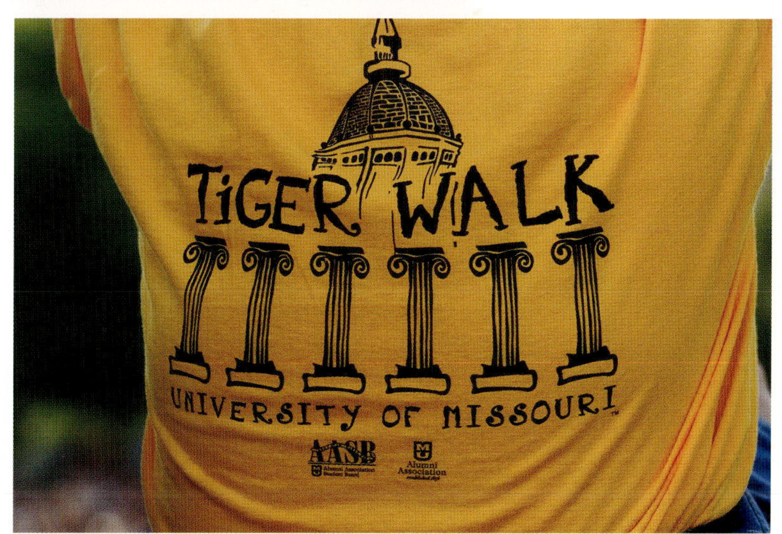

Faculty and staff don gold T-shirts to serve students Tiger Stripe ice cream.

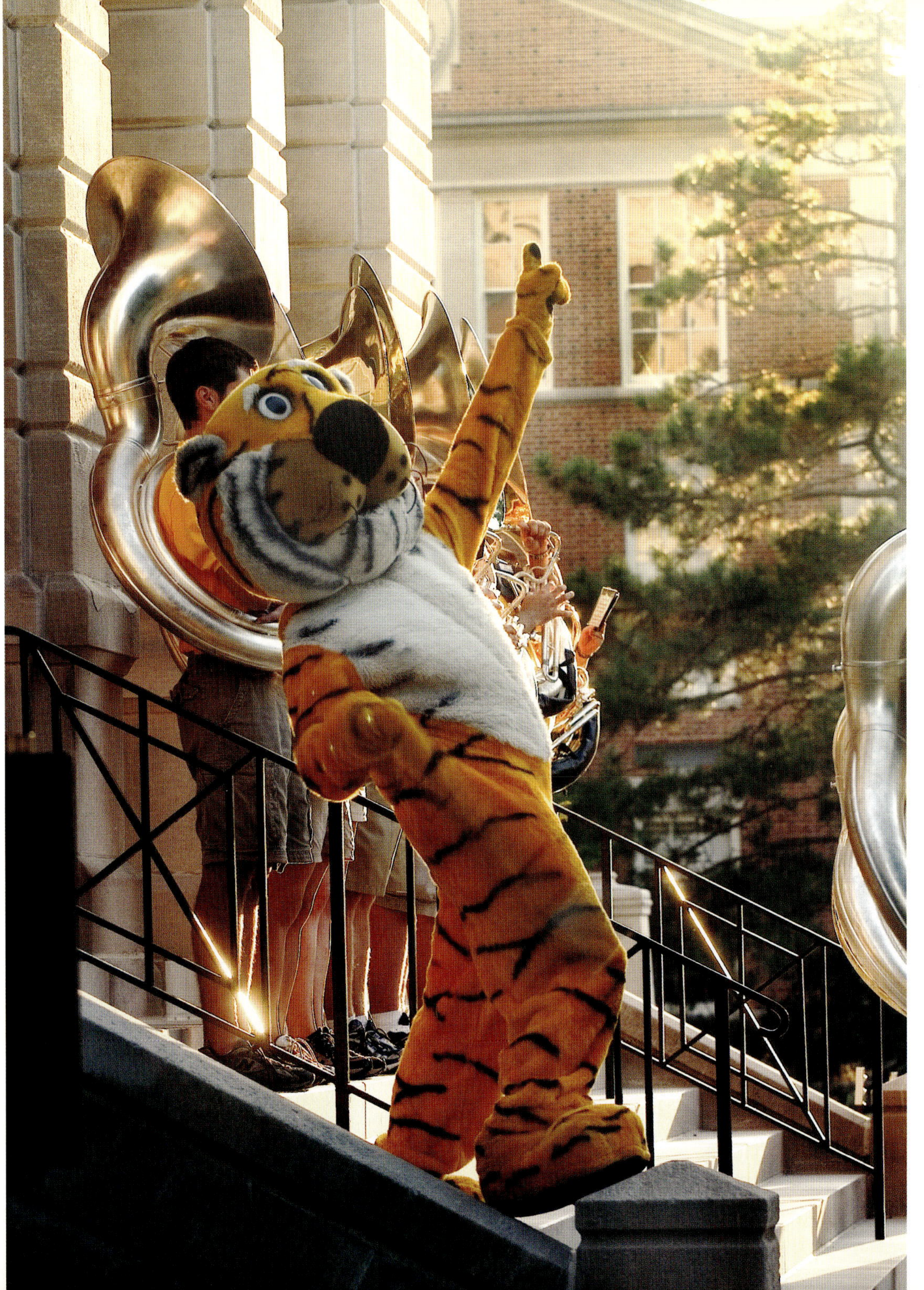

Truman dances to Marching Mizzou's music on the steps of Jesse Hall.

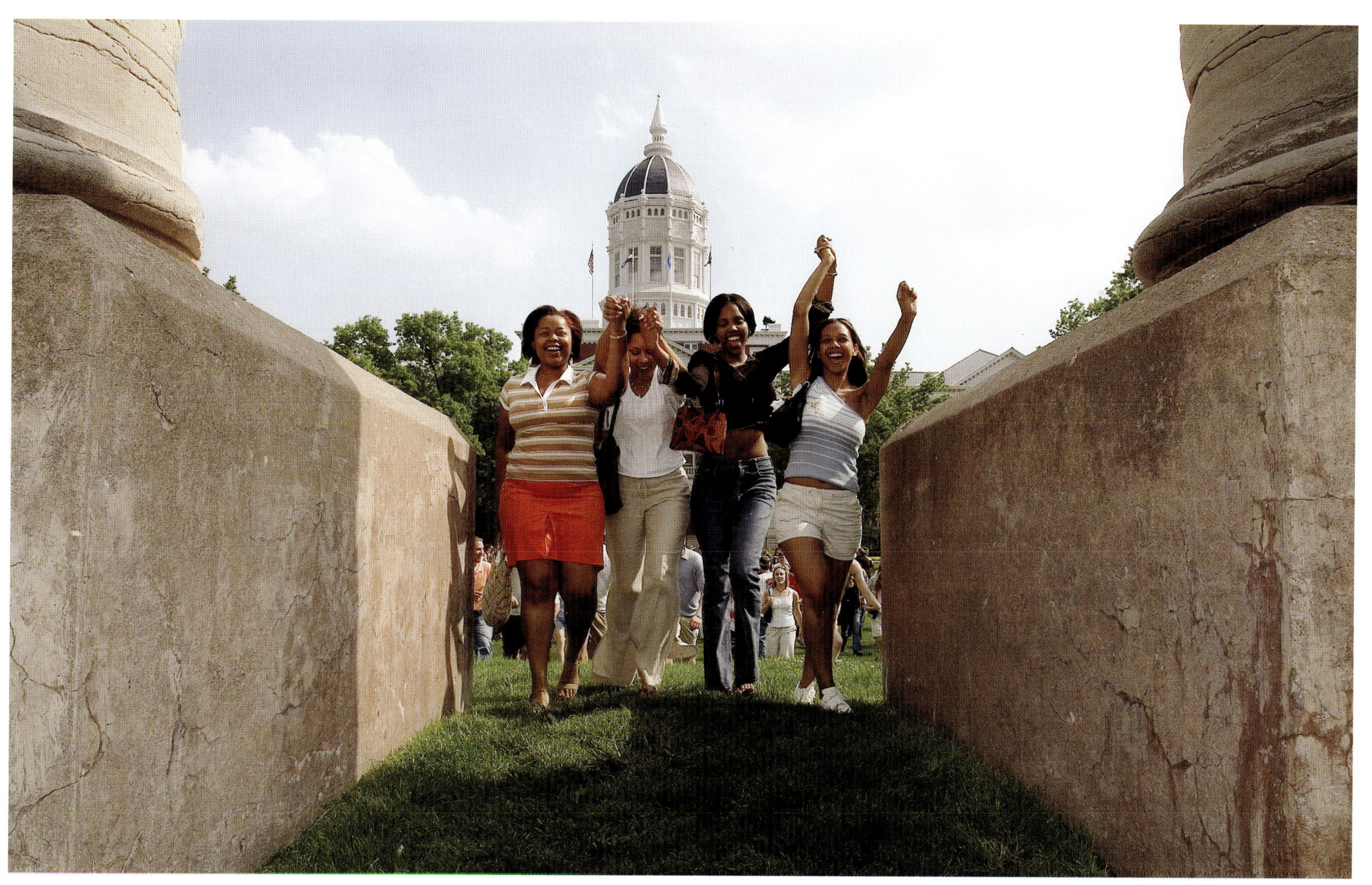

As graduation nears, students enjoy Tiger Prowl, essentially the reverse of Tiger Walk. For this event, students exit Francis Quadrangle through the Columns to signify their graduation.

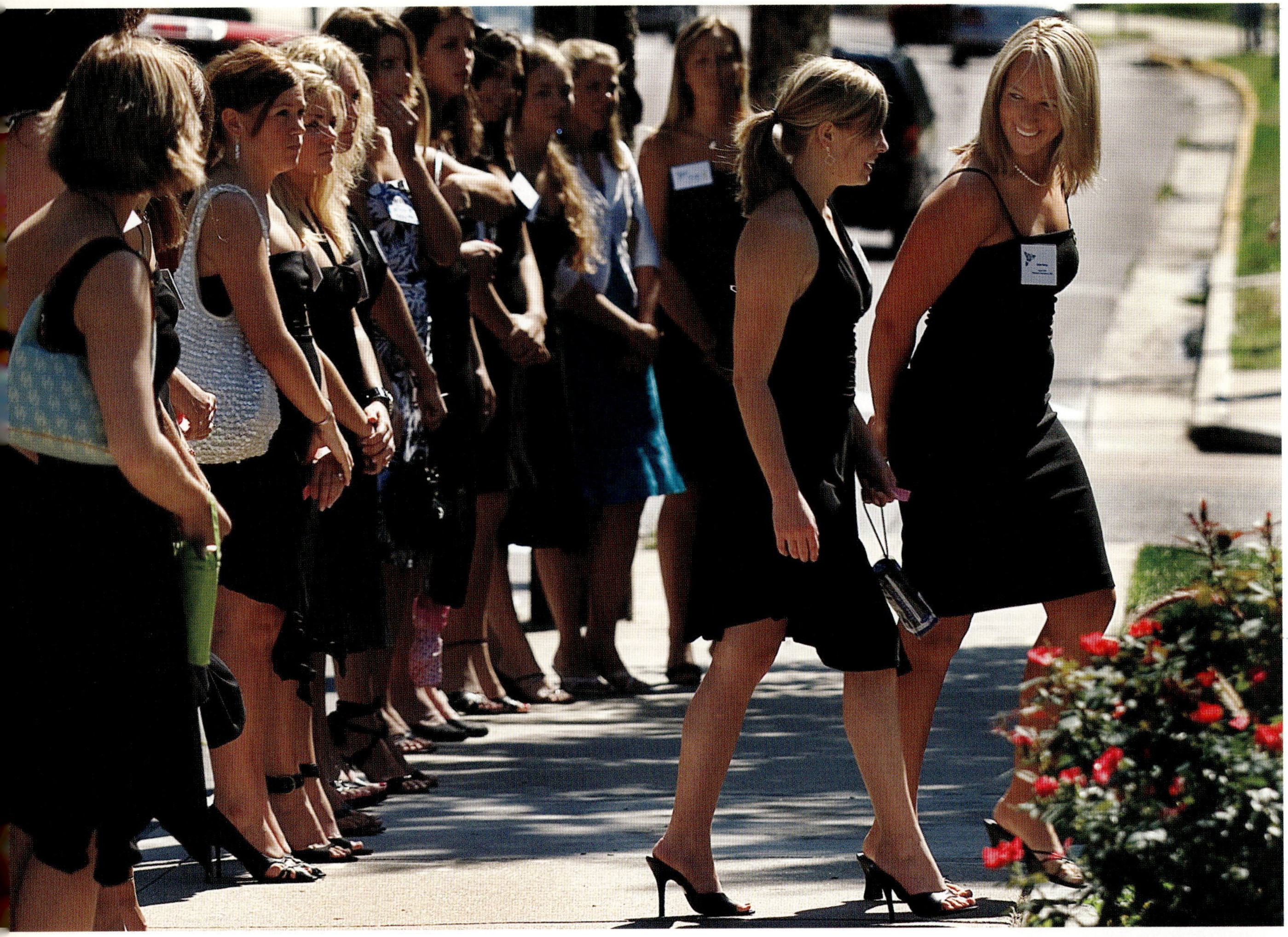

After a week of sorority house visits, bid day arrives. Pledge hopefuls wear the uniform: a little black dress and high-heeled shoes.

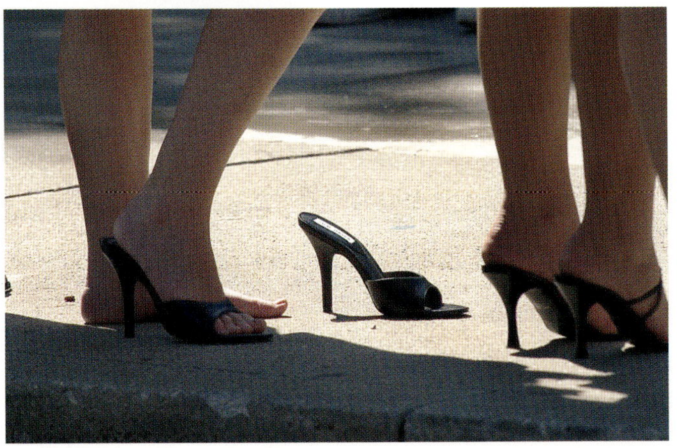

Rush week has taken its toll. A rushee tries to cool her feet, but the sidewalk is hot.

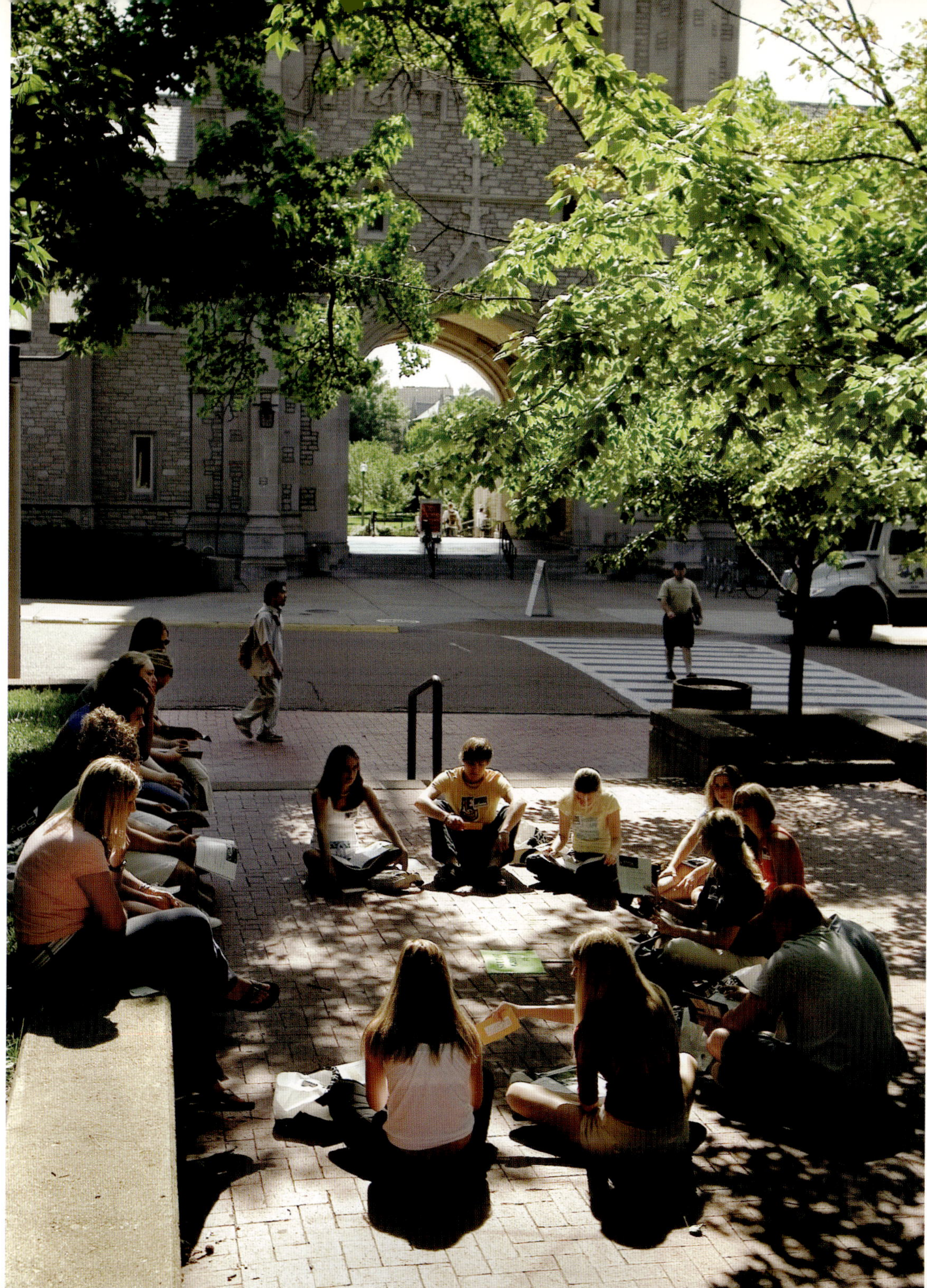

At orientation, a Summer Welcome leader gathers incoming freshmen in a circle under a red maple tree on Lowry Mall to answer their questions.

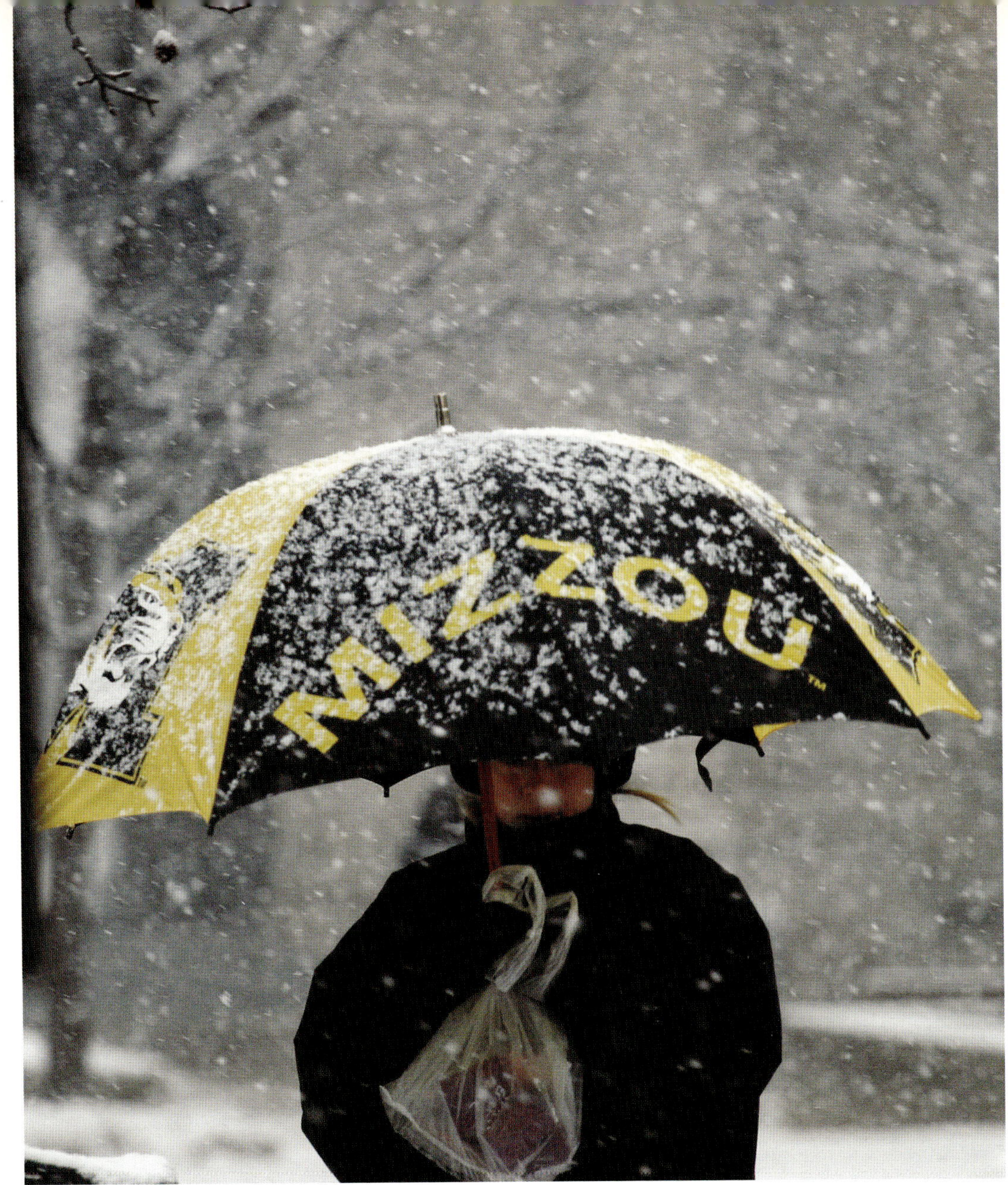

*H*at, coat, gloves, and umbrella shelter this pedestrian from a winter storm as she scurries across Lowry Mall.

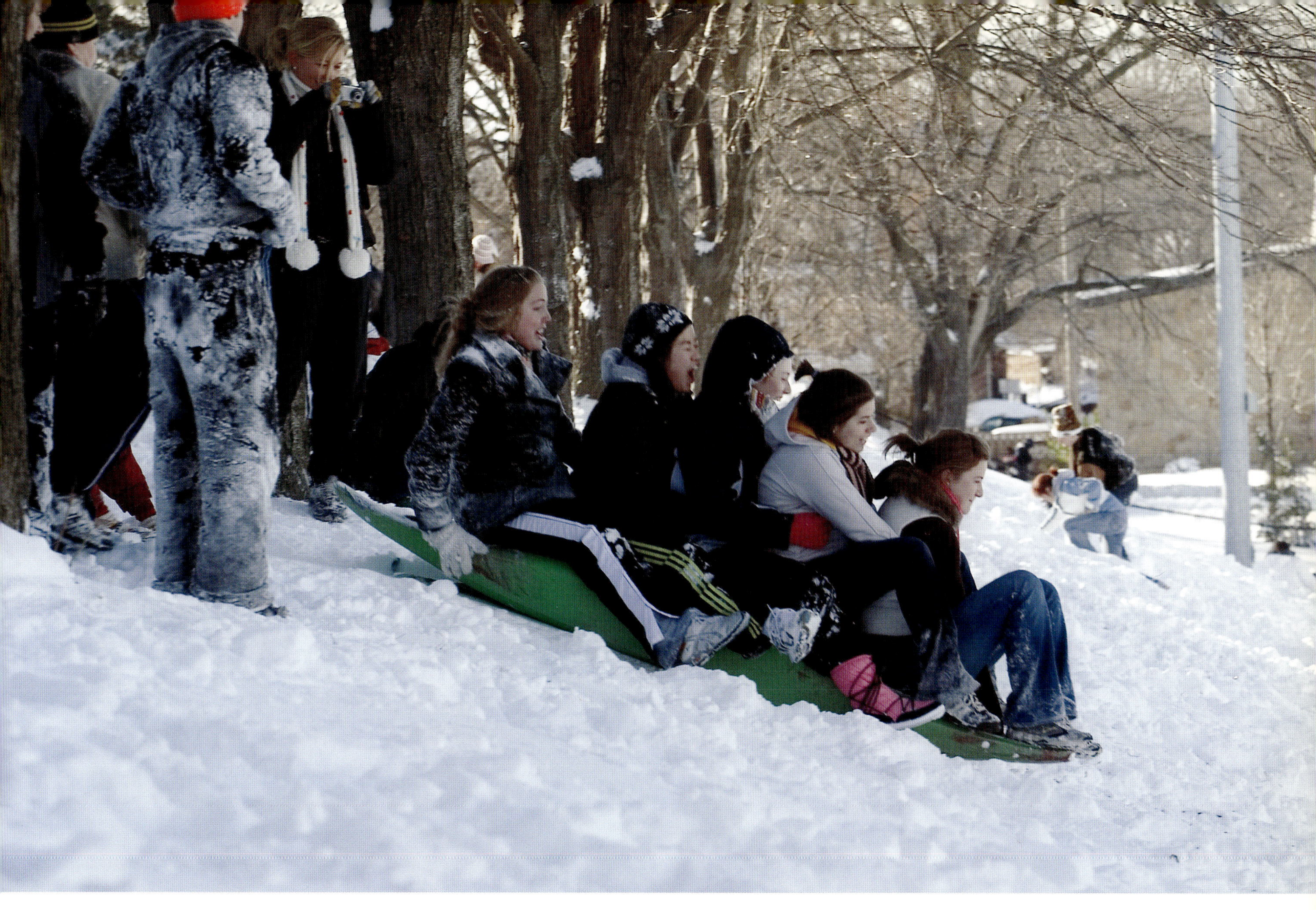

On December 1, 2006, fourteen inches of snow prompt a snow day on campus. A kayak doubles as a sled on a hill along Maryland Avenue near Stankowski Field.

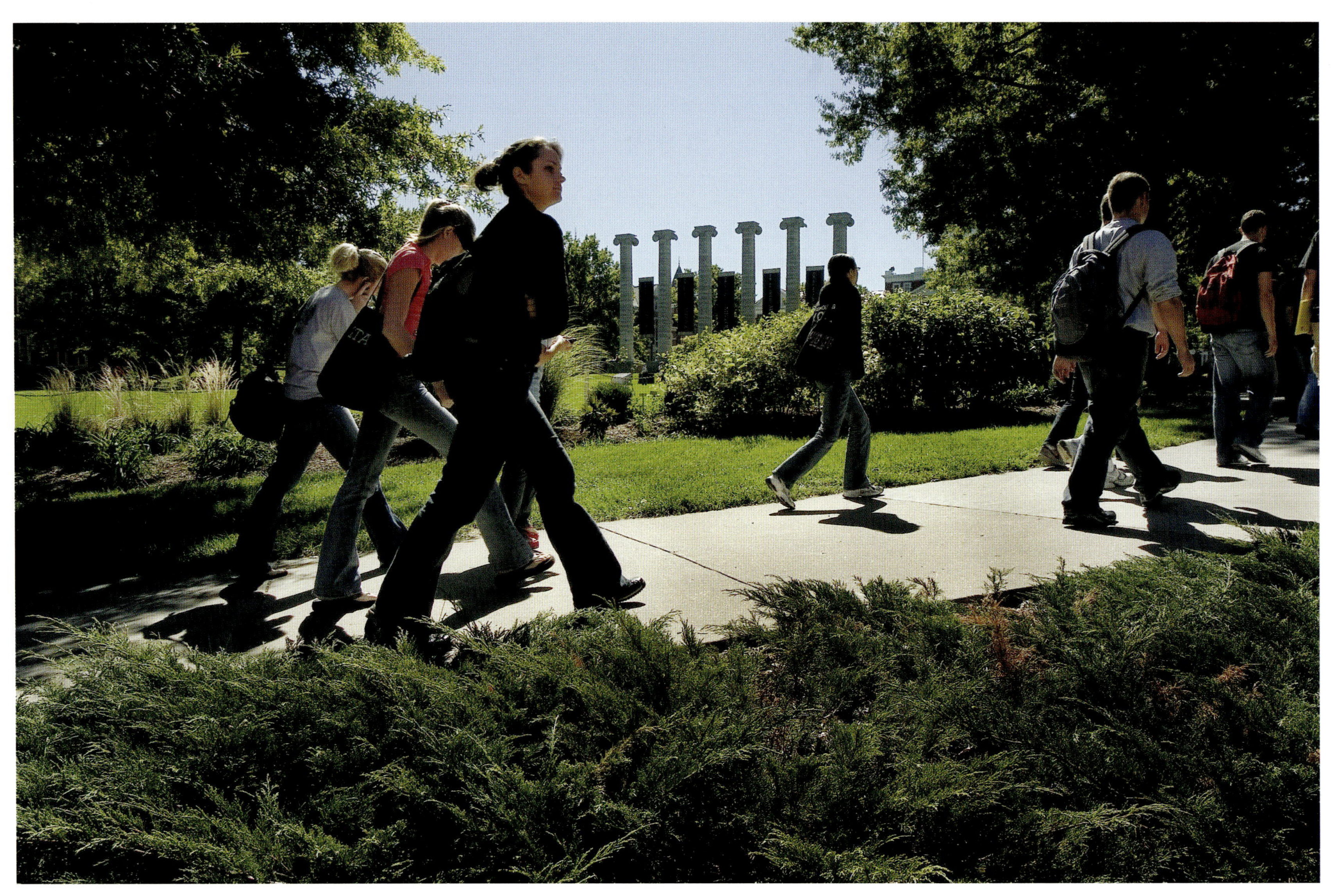

After class, students head from the Geological Sciences Building up a slight hill lined with junipers.

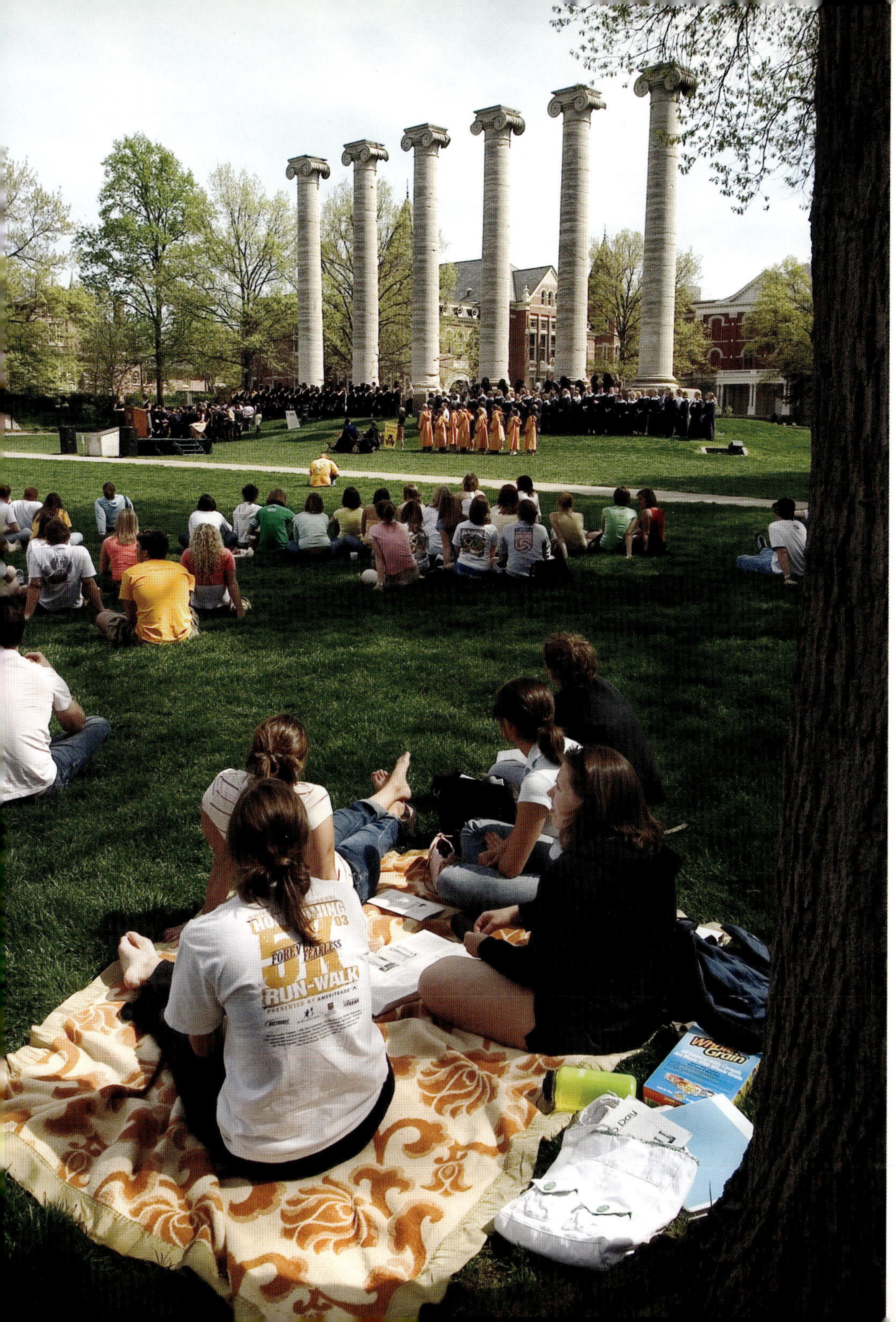

Family and friends gather to watch Tap Day ceremonies unfold at the base of the Columns.

Inductees into the Mystical 7 honorary society clasp hands before being introduced during Tap Day ceremonies honoring outstanding students, faculty, and alumni. The year 2007 marks the group's hundredth anniversary. It emphasizes leadership, integrity, scholarship, and service.

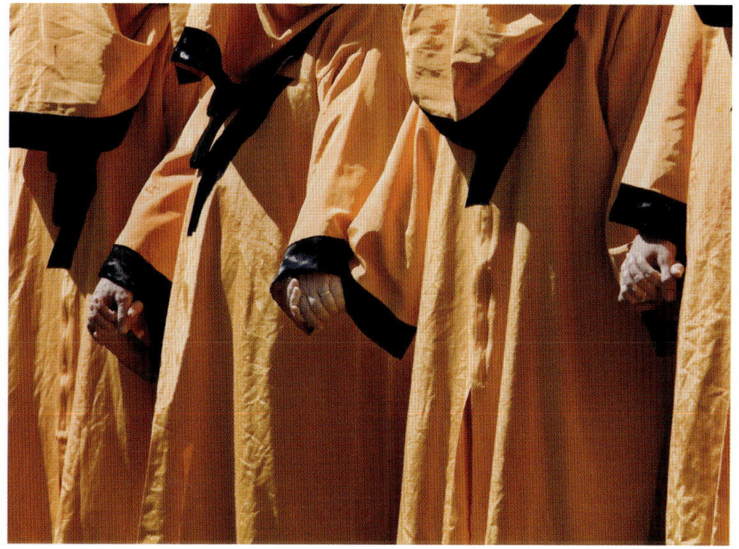

The swimming area in the Student Recreation Complex features a lazy river.

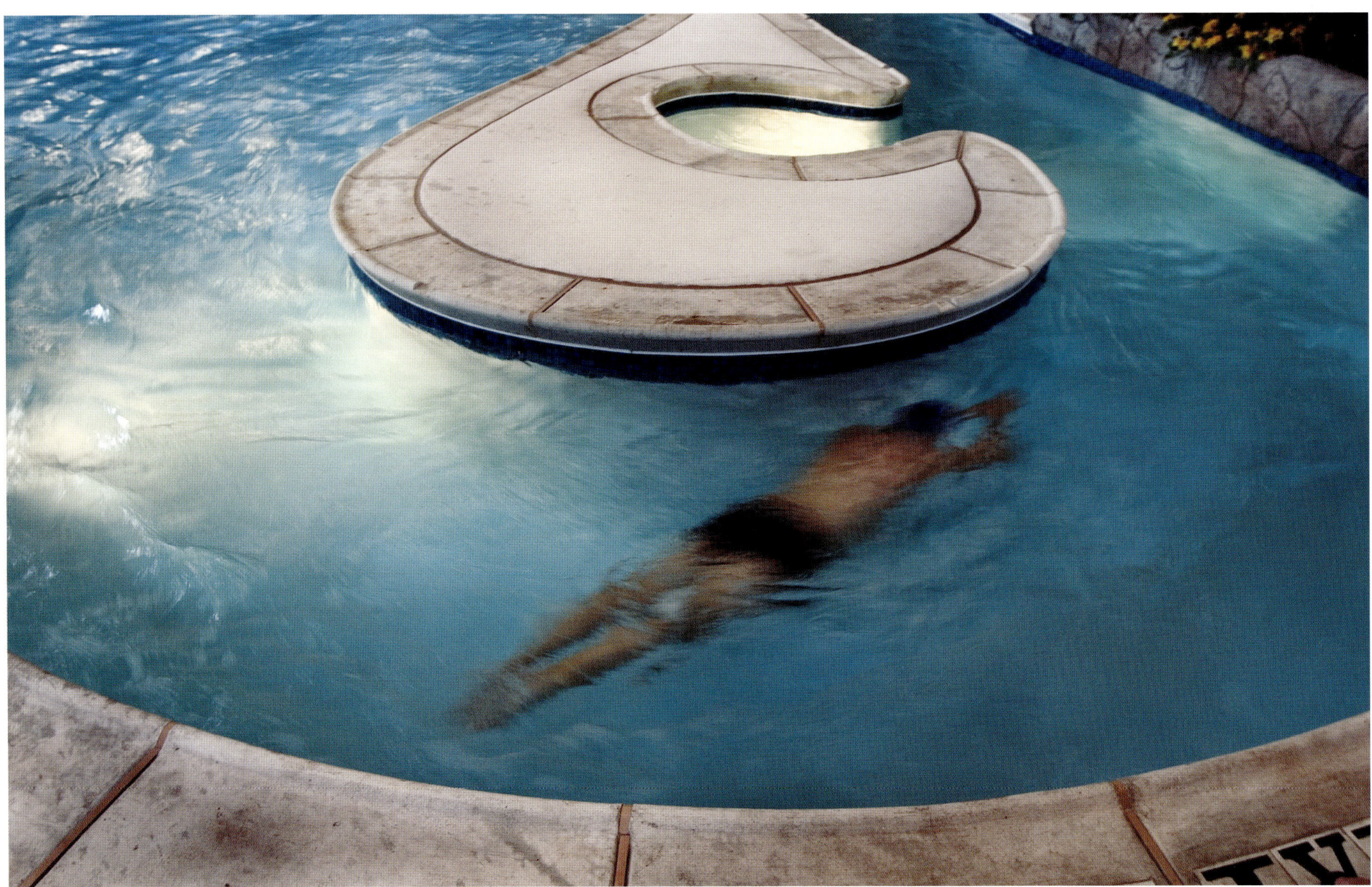

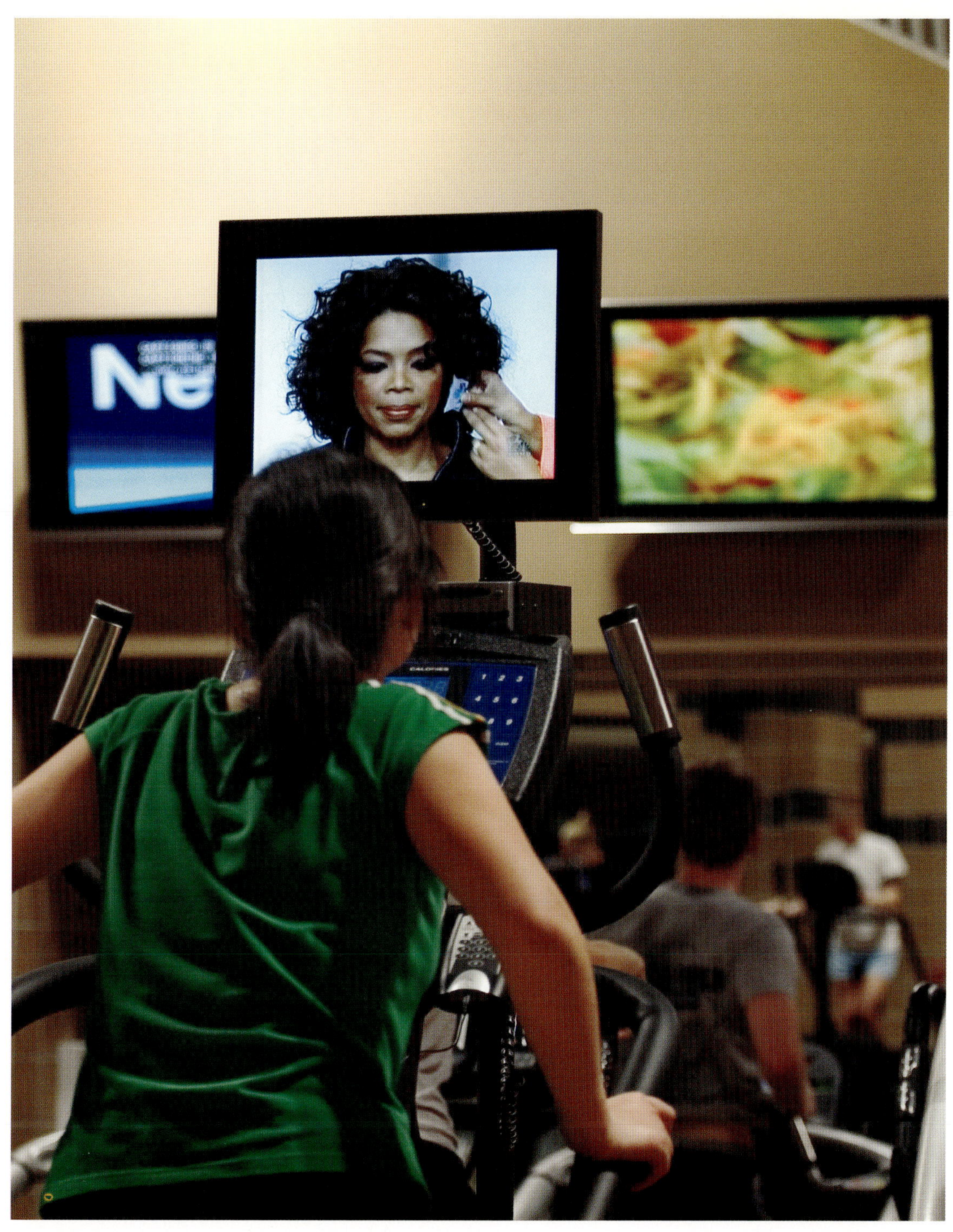

Watching *The Oprah Winfrey Show* on a flat-screen television keeps students focused during cardiovascular workouts in the Jungle Gym at the Student Recreation Complex.

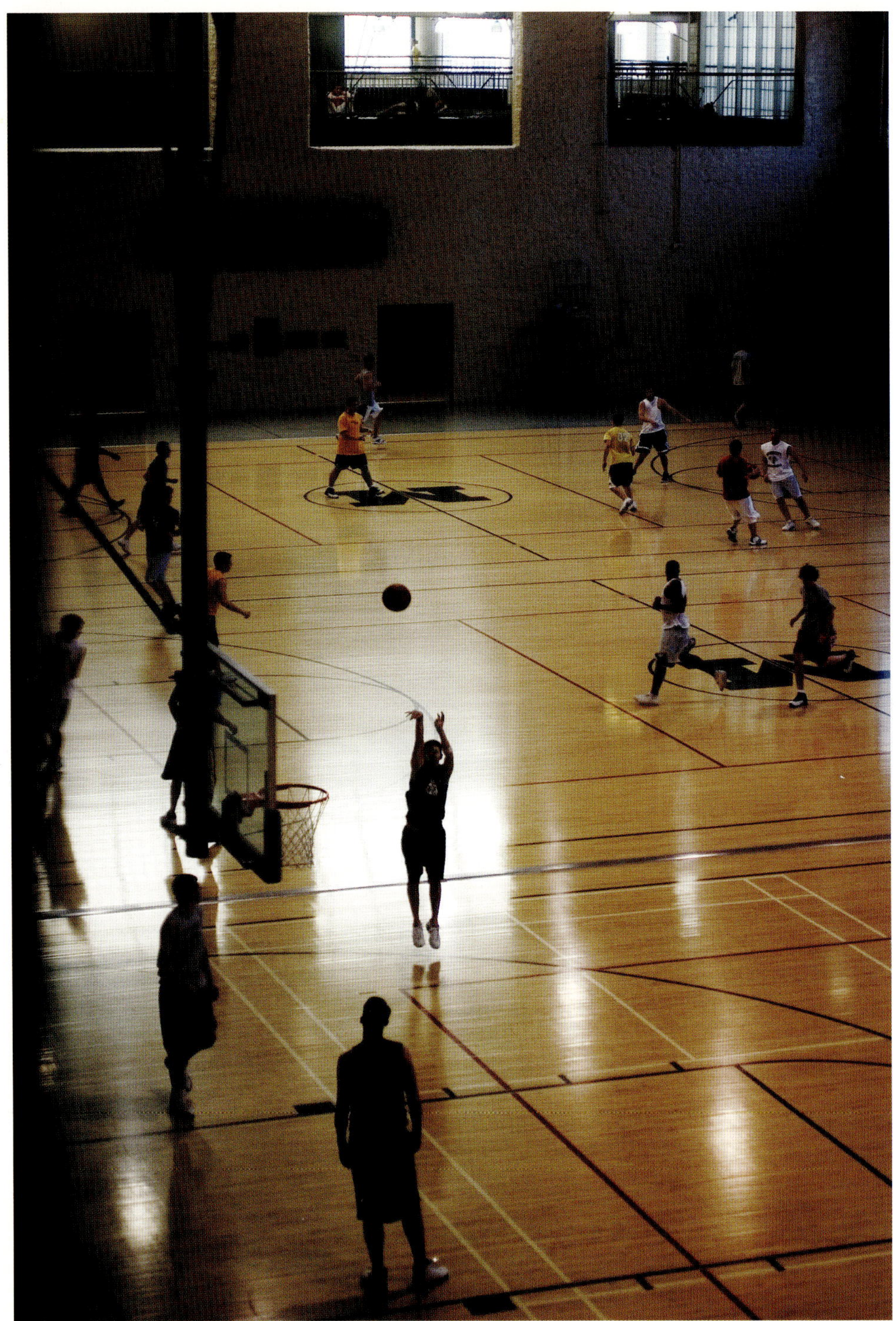

Pickup and intramural games occupy the ten basketball courts in the recreation center. These renovated courts are located in the original Brewer Feildhouse.

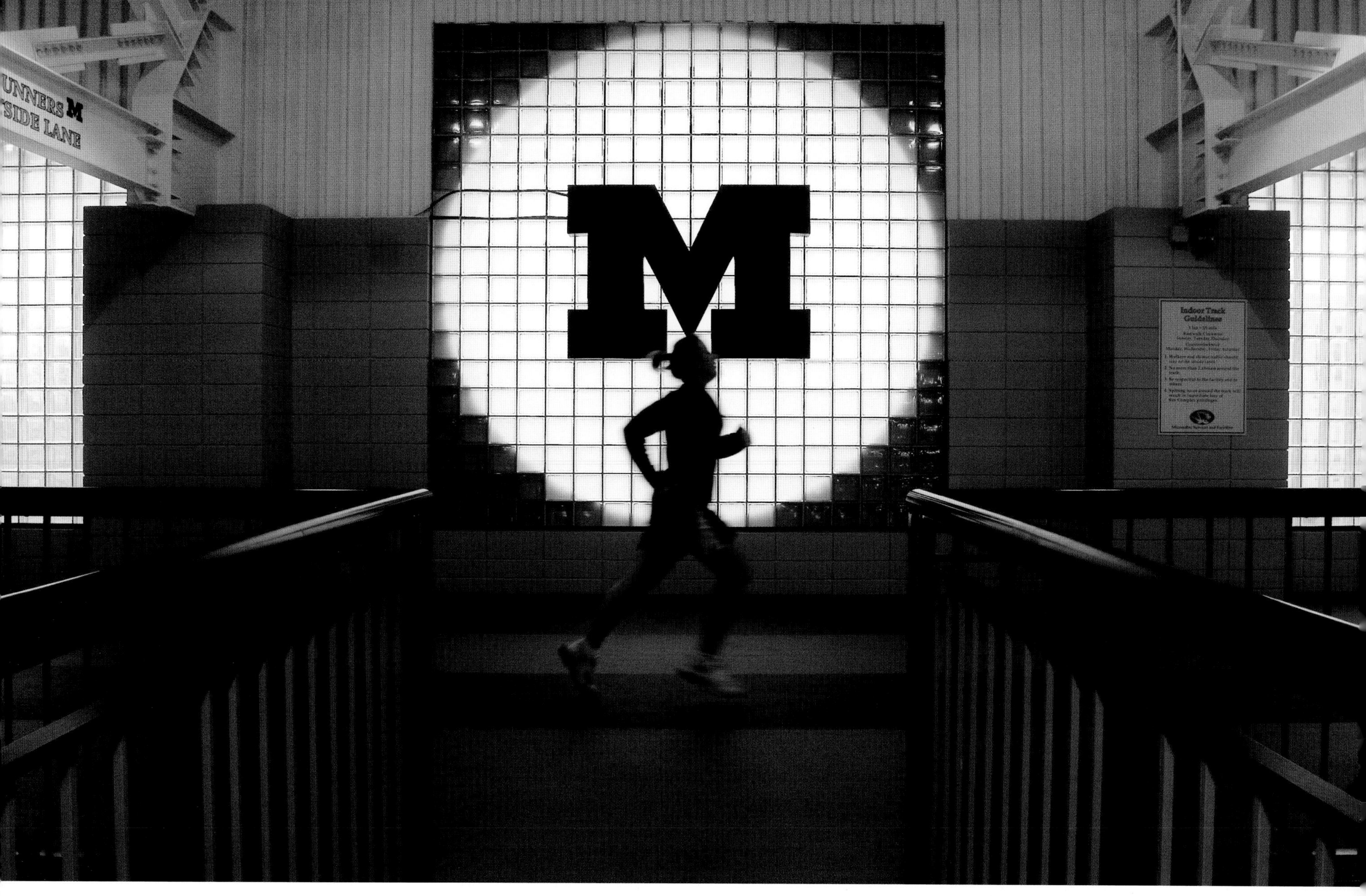

Runners, walkers, and people using wheelchairs are welcome on the elevated track of the recreation center.

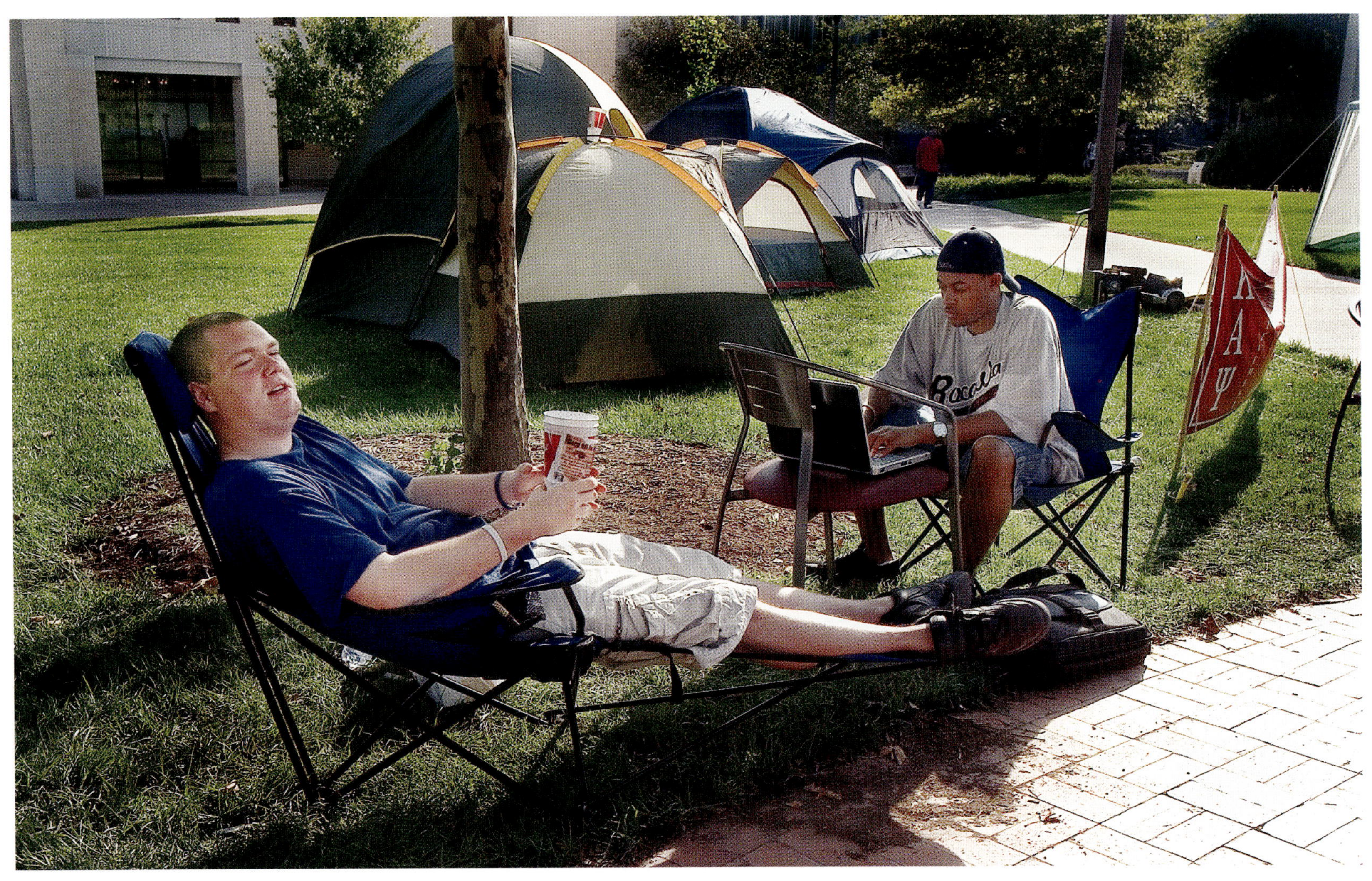

After Hurricane Katrina devastated the Gulf Coast in September 2005, members of Phi Beta Sigma and other fraternities camped out on Kuhlman Court to raise money for relief efforts.

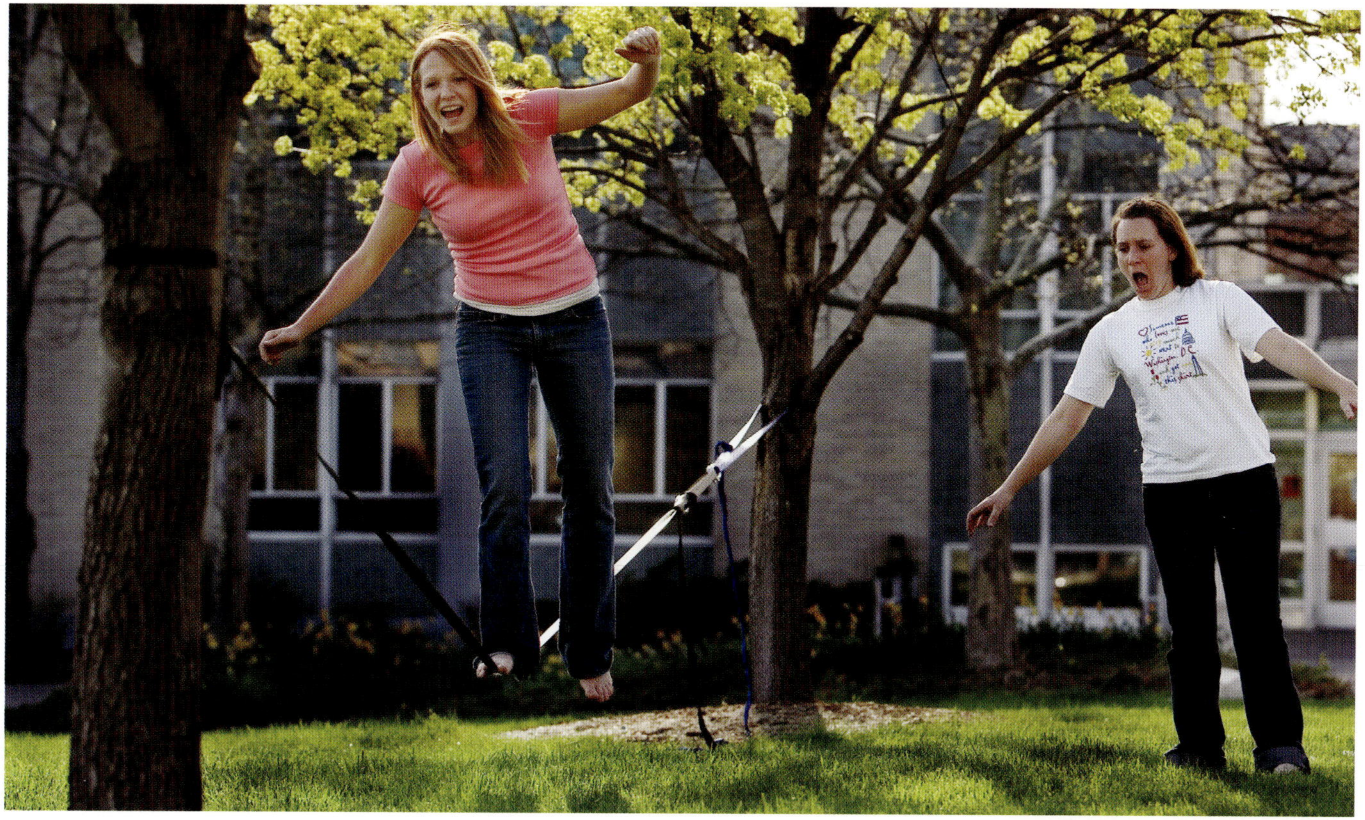

The fall wouldn't be far, but balance is crucial. Students Emily Hoel (*left*) and Abigail Havens practice balancing on a slack line tied to linden trees east of the Arts and Science Building on Kuhlman Court.

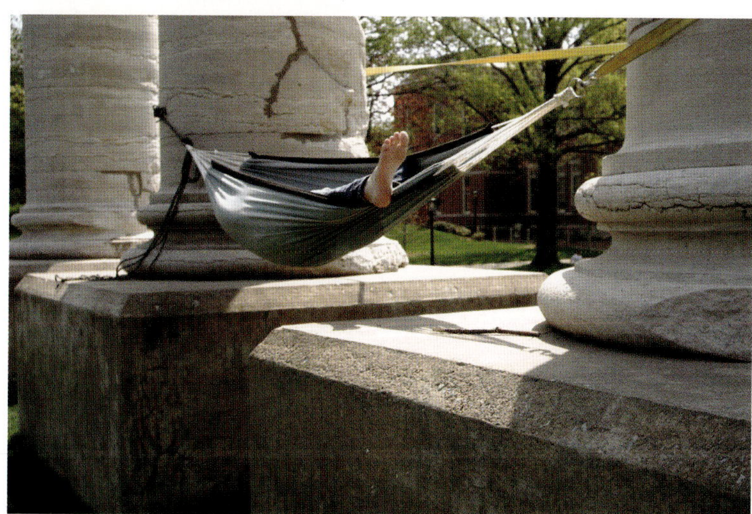

Perpetually tired college students can nap almost anywhere. This one uses the Columns to support his hammock.

*E*mily Moorkamp (*left*) and Emily Jones wait for friends in Brady Commons.

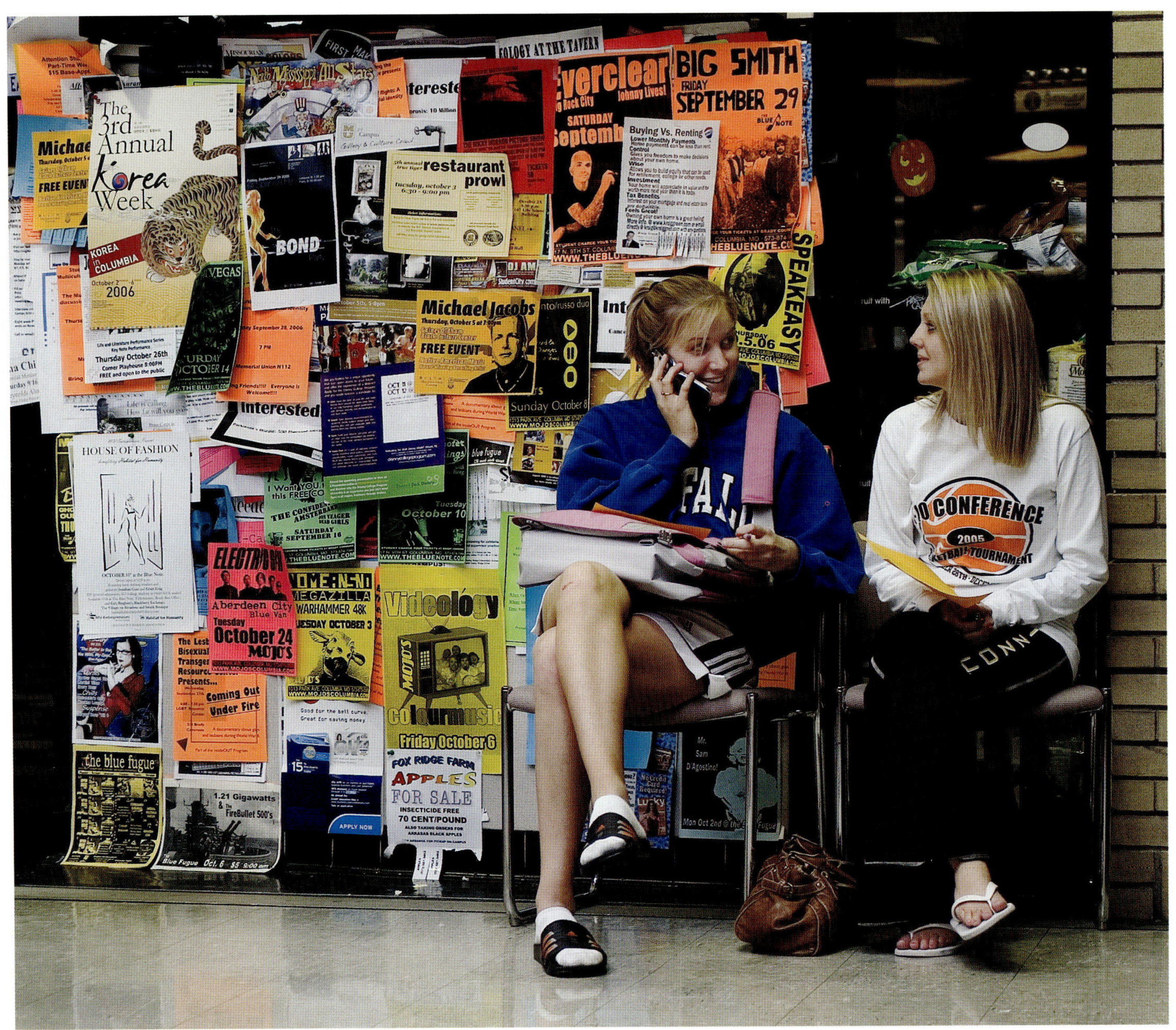

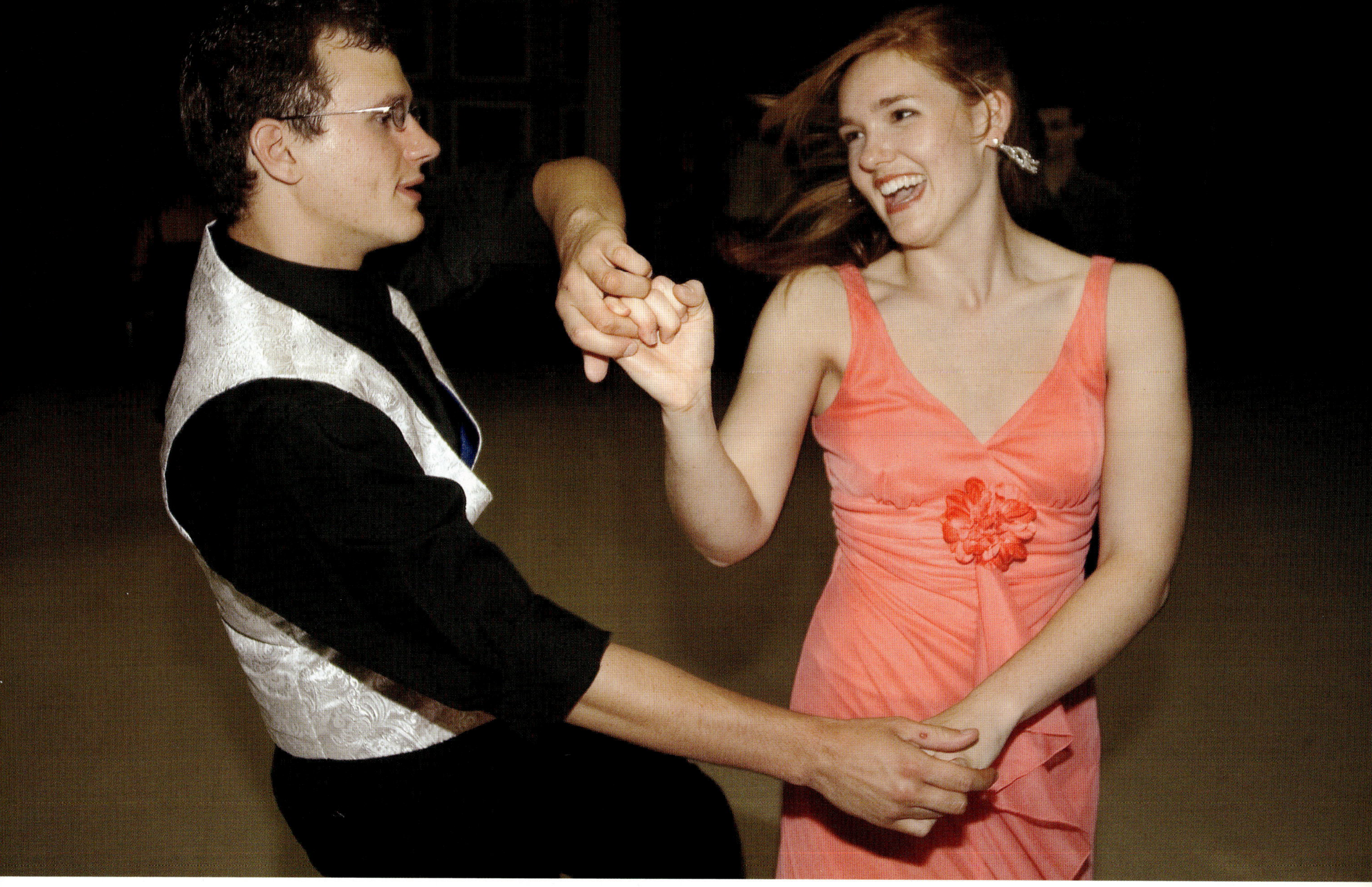

After months of practice, Lucas Naeger and Louise Allen show off their dance skills at the spring semiformal held by Mizzou Ballroom Dance, a student club, on April 30, 2006.

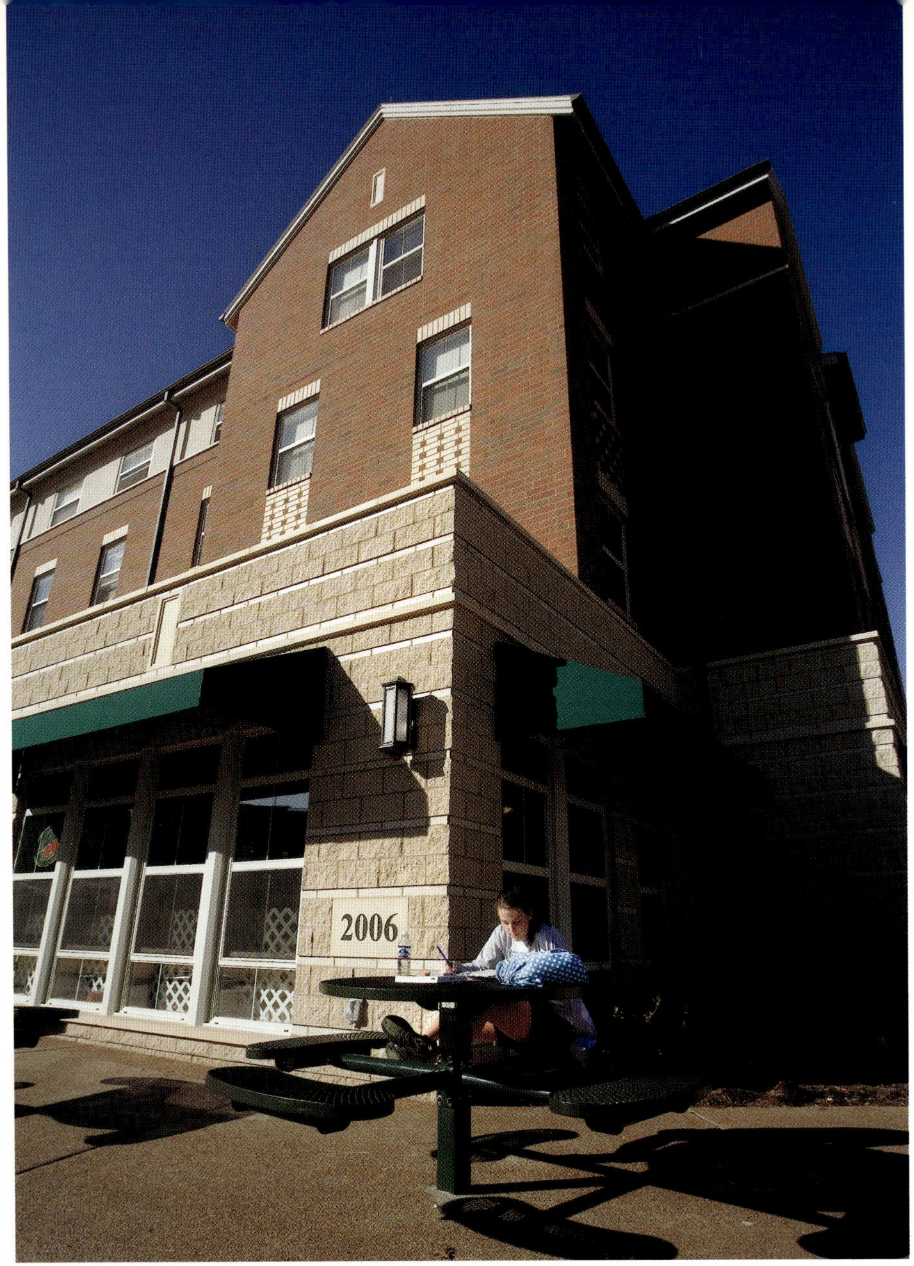

Elaine Delph finds her place in the sun outside Southwest Campus Housing, Providence Road and Stadium Boulevard. Three halls—North, Center, and South—opened in fall 2006 and offer suite-style rooms.

Architectural details such as an open book are included on Southwest Campus Housing buildings.

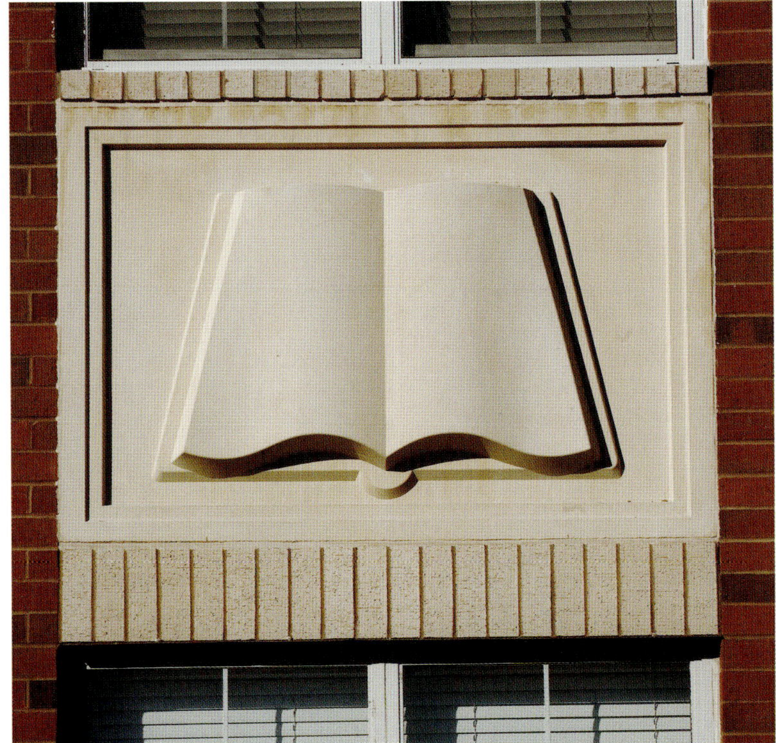

*M*ultiple computers, televisions, a microwave, and a mini refrigerator complete dorm life for students in Hatch Hall.

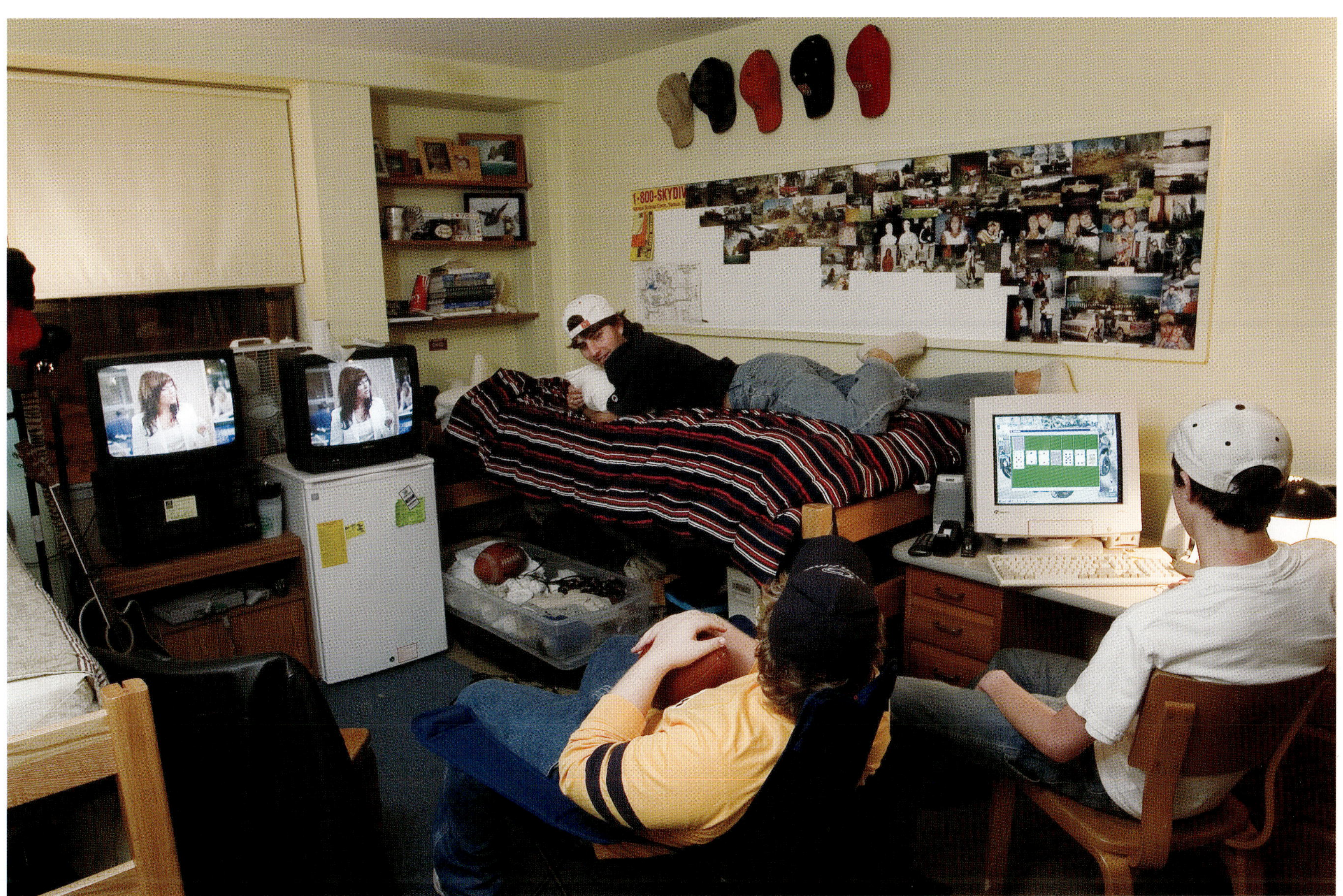

*D*ennis Priest maneuvers a riding lawn mower around flowering red dogwoods in front of Gwynn Hall. The student works for Landscape Services.

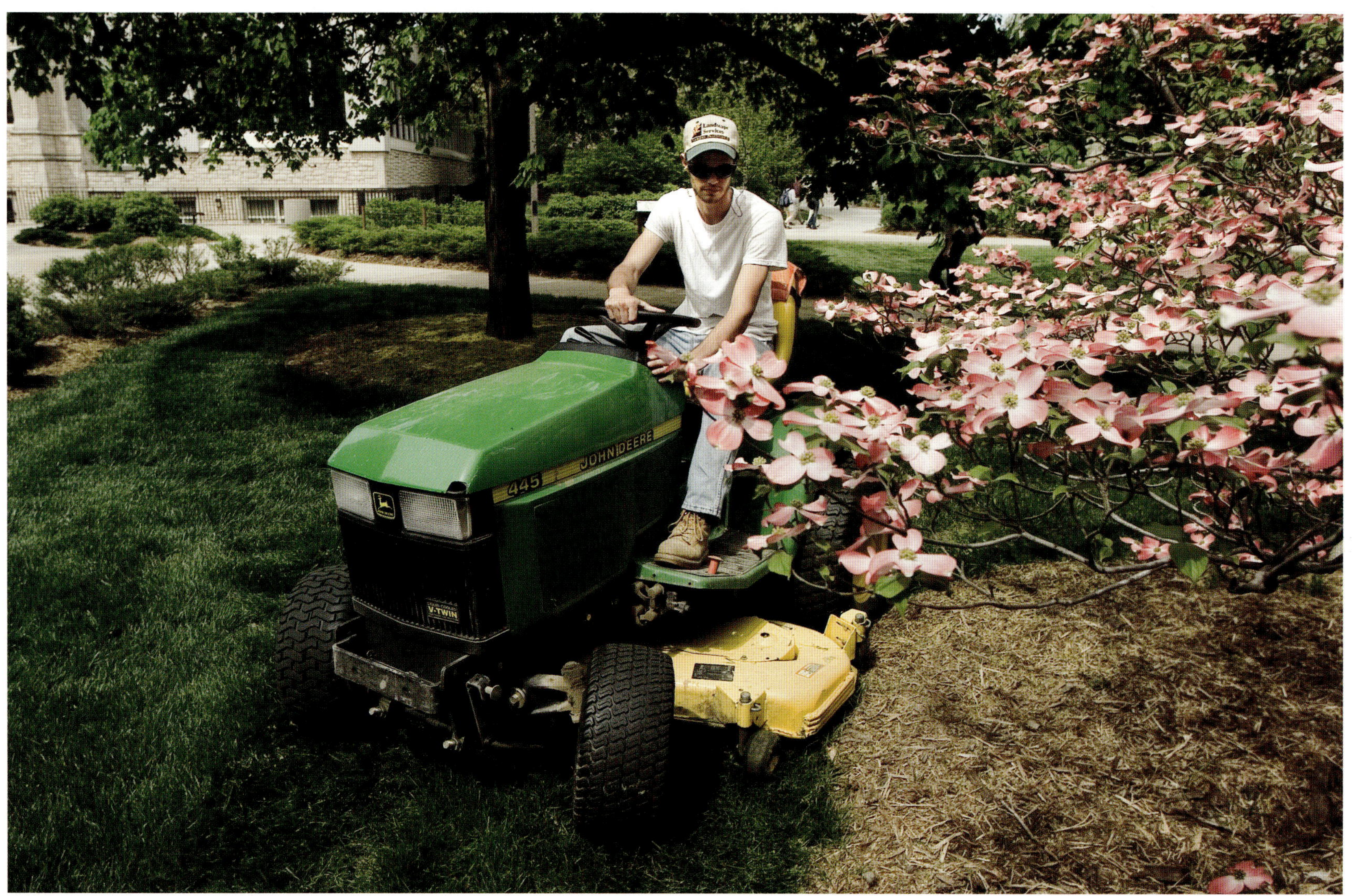

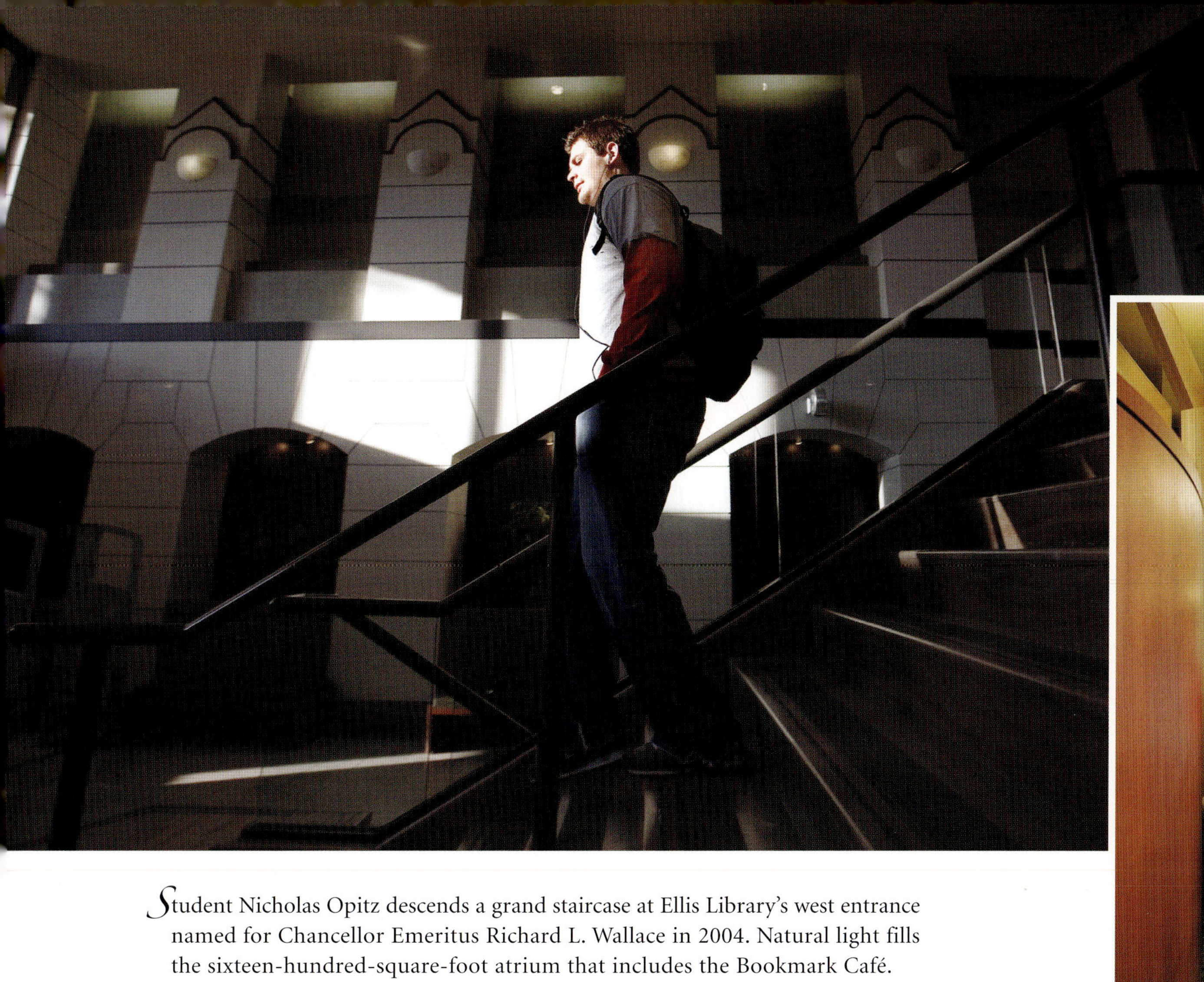

Student Nicholas Opitz descends a grand staircase at Ellis Library's west entrance named for Chancellor Emeritus Richard L. Wallace in 2004. Natural light fills the sixteen-hundred-square-foot atrium that includes the Bookmark Café.

David Smith uses his laptop computer to connect to the Internet in Ellis Library. Since the fall of 2004, the James B. Nutter Family Information Commons has offered students computer workstations and study rooms where they can work independently or in small groups.

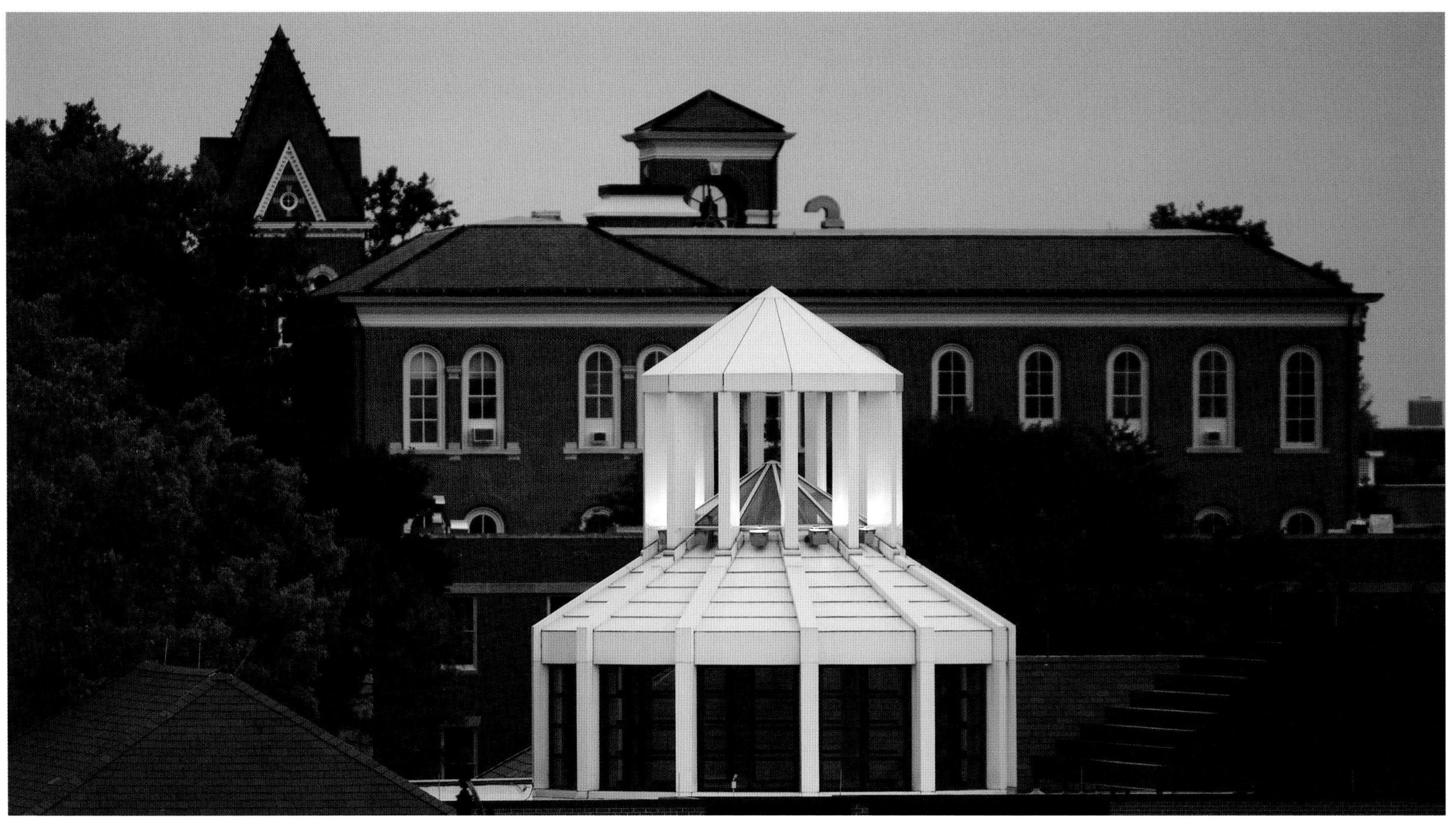

The light from the dome of Lee Hills Hall punctuates the campus skyline. The roof of Switzler Hall, Mizzou's oldest academic building, built in 1871, can be seen in the background.

The interior of the Lee Hills Hall dome inspires students to reach their potential in the field of journalism. Dedicated in 1995 in honor of the journalist Lee Hills, who studied at Mizzou from 1927 to 1929, the structure is one of four School of Journalism buildings, along with Walter Williams, Neff, and Gannett halls. Renovation of Walter Williams and the nearby Sociology Building, with new construction connecting the two, will form the Donald W. Reynolds Journalism Institute. The work is scheduled for completion in June 2008.

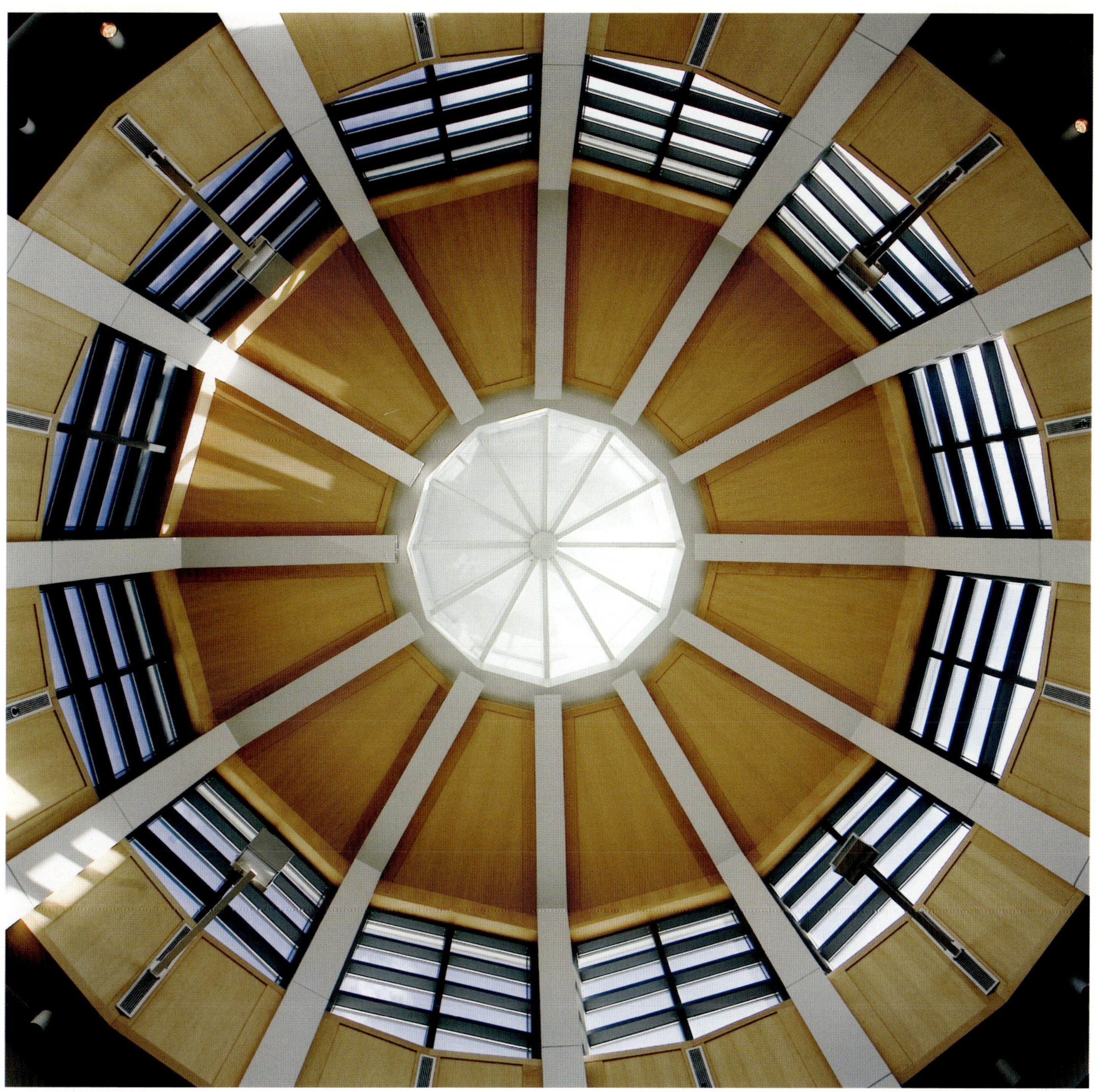

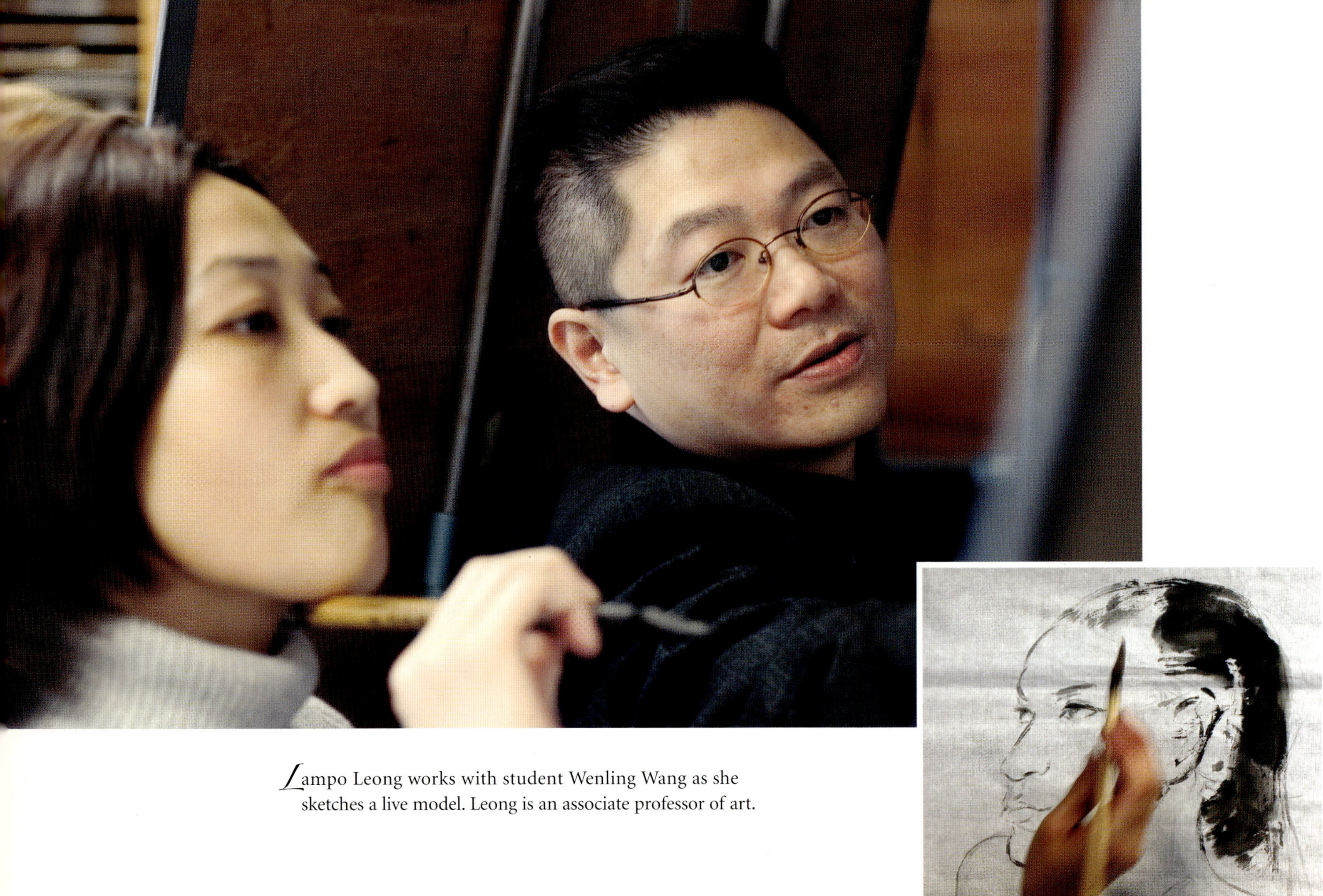

Lampo Leong works with student Wenling Wang as she sketches a live model. Leong is an associate professor of art.

Dedicated in 2002, Cornell Hall brought all of the faculty and academic units of the College of Business under one roof. The grand staircase in its sunlit atrium provides a natural crossroads for business students.

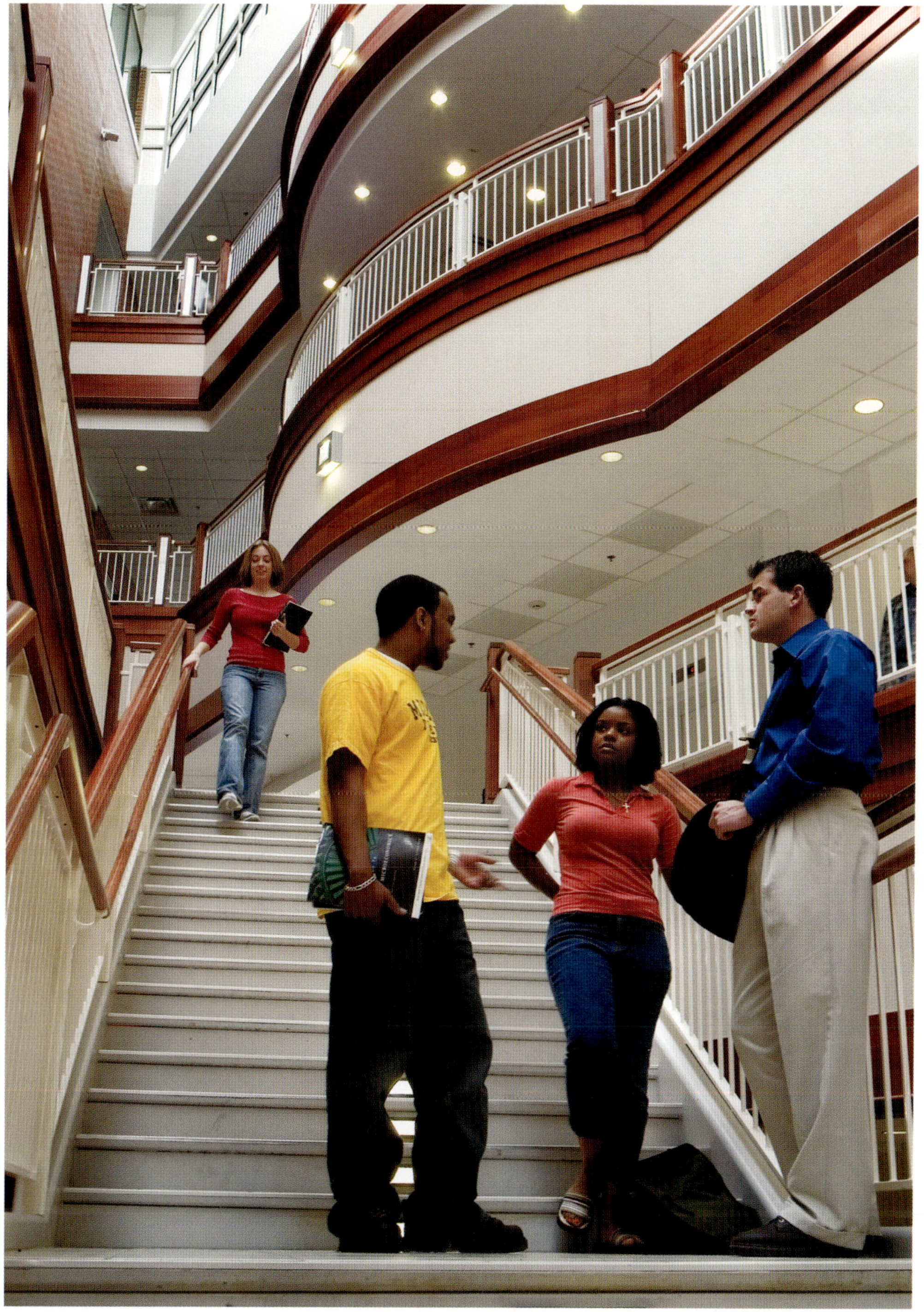

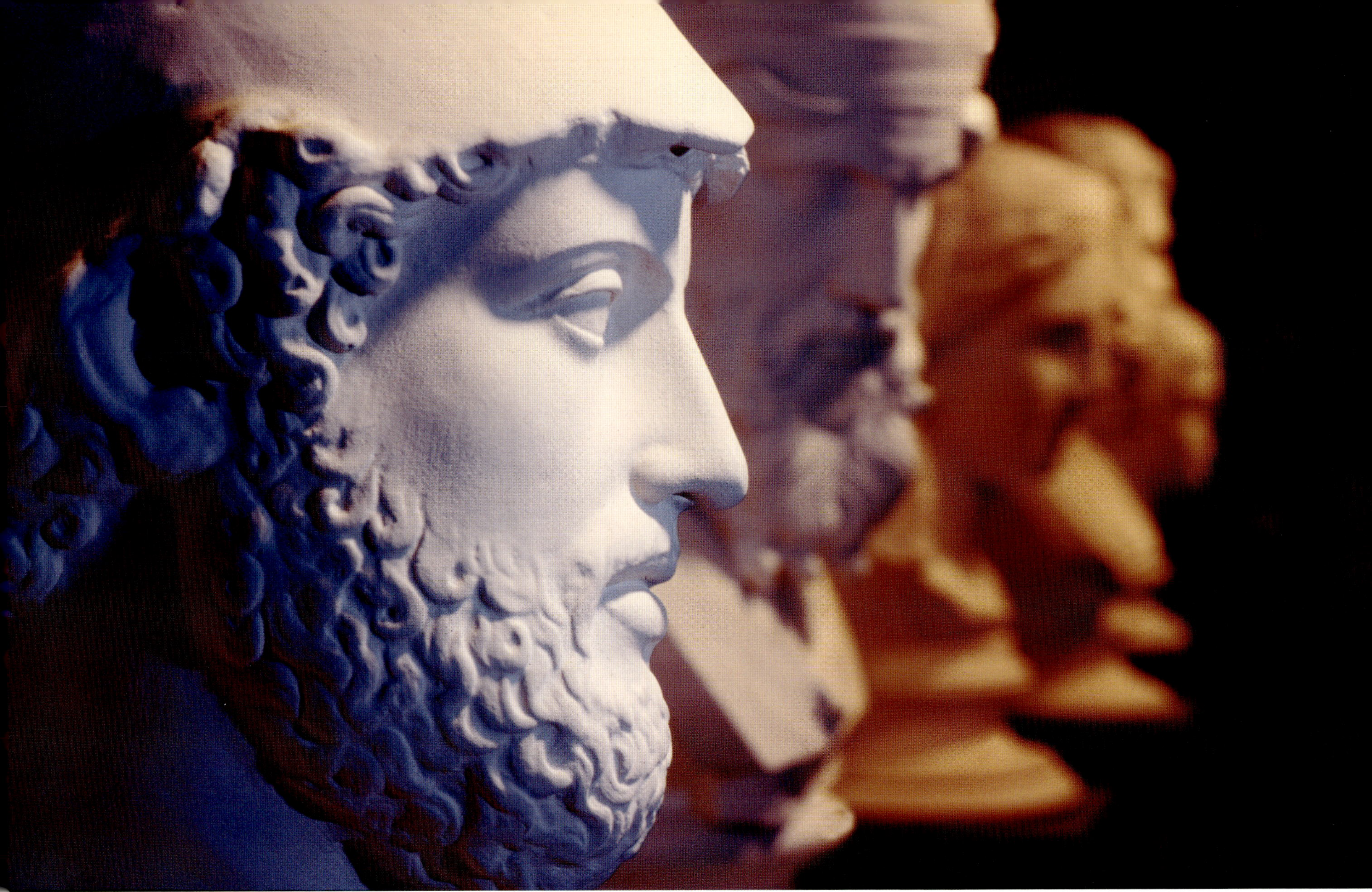

Casts of Greek and Roman sculptures occupy a gallery on the first floor of the Museum of Art and Archaeology in Pickard Hall. The casts, acquired in the 1890s, are used as models for drawing classes as well as for teaching about Greek and Roman art and architecture. The year 2007 marks the museum's fiftieth anniversary.

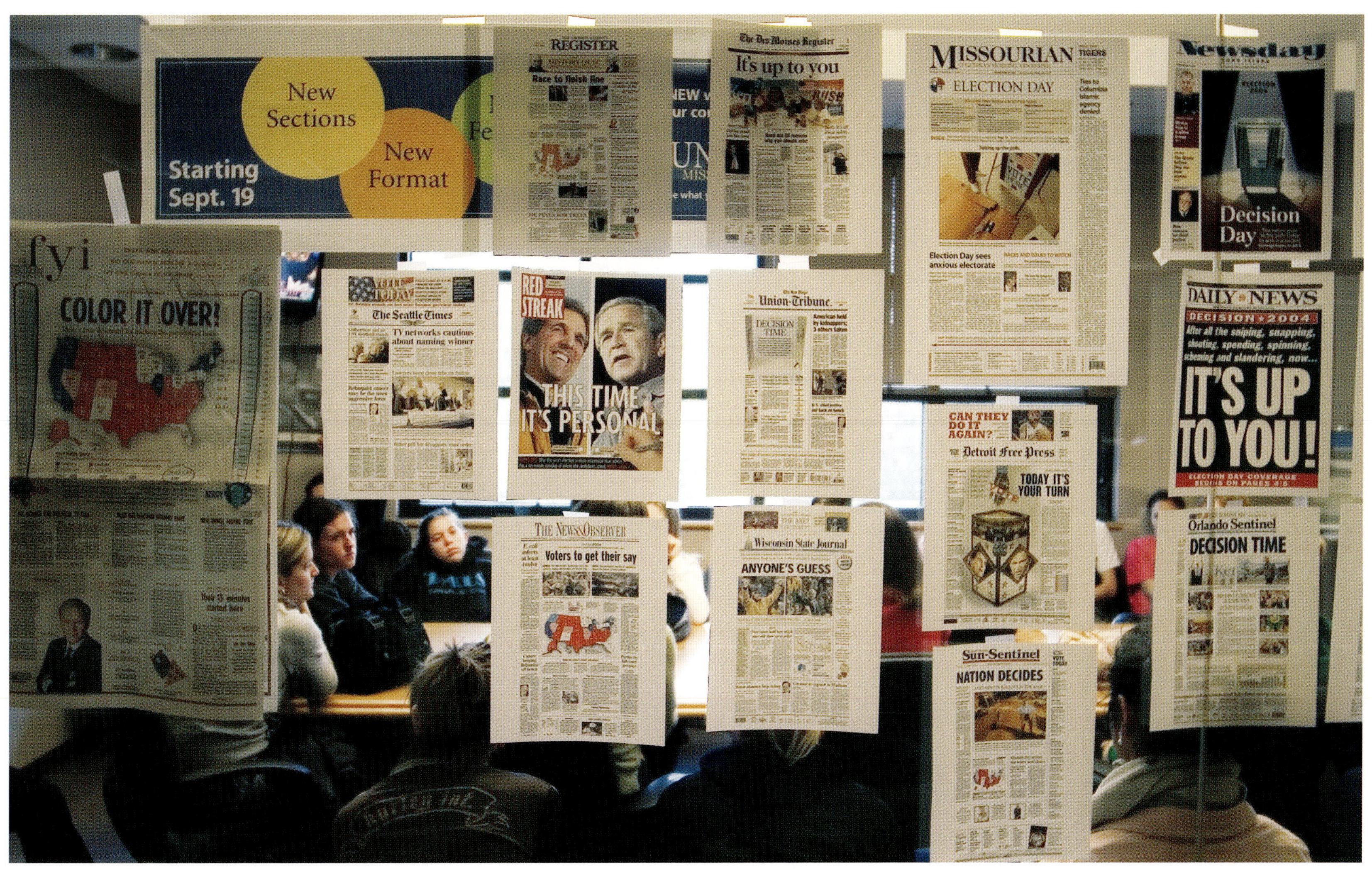

Election coverage is displayed in the *Columbia Missourian* newsroom in Lee Hills Hall on Election Day 2004. Hands-on media work is a hallmark of the School of Journalism, established in 1908.

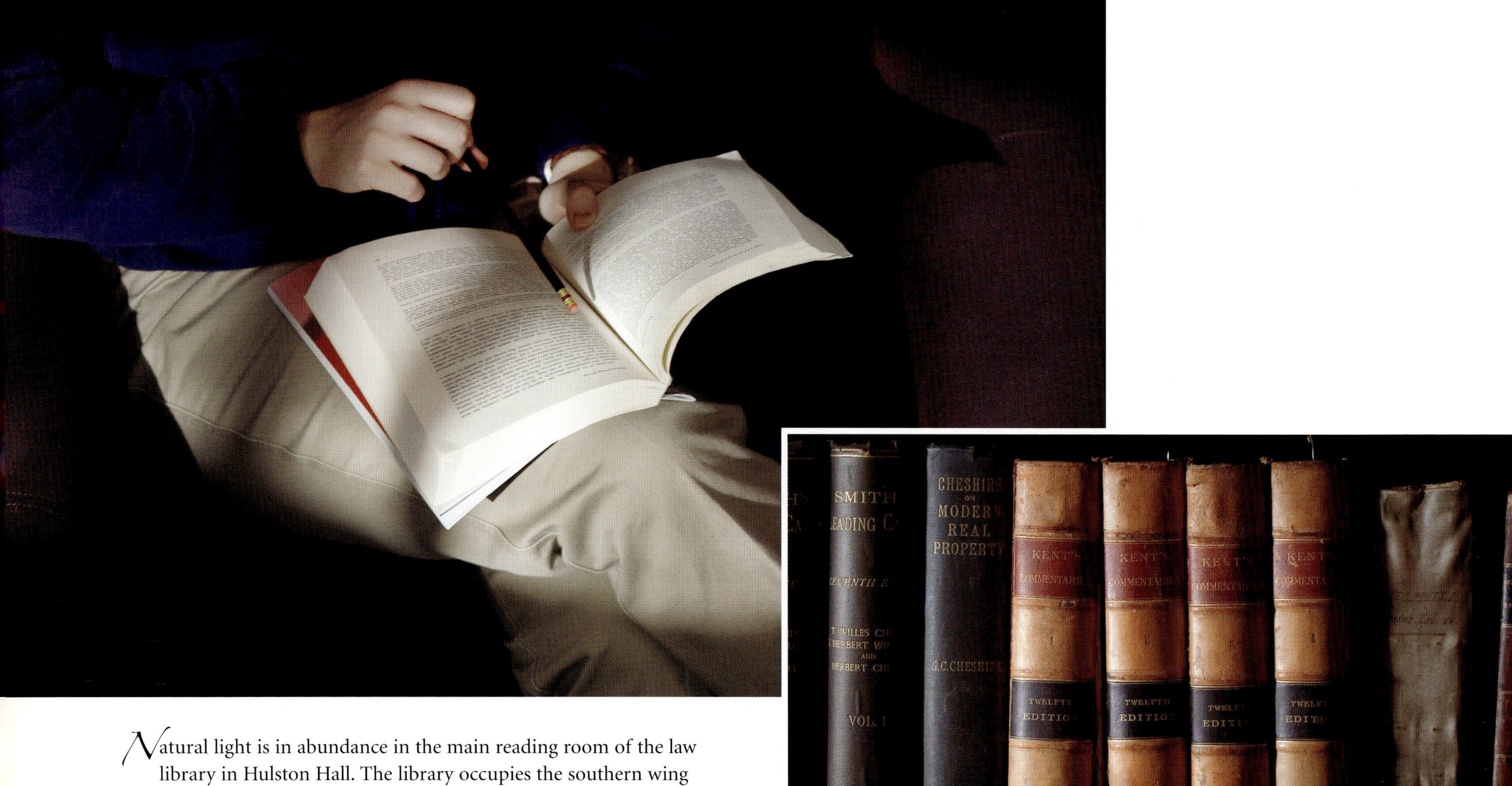

*N*atural light is in abundance in the main reading room of the law library in Hulston Hall. The library occupies the southern wing on all four levels of the building, which was dedicated in 1988.

*F*rom the late Professor William F. Fratcher's private library come these volumes housed in the law library's rare-book room, which carries his name. The climate-controlled room contains a collection of early law books and manuscripts, as well as the famous Lawson Collection of materials on eighteenth- and nineteenth-century trials.

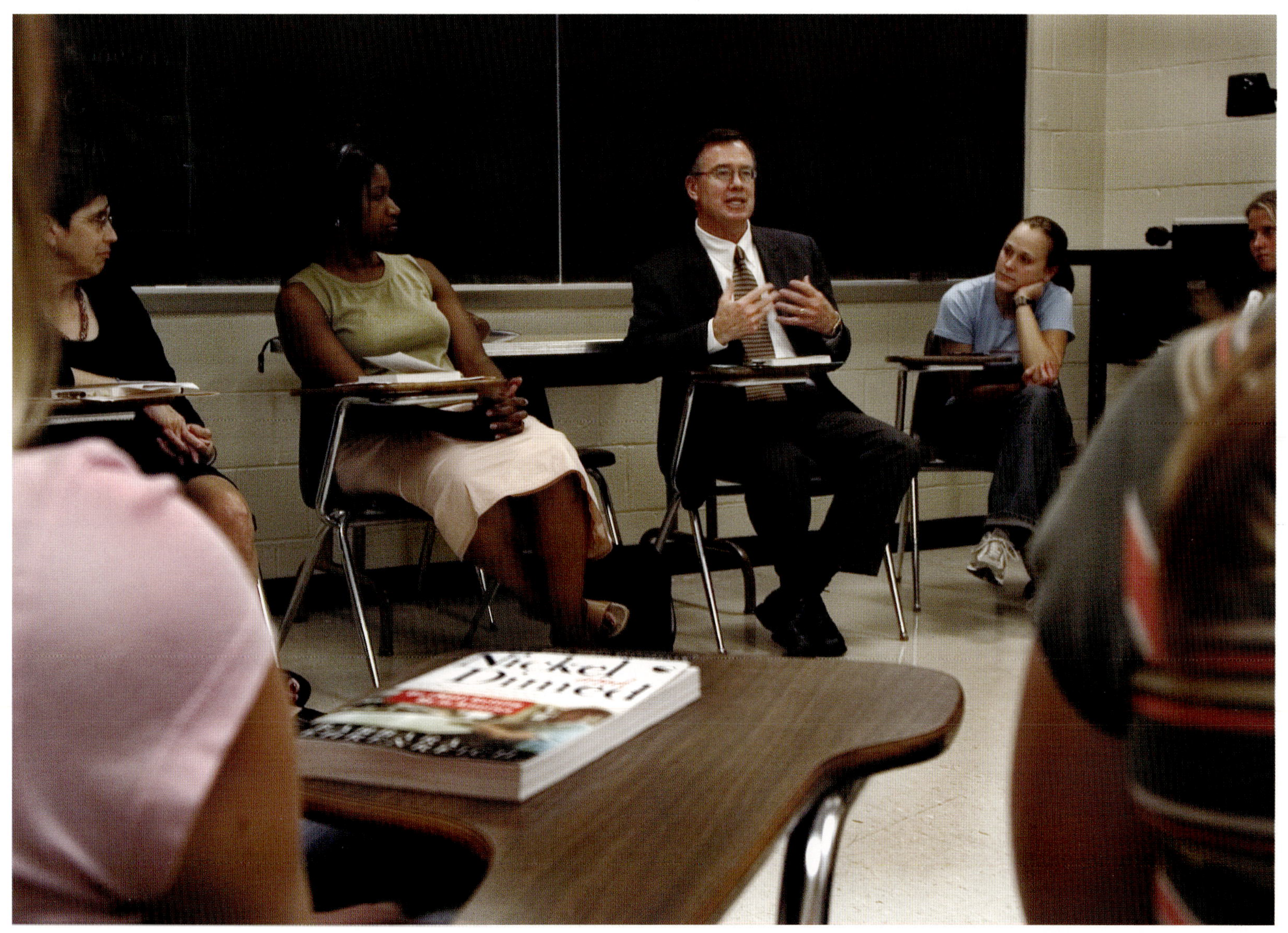

Chancellor Brady Deaton leads a group of new students in a discussion of Barbara Ehrenreich's book *Nickel and Dimed* in August 2004. Deaton was named chancellor on October 1 of that year.

The Sears Plant Growth Facility, located southeast of Memorial Union, was named for the husband-wife geneticist team of Ernie and Lotti Sears in 2001. They helped create a strain of wheat that is resistant to rust disease.

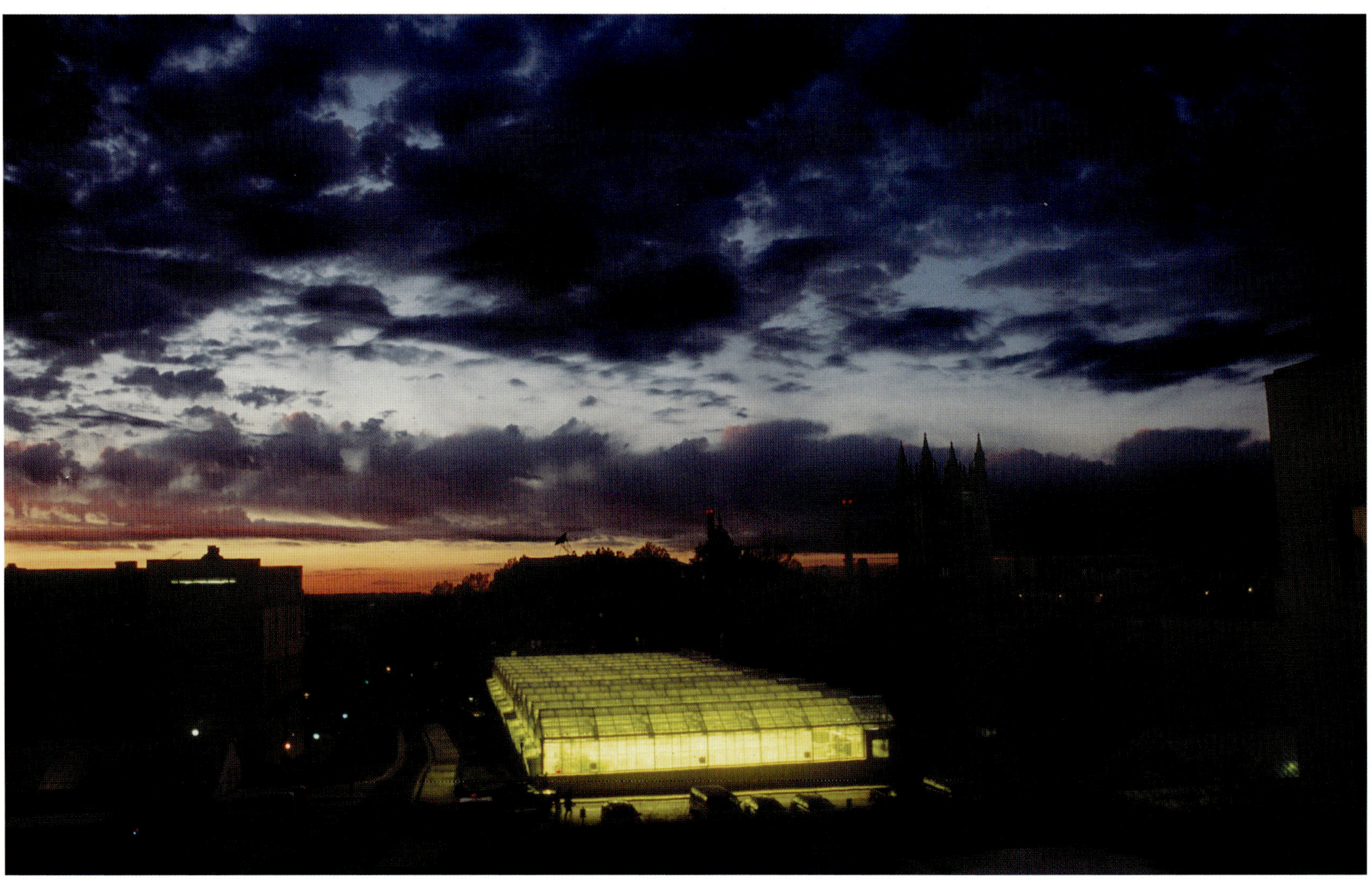

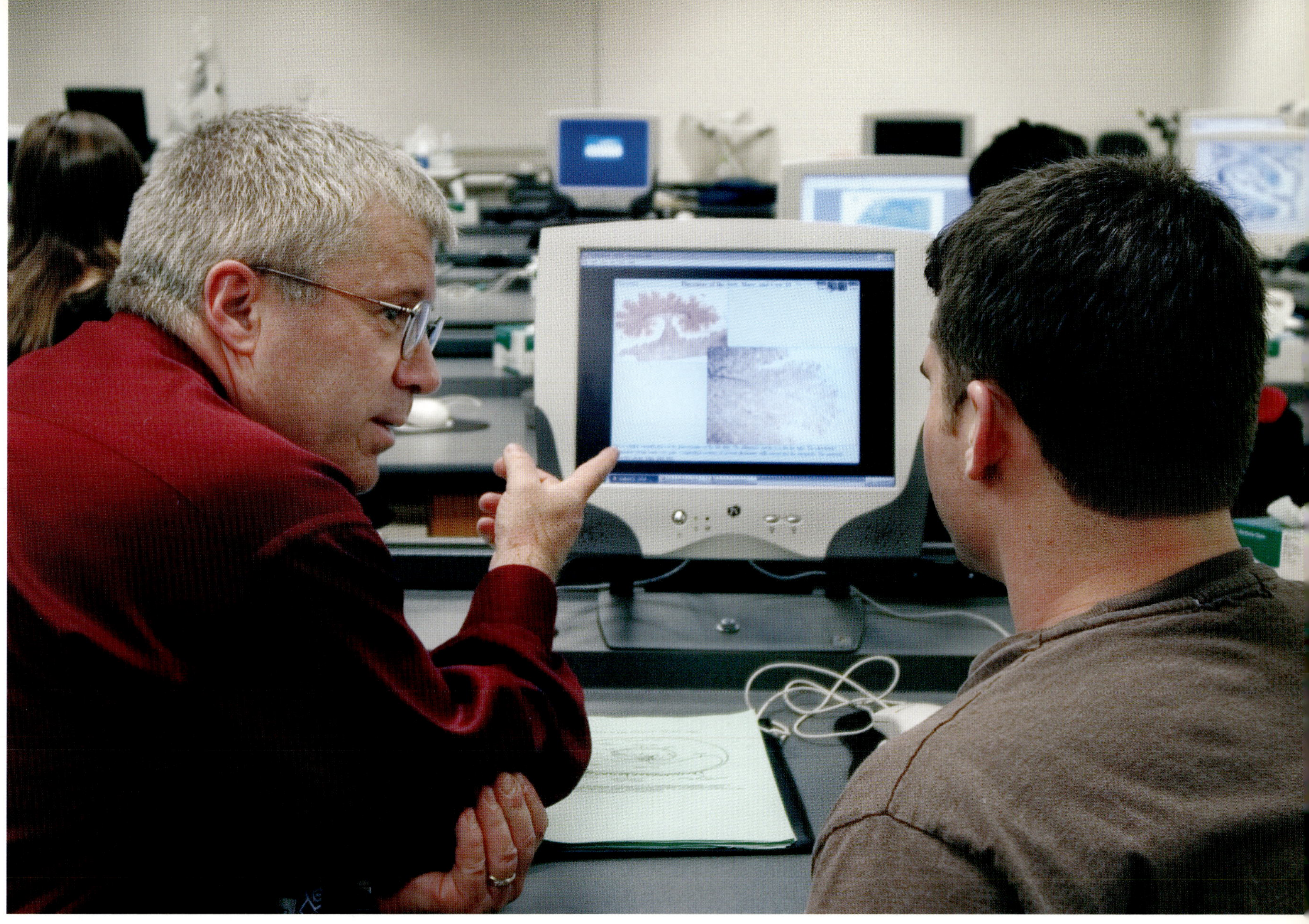

*I*n the microscopic anatomy lab, Brian Frappier helps student Tom Millis identify vascular networks discussed in an earlier lecture. Frappier is a clinical associate professor of biomedical sciences.

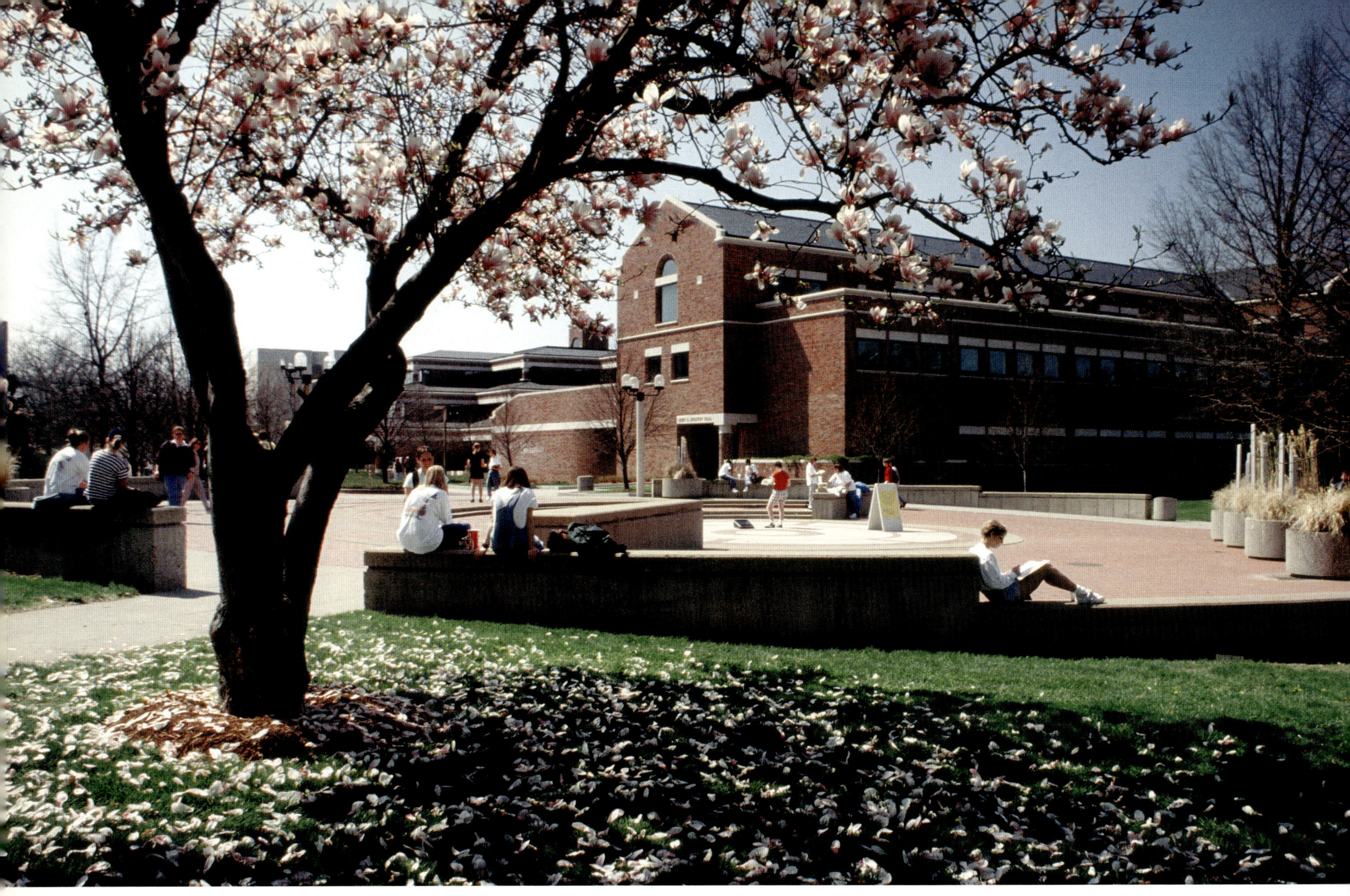

Opinions of students and others resonate from Speakers Circle near Hulston Hall, home of the law school. In early spring, saucer magnolia trees flower with large, fragrant blooms.

In a women's self-defense class in McKee Gymnasium, College of Education instructor Renata Maiorino demonstrates to a student how to defend against an attacker from behind.

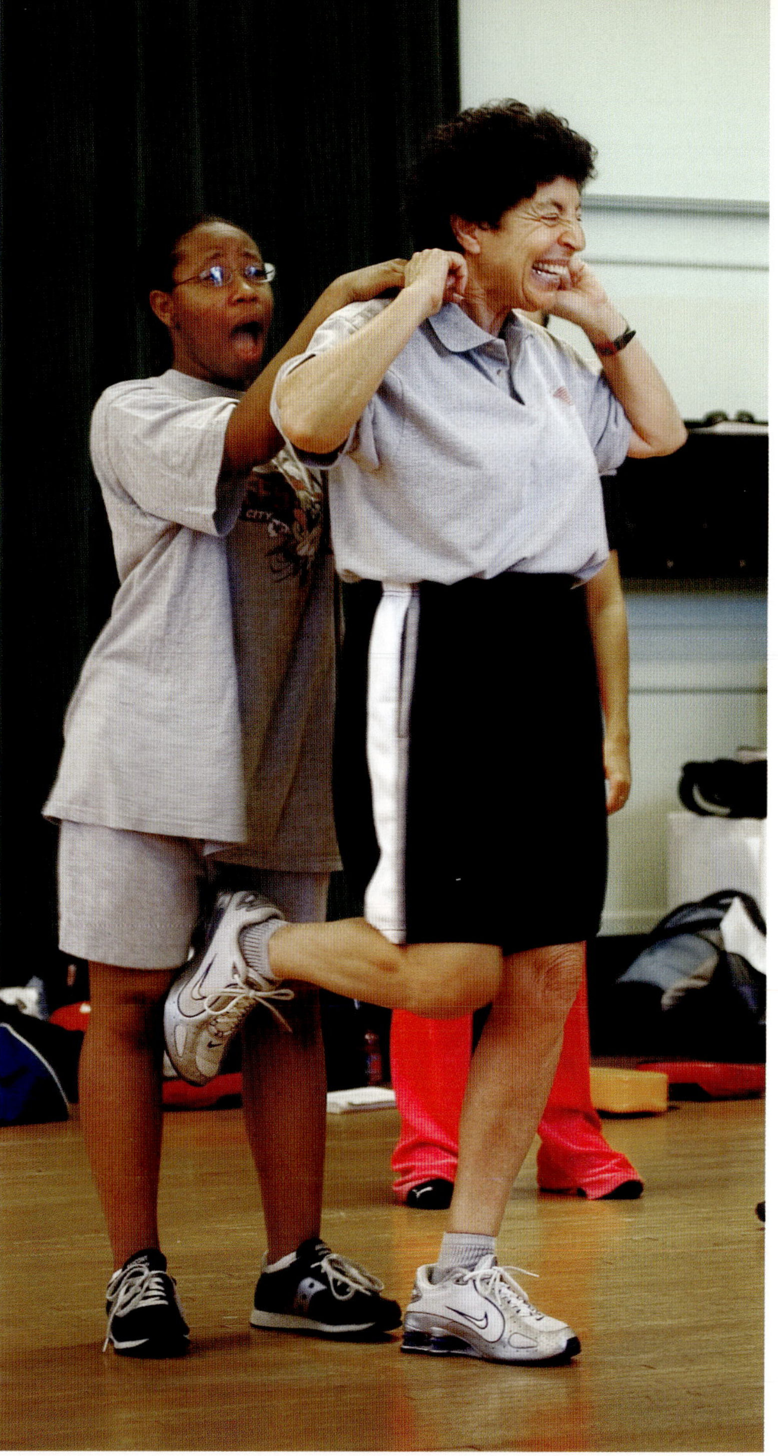

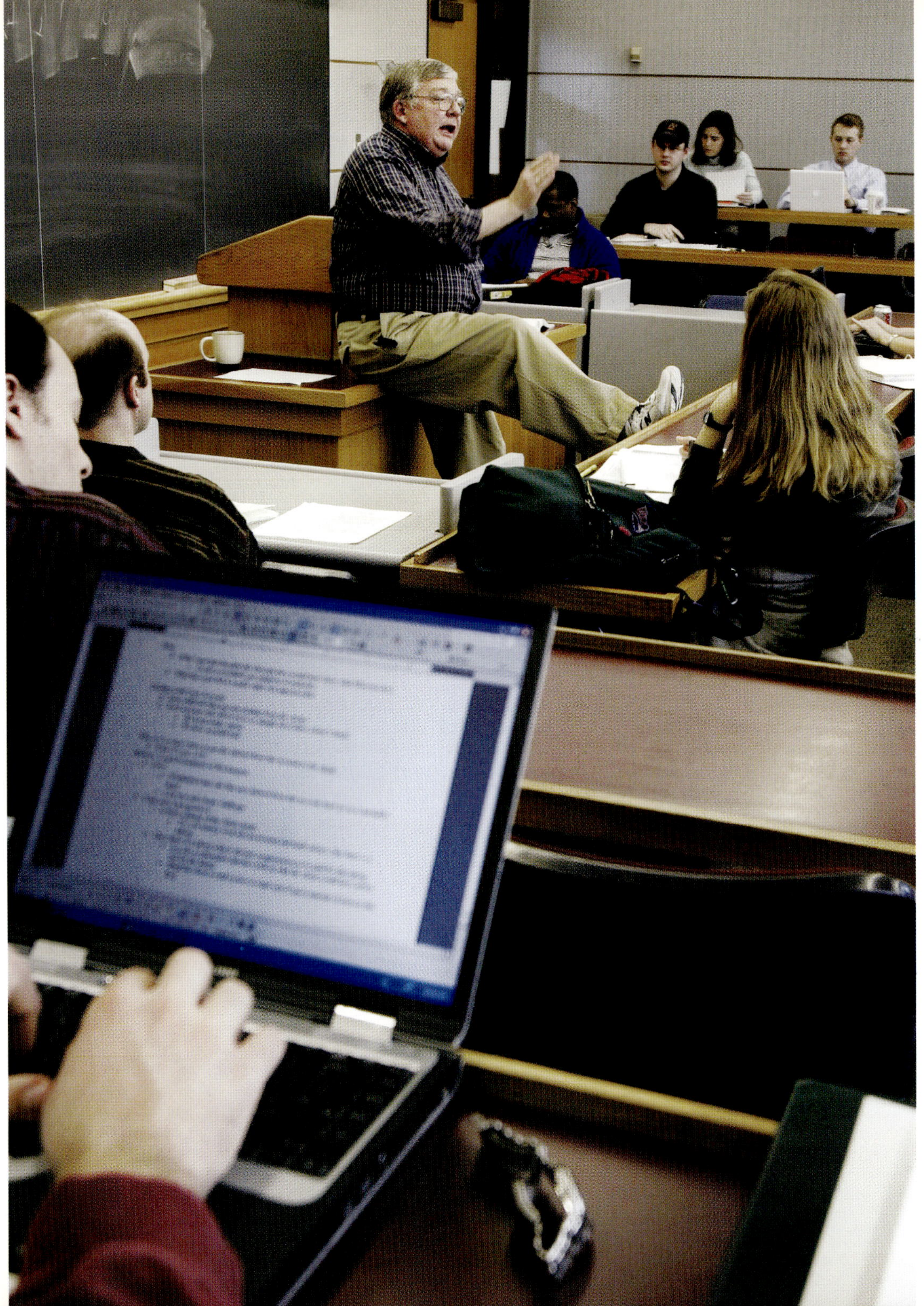

Technology and teaching commingle as a student takes notes on a laptop computer during James Devine's professional responsibility class in Hulston Hall. Devine is the David Ross Hardy professor of law and trial practice.

Lindsey Vansandt studies the skeletal structure of a chicken in a gross-anatomy lab.

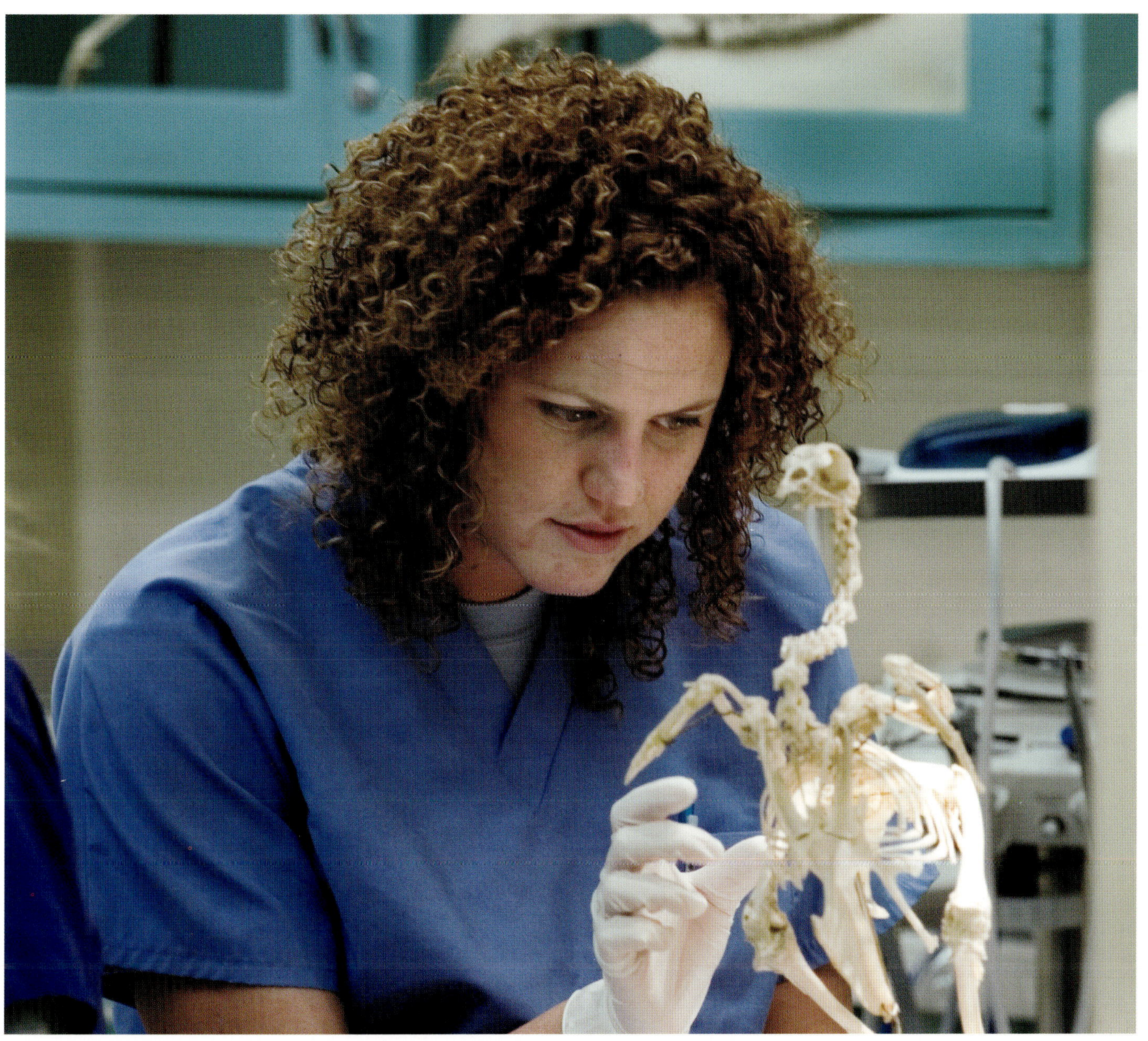

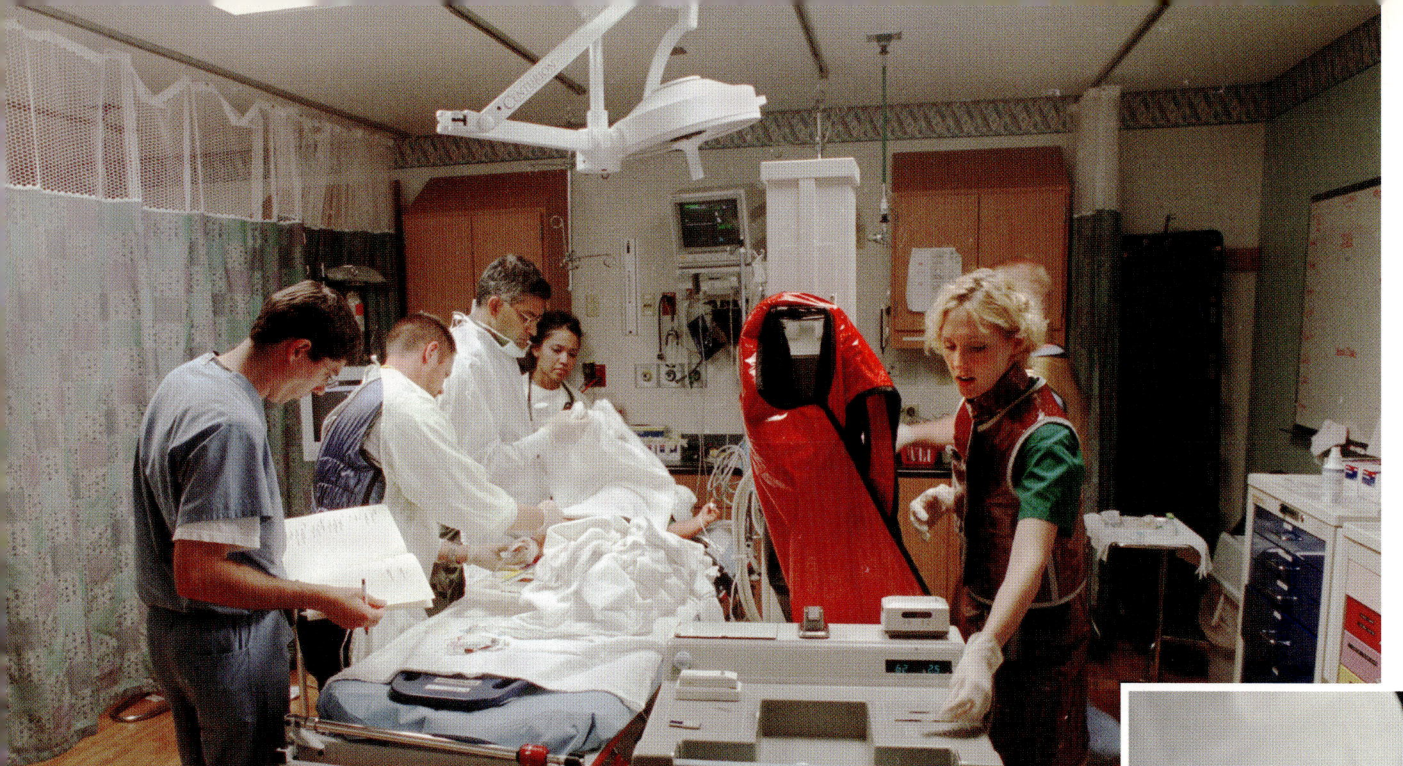

A trauma team at University Hospital responds to a patient in the emergency room. In fiscal year 2006, the University counted 39,366 patient visits through its emergency services and the Frank L. Mitchell Jr. Trauma Center.

Doctors and nurses check responses of extremities in a head-injury patient.

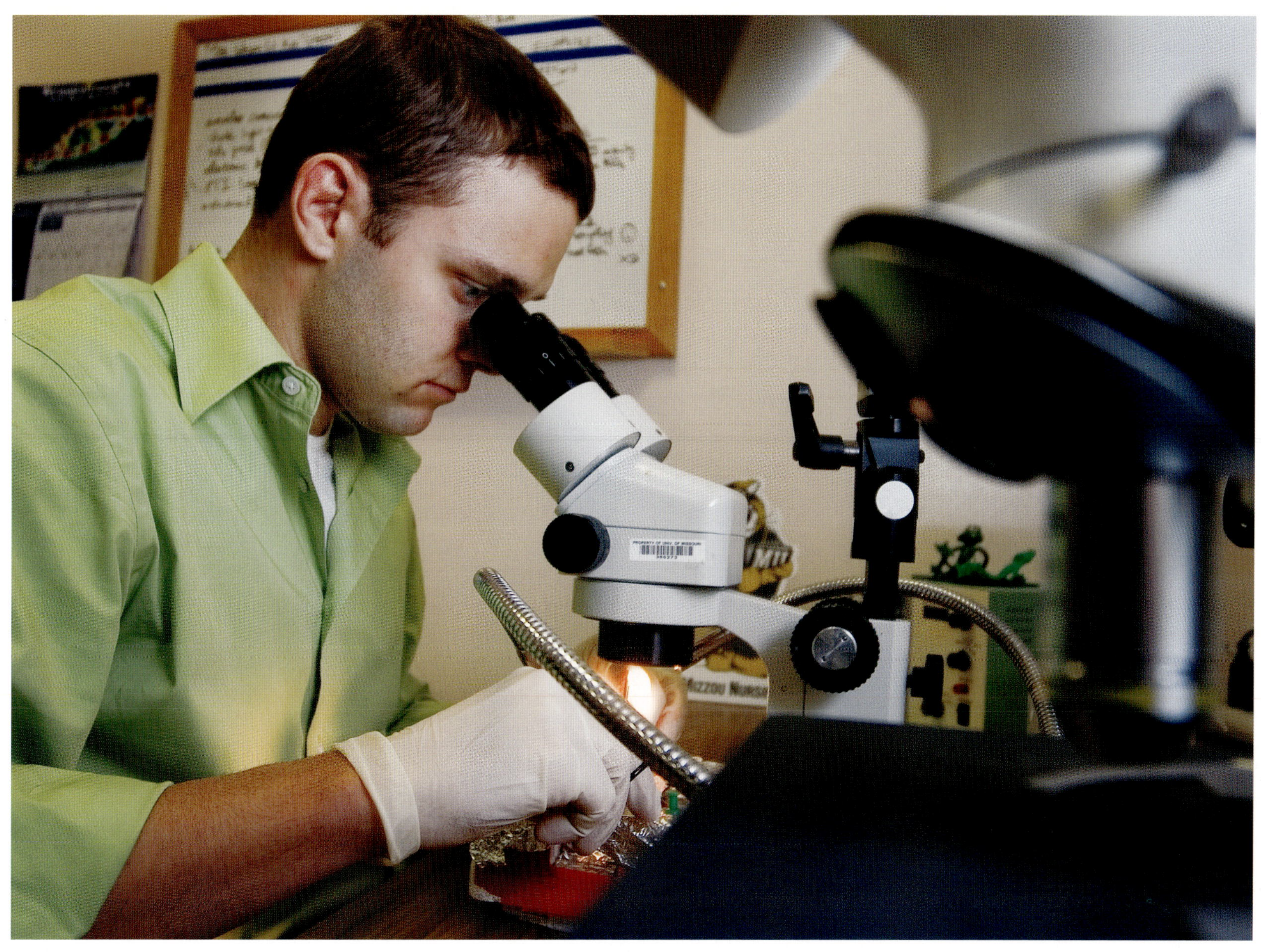

Nursing student Curt Canine uses a microscope to study microcirculation in a frog in a lab at MU's Sinclair School of Nursing.

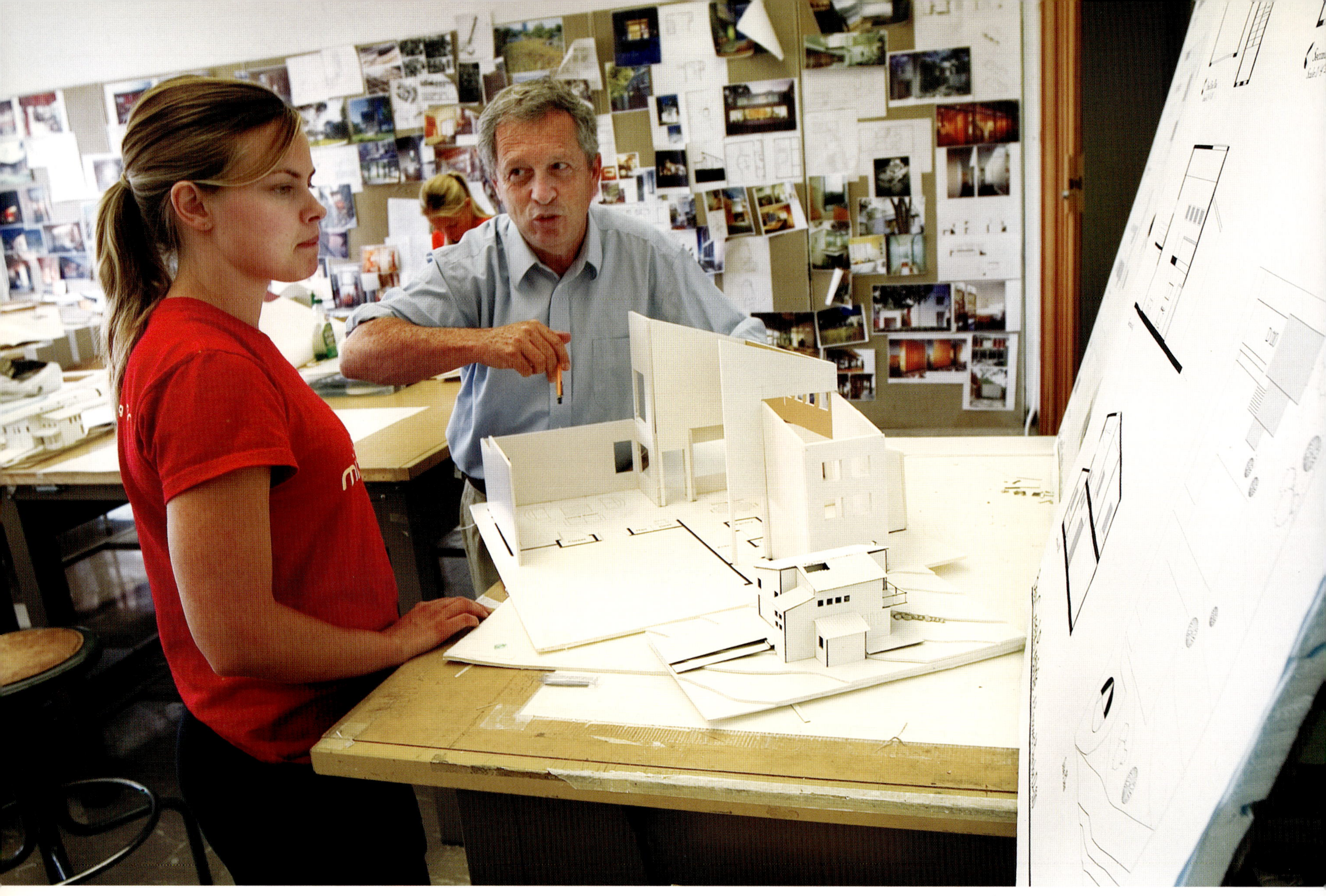

Benyamin Schwarz, professor of environmental design, critiques student Karissa Kramer's three-dimensional house design. The College of Human Environmental Sciences class proposed ideas for Columbia's Bear Creek Prairie neighborhood.

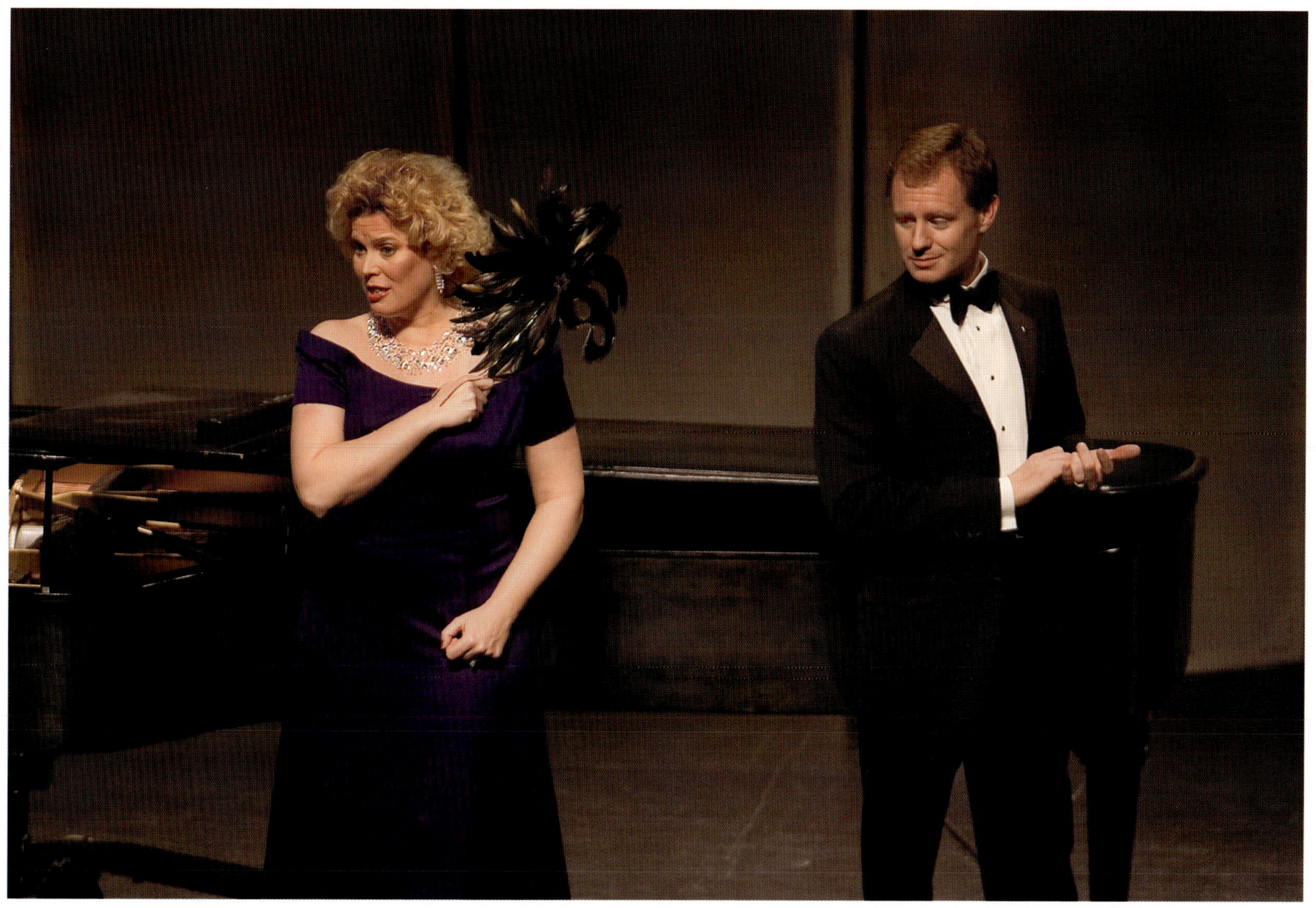

Graduates Caroline Worra and Ryan MacPherson perform the "Watch" duet from *Die Fledermaus* by Johann Strauss on January 29, 2006, in Jesse Hall. The event was a warm-up for a Carnegie Hall performance as part of the sixth annual Mizzou on Tour in New York.

Dr. Linda Headrick (*second from left*), professor of internal medicine, paces first-year medical students through taking a blood-pressure reading. The senior associate dean for medical education and faculty development is a national expert in improving physician education and patient care.

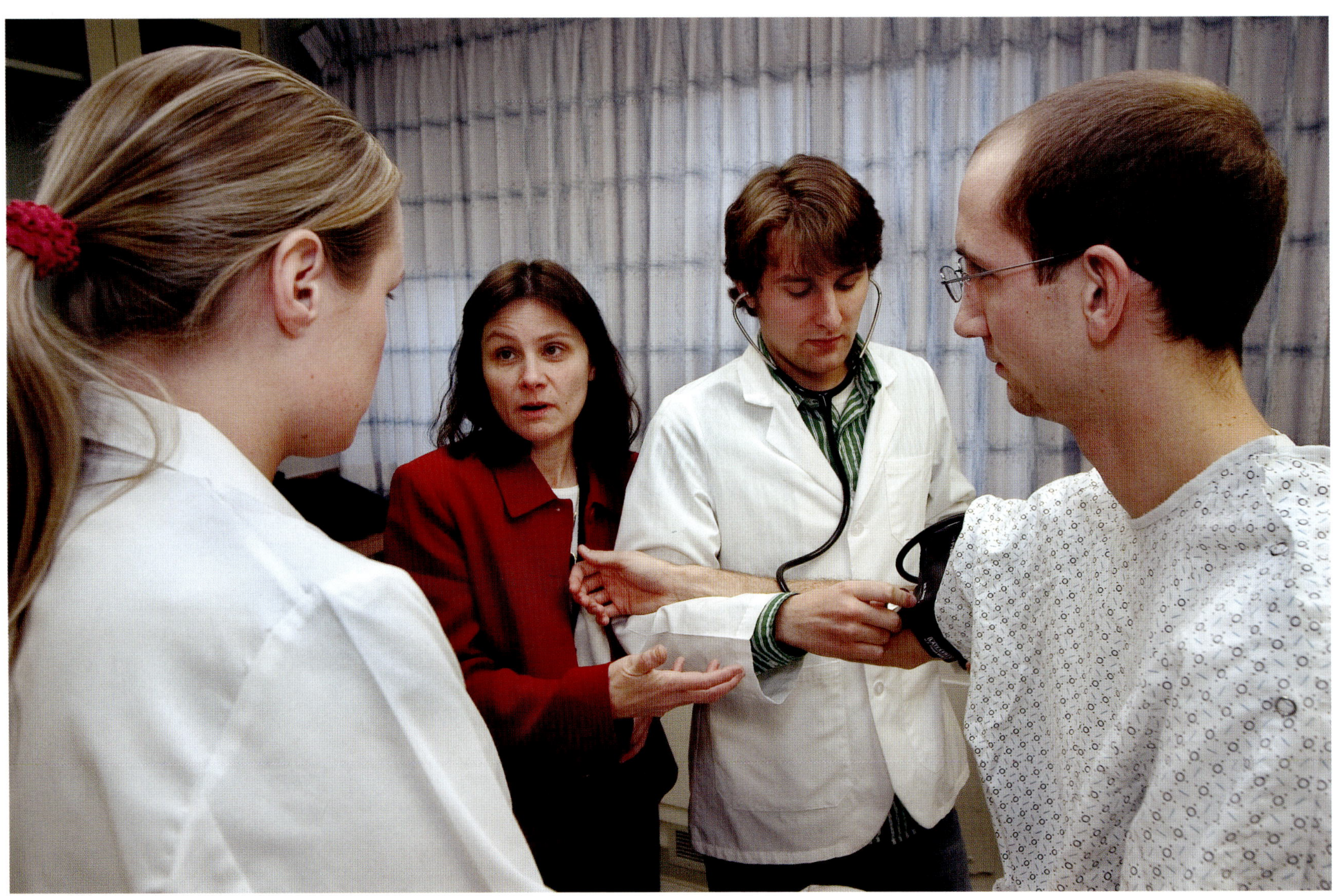

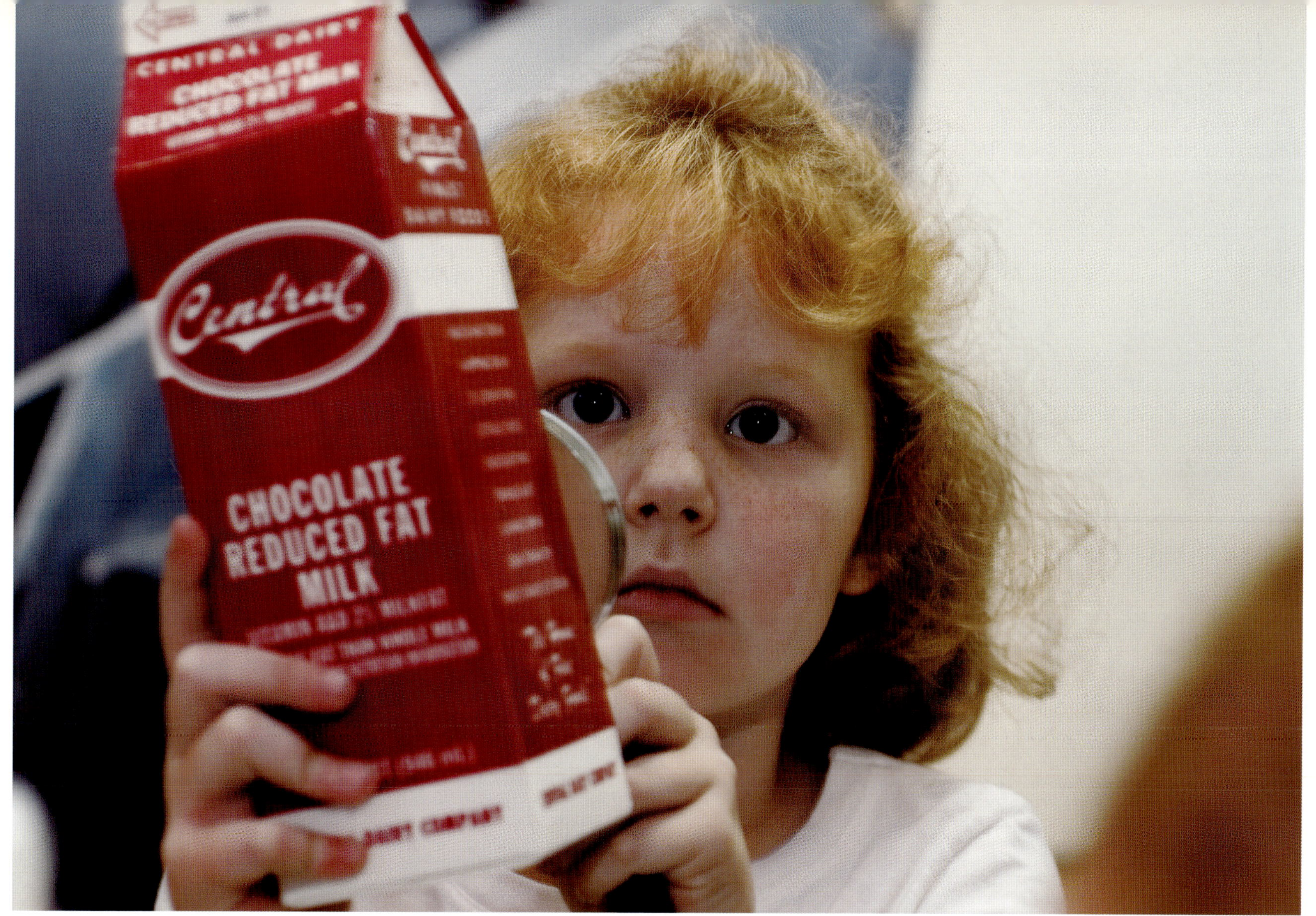

The nutritional value of chocolate milk is the focus of an elementary student in Tipton, Missouri. The activity is part of the Food Power nutrition program offered to public schools by University of Missouri Extension and MU's Nutritional Sciences Department.

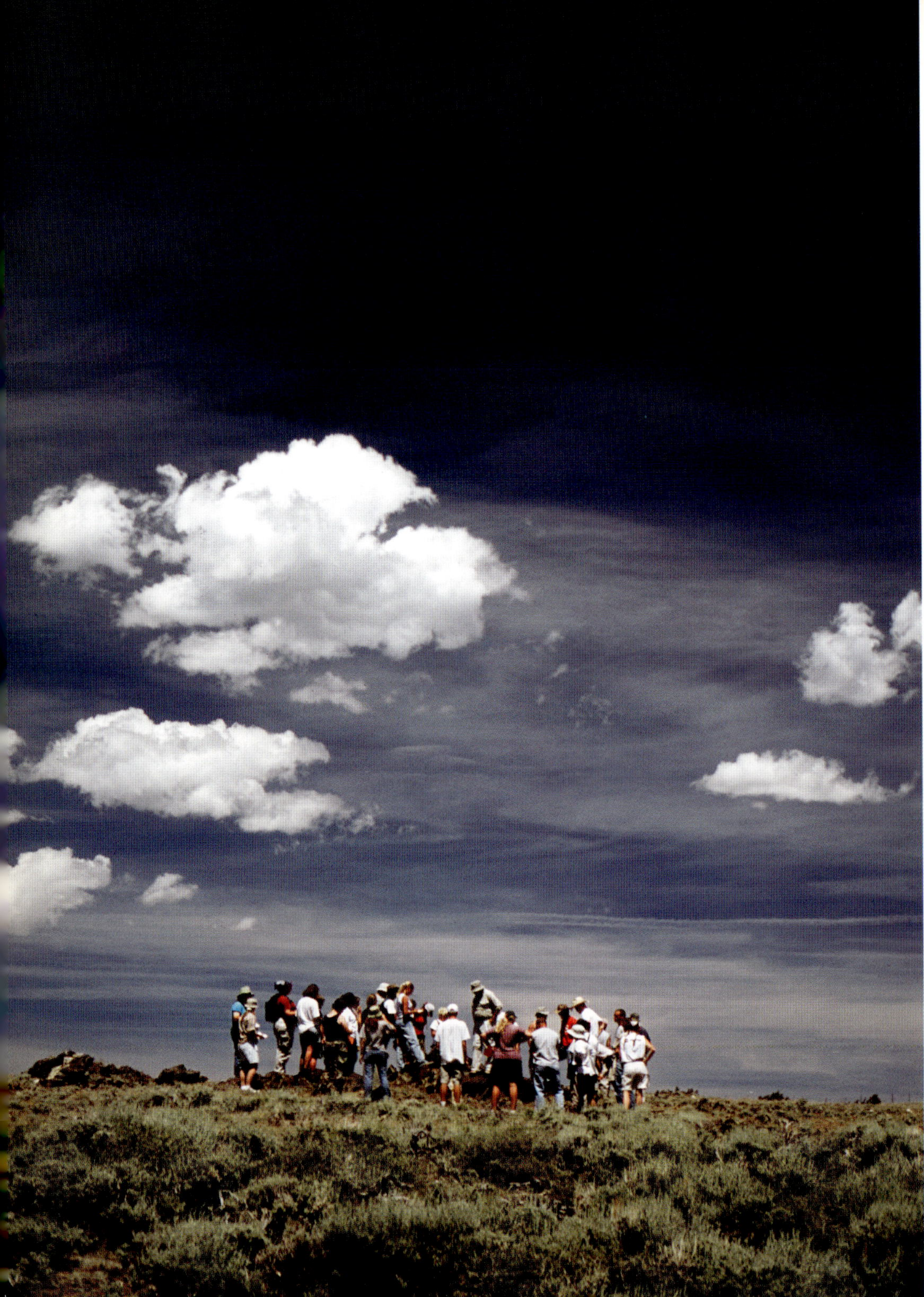

Associate Professor Robert Bauer leads a class of the Department of Geology's Camp Branson near Lander, Wyoming. Founded in 1911, the summer camp attracts students from all over the country to study geology field techniques.

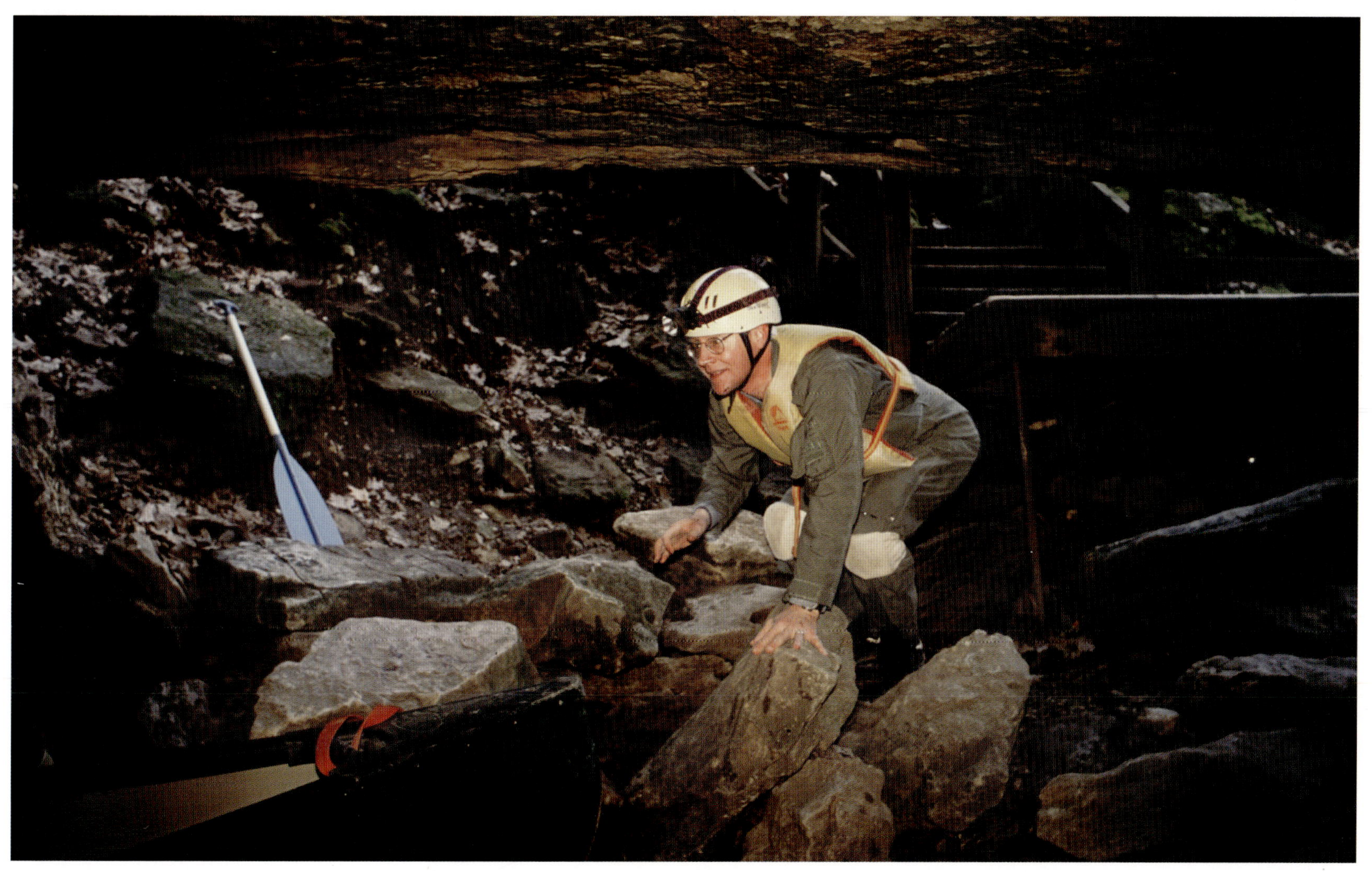

Professor of geography Joseph Hobbs, a noted authority on caves, leads a class touring the Devil's Icebox in Rock Bridge Memorial State Park, seven miles south of Columbia.

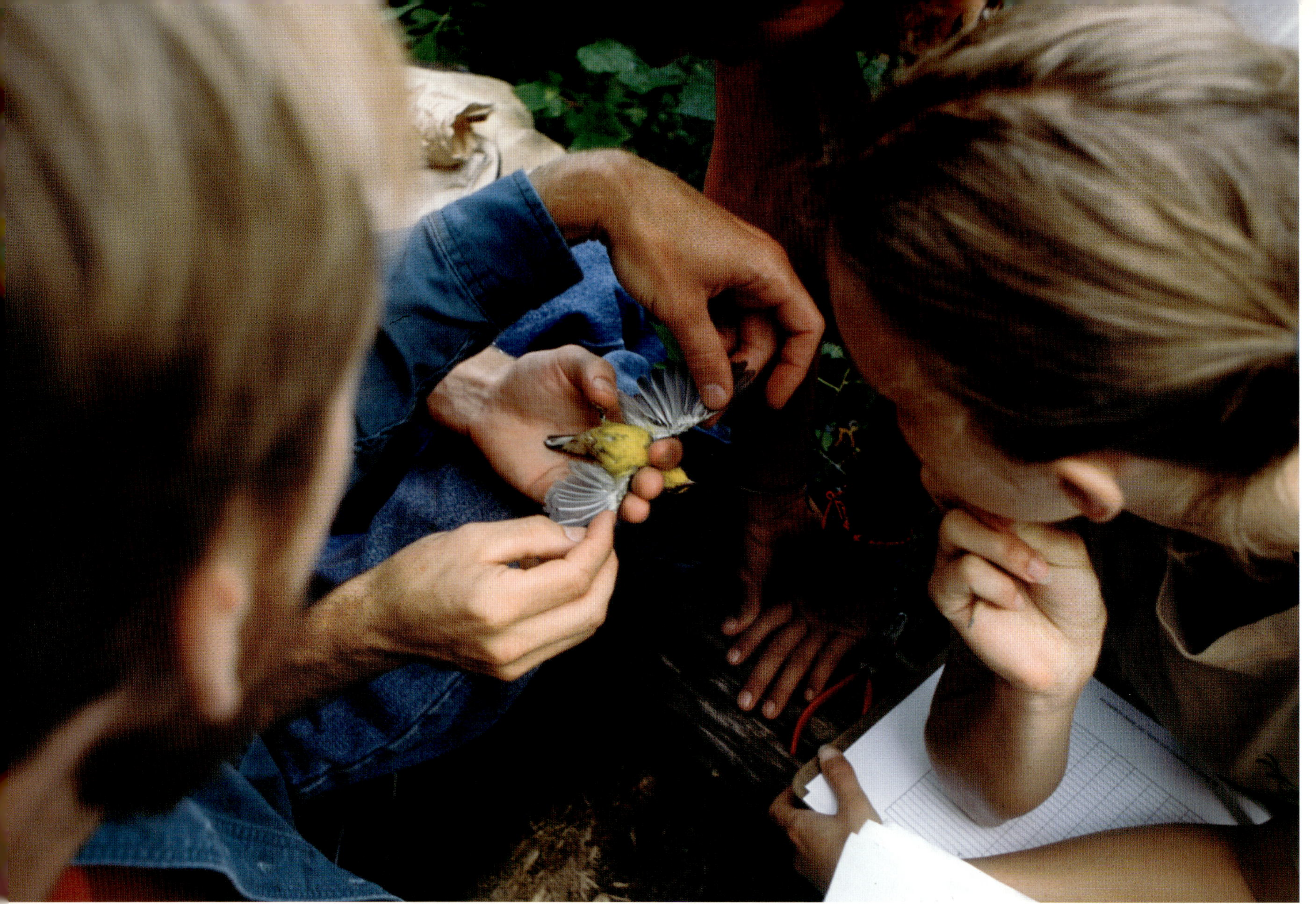

Students of John Faaborg determine the age of a songbird for a long-range environmental study gauging songbird populations in the Ozarks. Faaborg, a professor of biological science and fisheries and wildlife, conducts research in North and Central America.

A fisheries and wildlife student studies spotted salamanders in Warren County, Missouri. The study attempts to better determine how human activity has affected amphibian survival prospects. Students gather salamanders in pond traps to record their length, age, and sex.

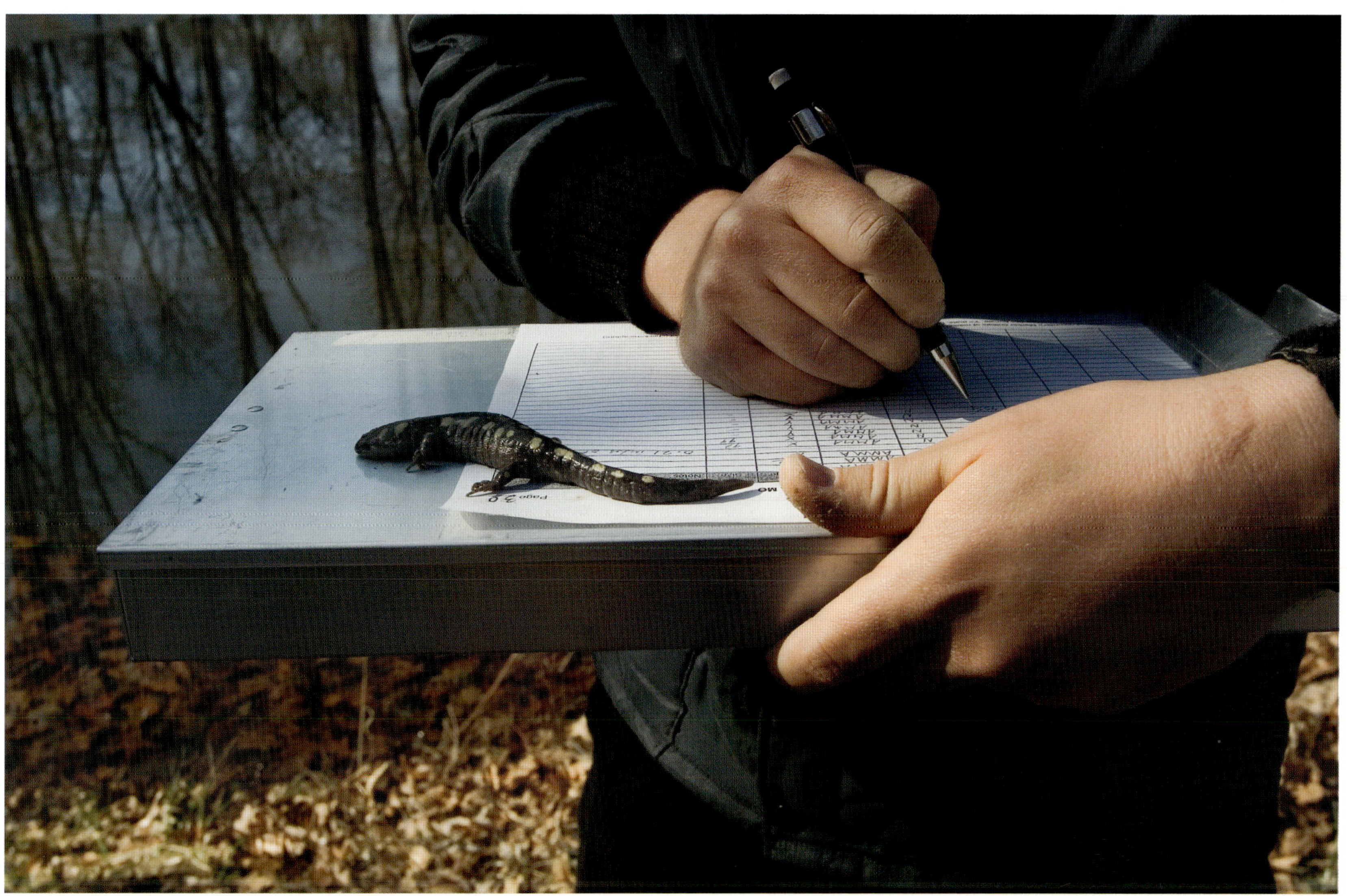

Television host Hunter Ellis delivers a fiery introduction for a Discovery Channel television show during a staged aircraft fire in a simulator at Columbia Regional Airport. The Fire and Rescue Training Institute, part of University of Missouri Extension, uses the simulator to train firefighters from across the country.

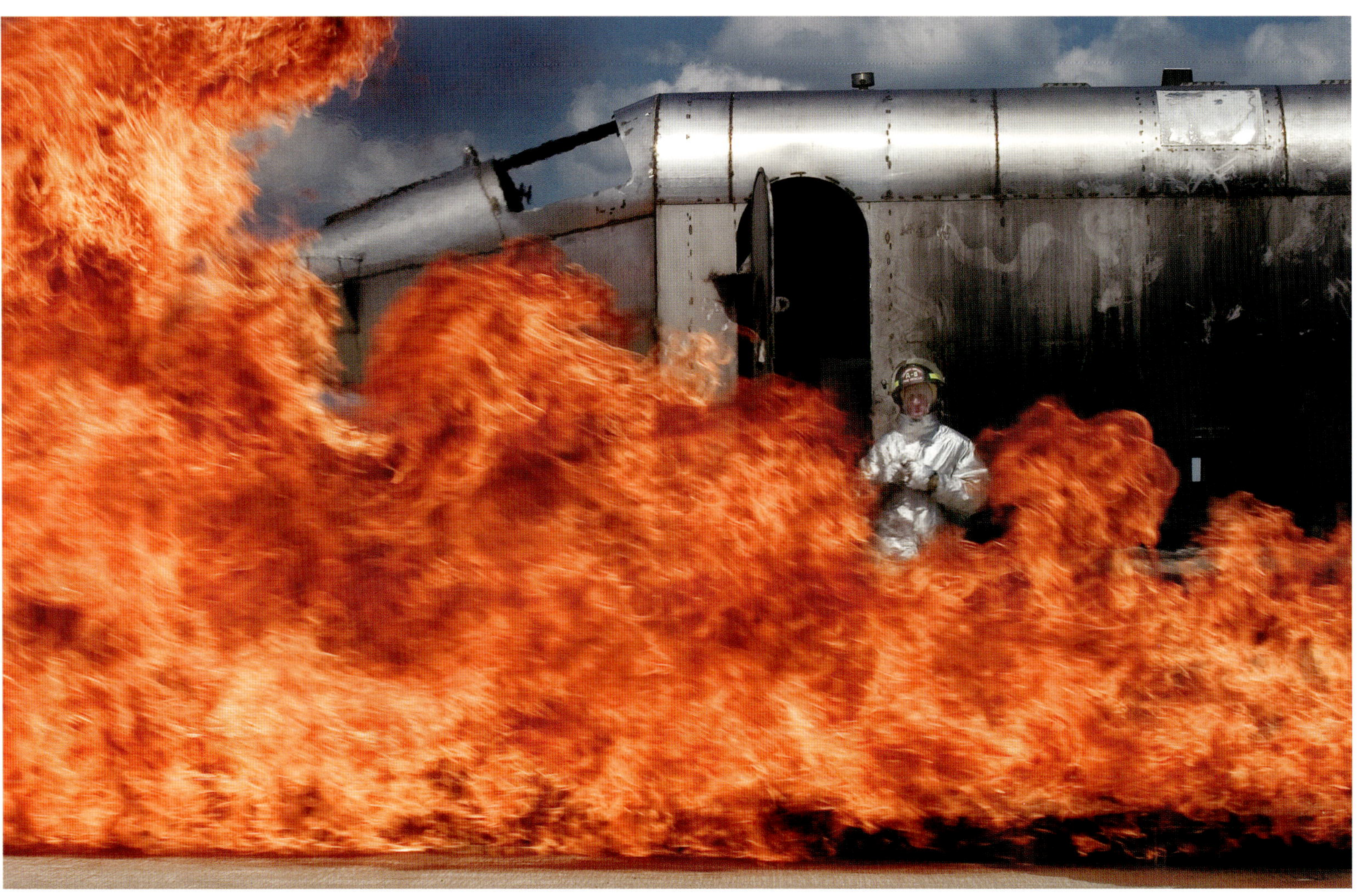

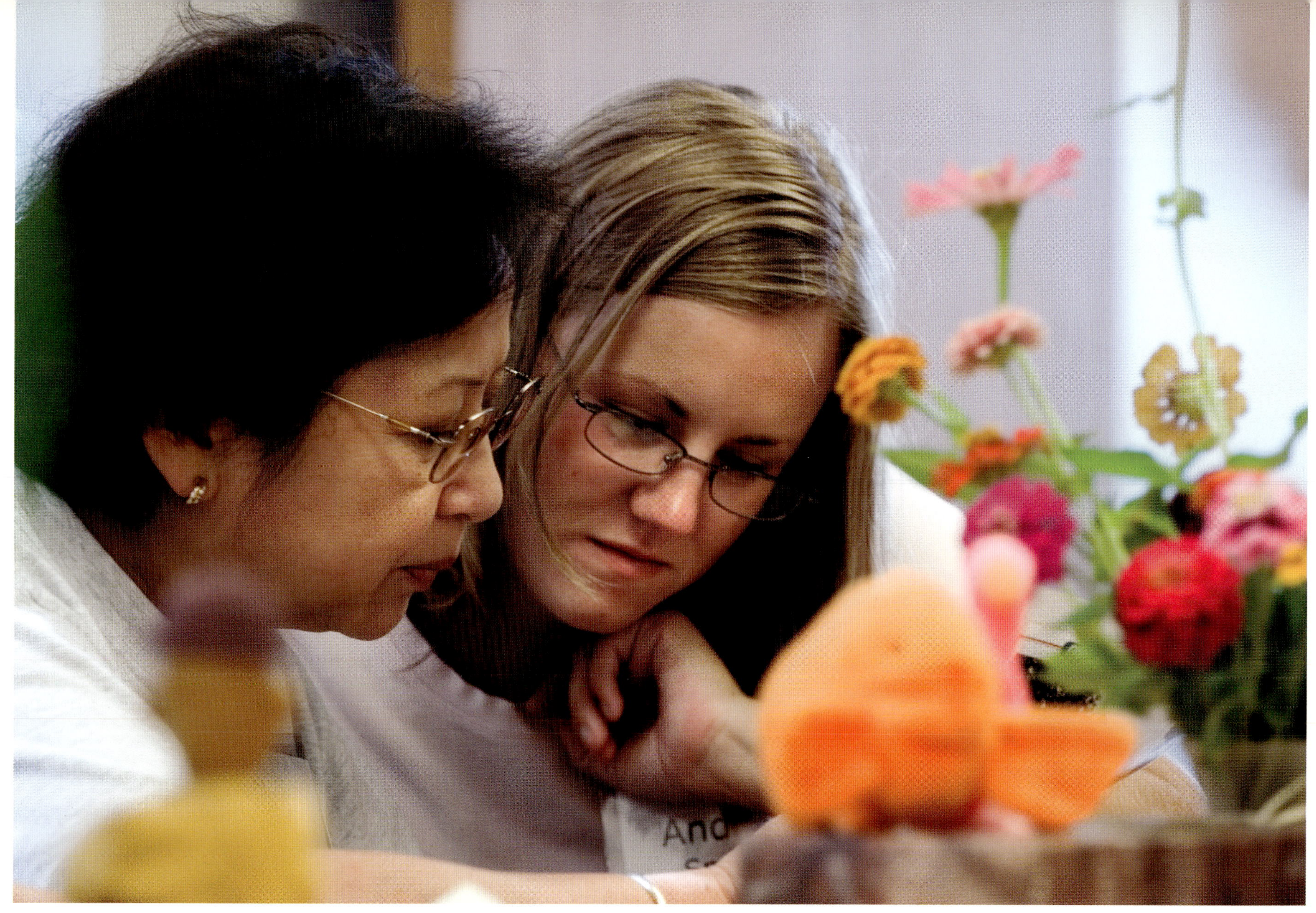

Flowers and friendship brighten days at Adult Day Connection, a School of Health Professions program that provides nursing care and therapeutic activities for older adults as well as learning experiences for students.

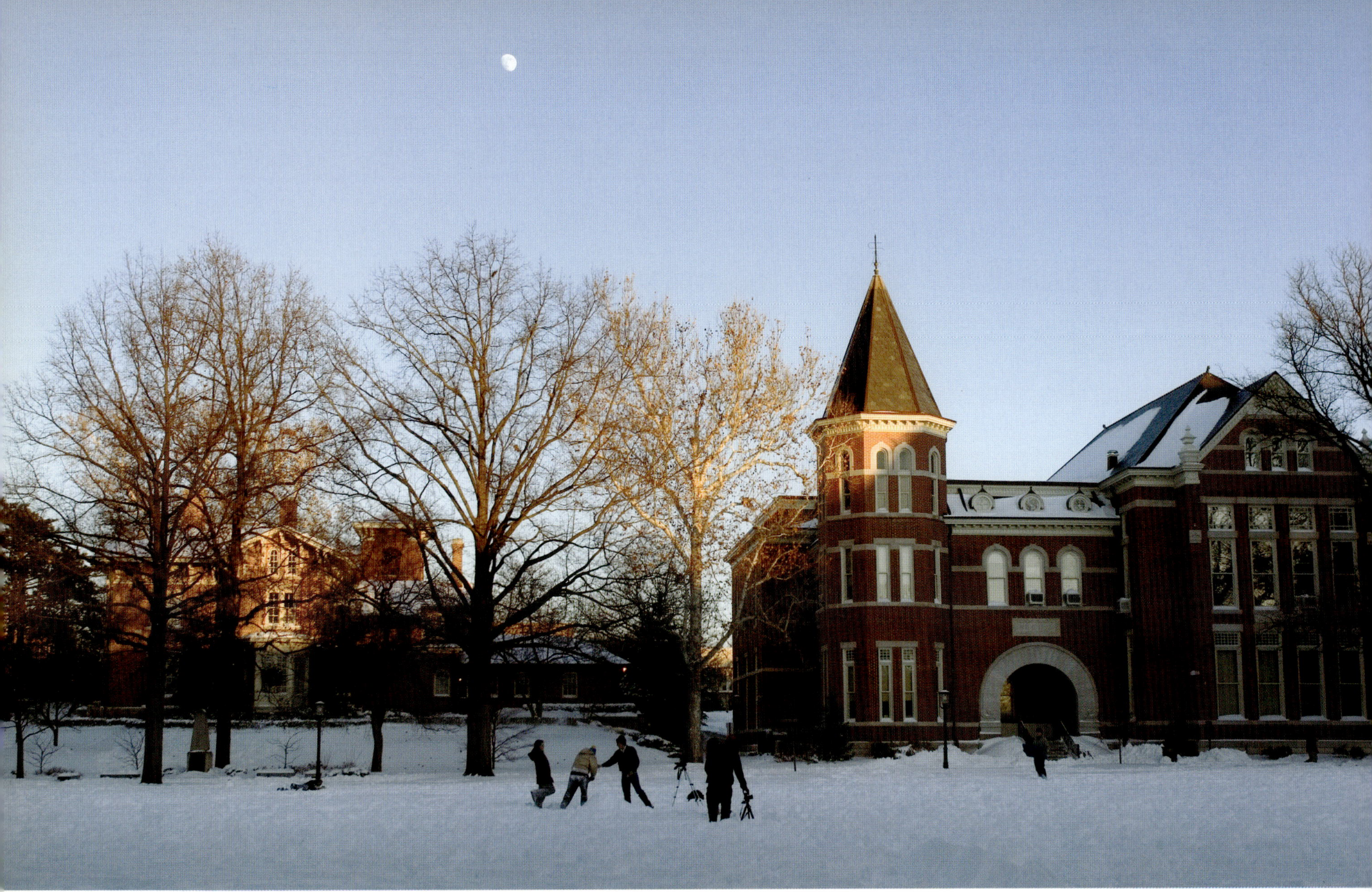

The setting sun highlights snow-frosted pin oaks on Francis Quadrangle on December 1, 2006, after Mother Nature had delivered fourteen inches of snow and classes were canceled for the first time in eleven years.

Only the tracks of a venturesome rabbit disturb the fresh snow on the lawn of the Residence on Francis Quadrangle, where Chancellor Brady Deaton and his wife, Anne, live.

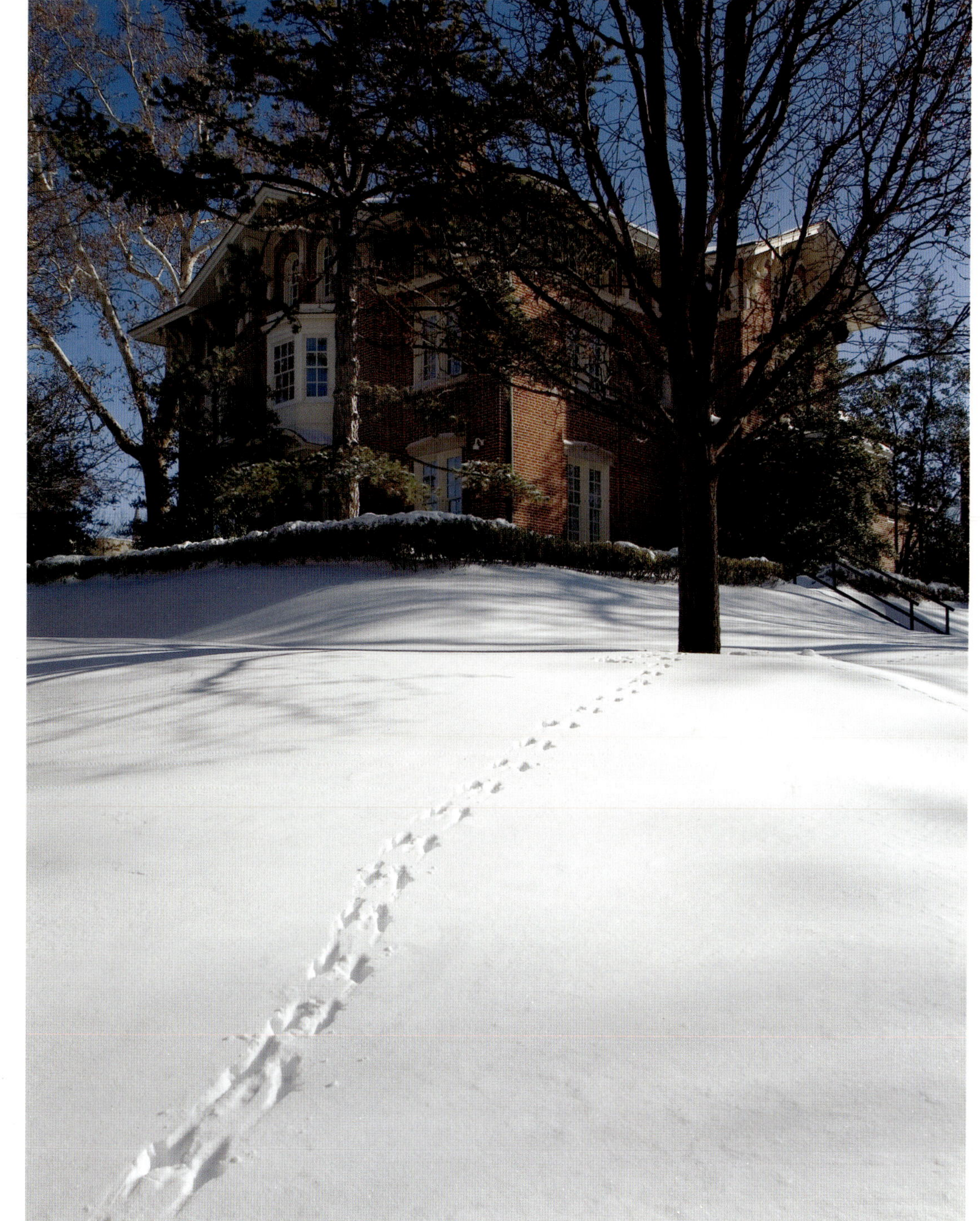

A student heads to class across Carnahan Quadrangle, where dormant maiden grass lines sidewalks in late winter.

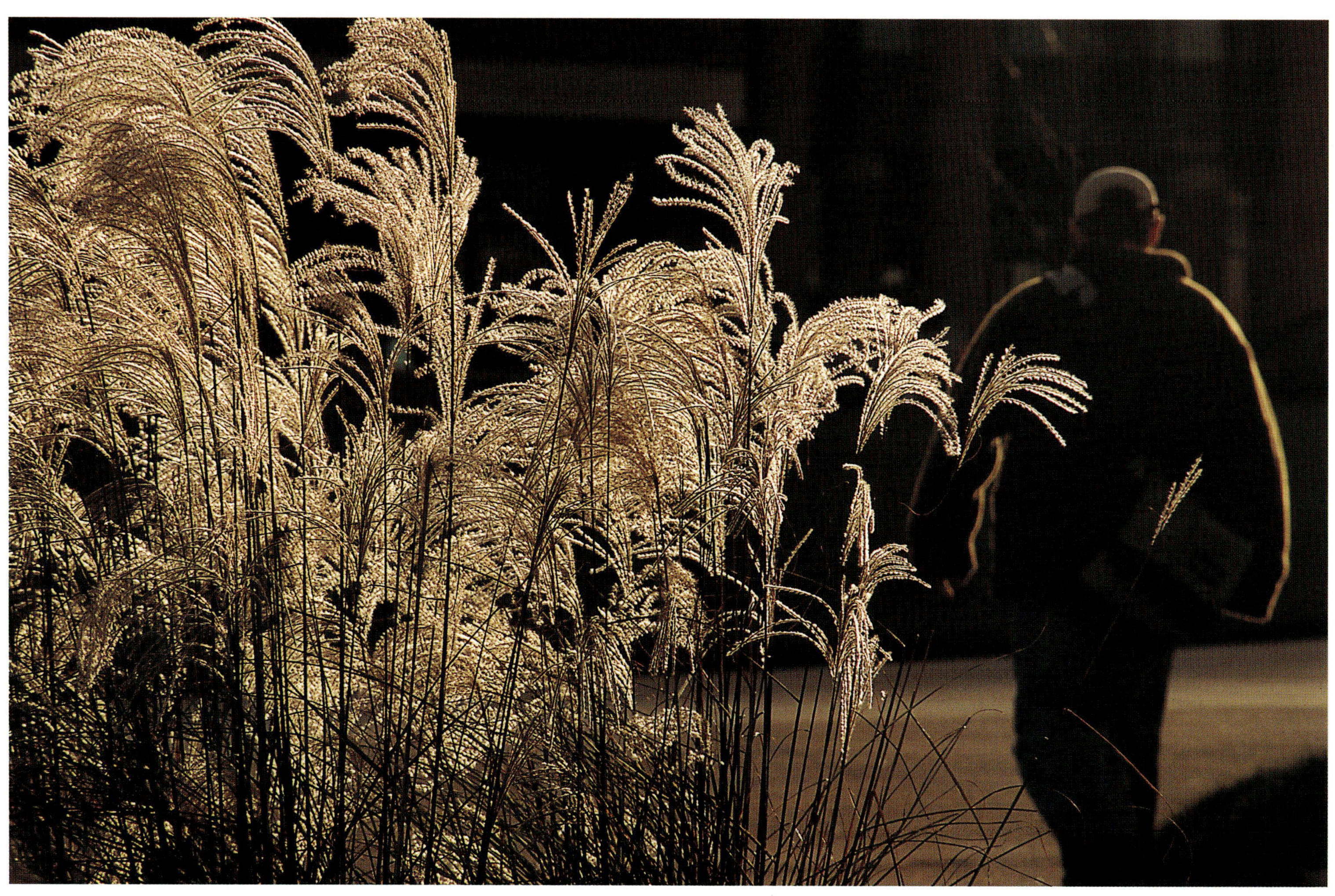

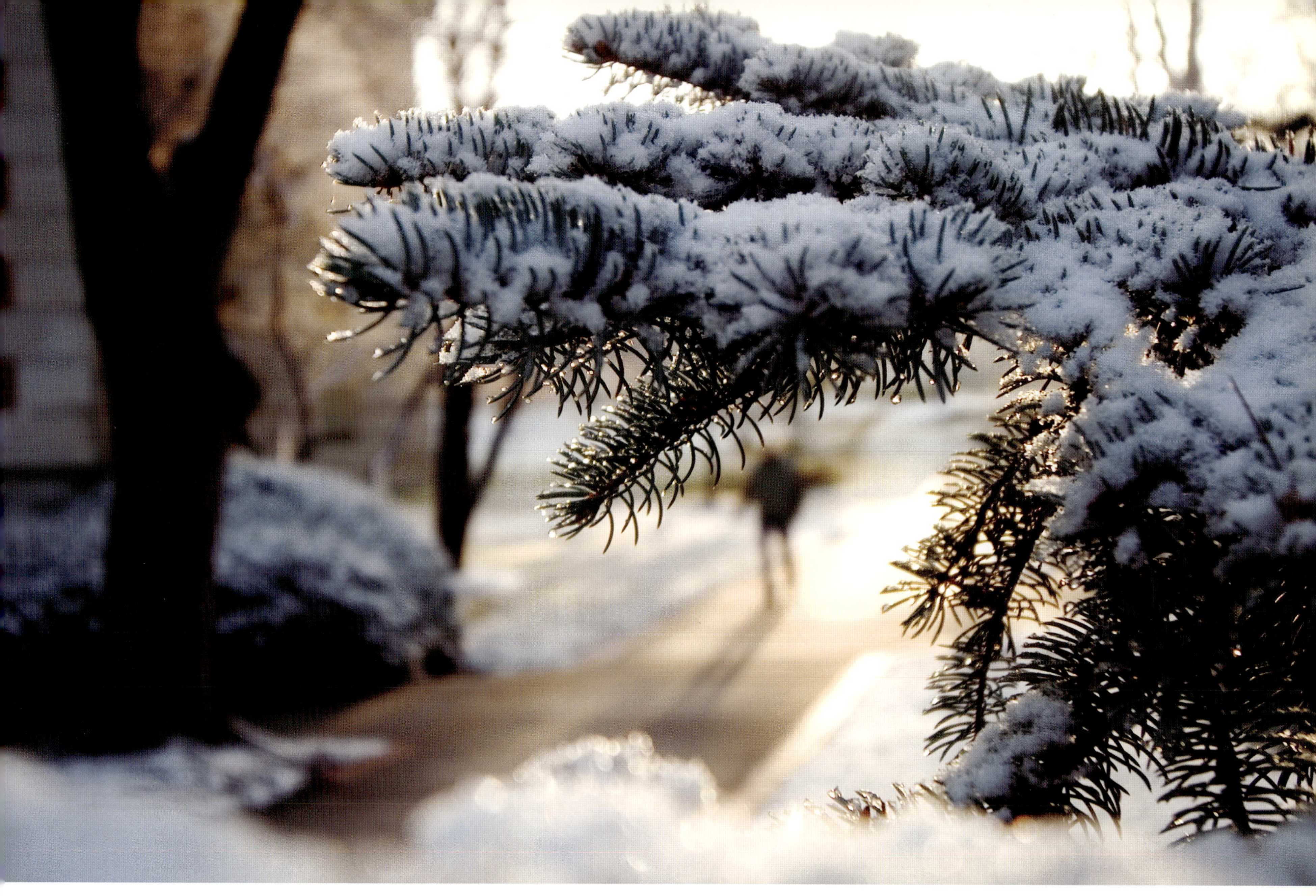

The early morning sun lights a snow-covered spruce tree near Tate Hall and Speakers Circle.

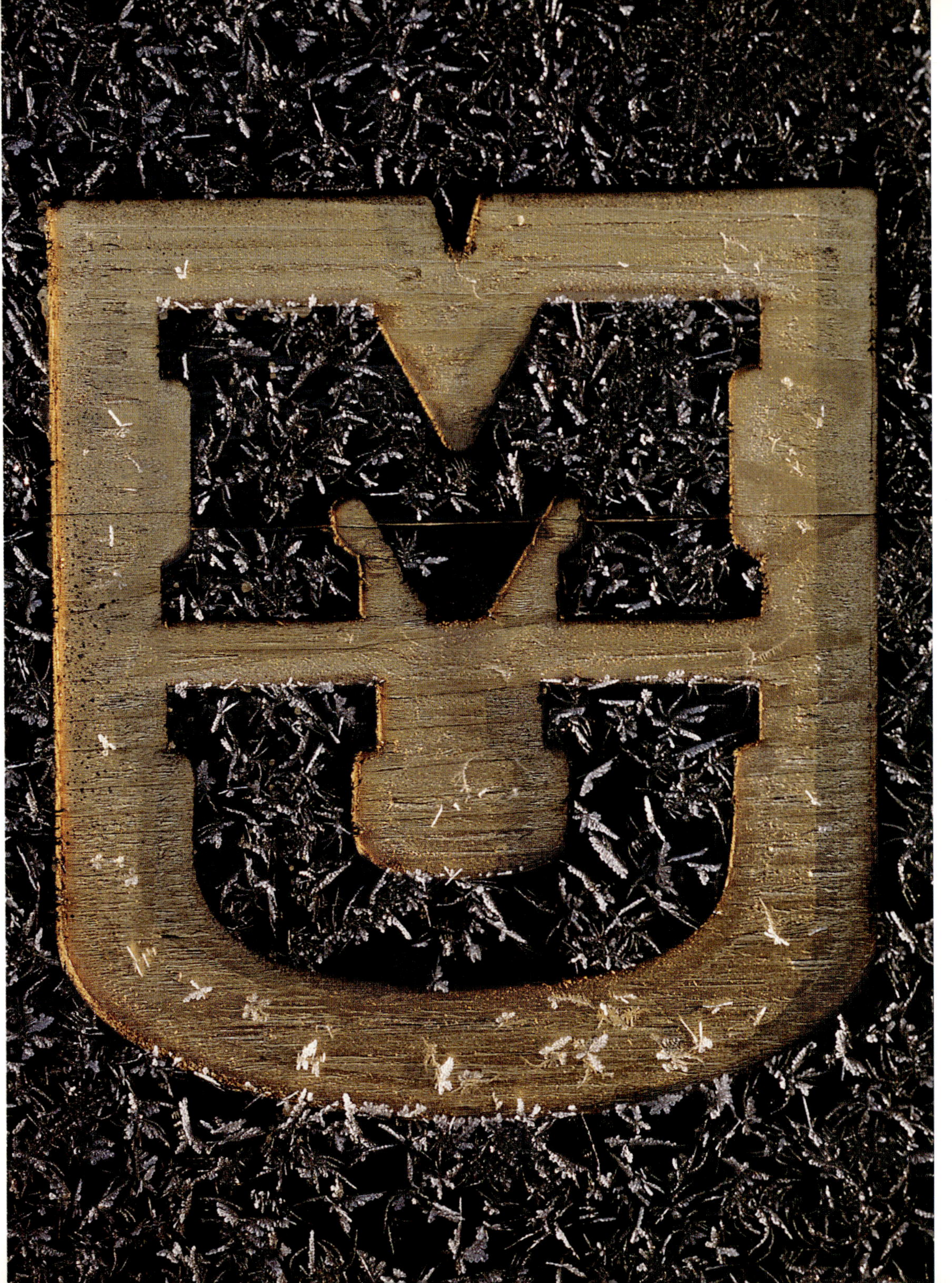

Frost settles on the MU logo in the valley near the Green Tennis Center at Epple Field. The facility was built in 2002.

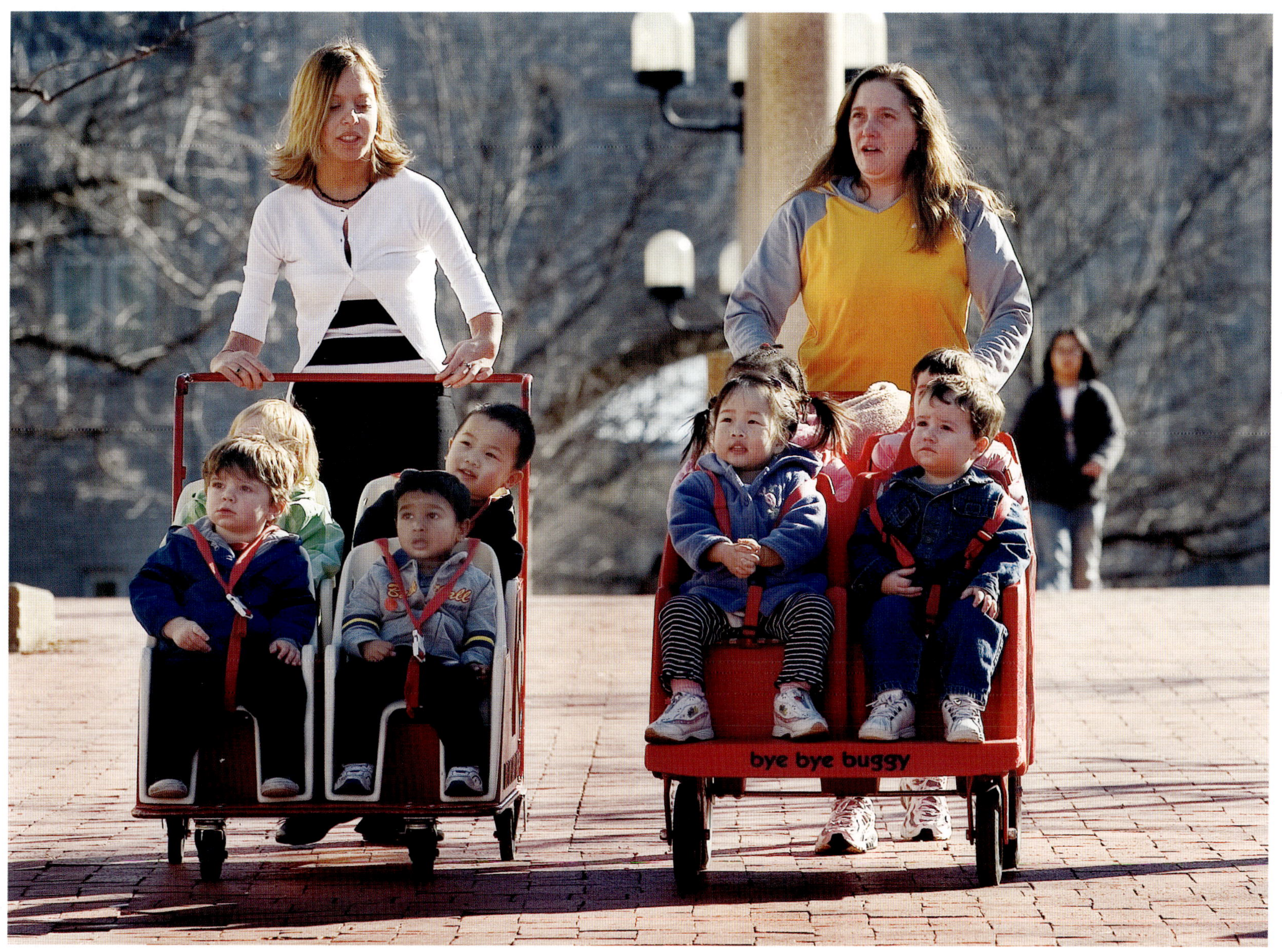

Eight tykes from the Child Development Laboratory (part of the College of Human Environmental Sciences) take a stroller trip from Stanley Hall across Lowry Mall. The adults in charge are headed to Stankowski Field, where the children can run and play.

Finials decorate a number of Memorial Union's small towers, or tourelles. Gothic arcades, or pointed arches, form openings far above the ground. In the early 1900s, architect James Jamieson invoked the revival of English collegiate Gothic architecture—the likes of Cambridge and Oxford—to design White Campus buildings. The model was less formal than that used for the Red Campus buildings and included surprising details.

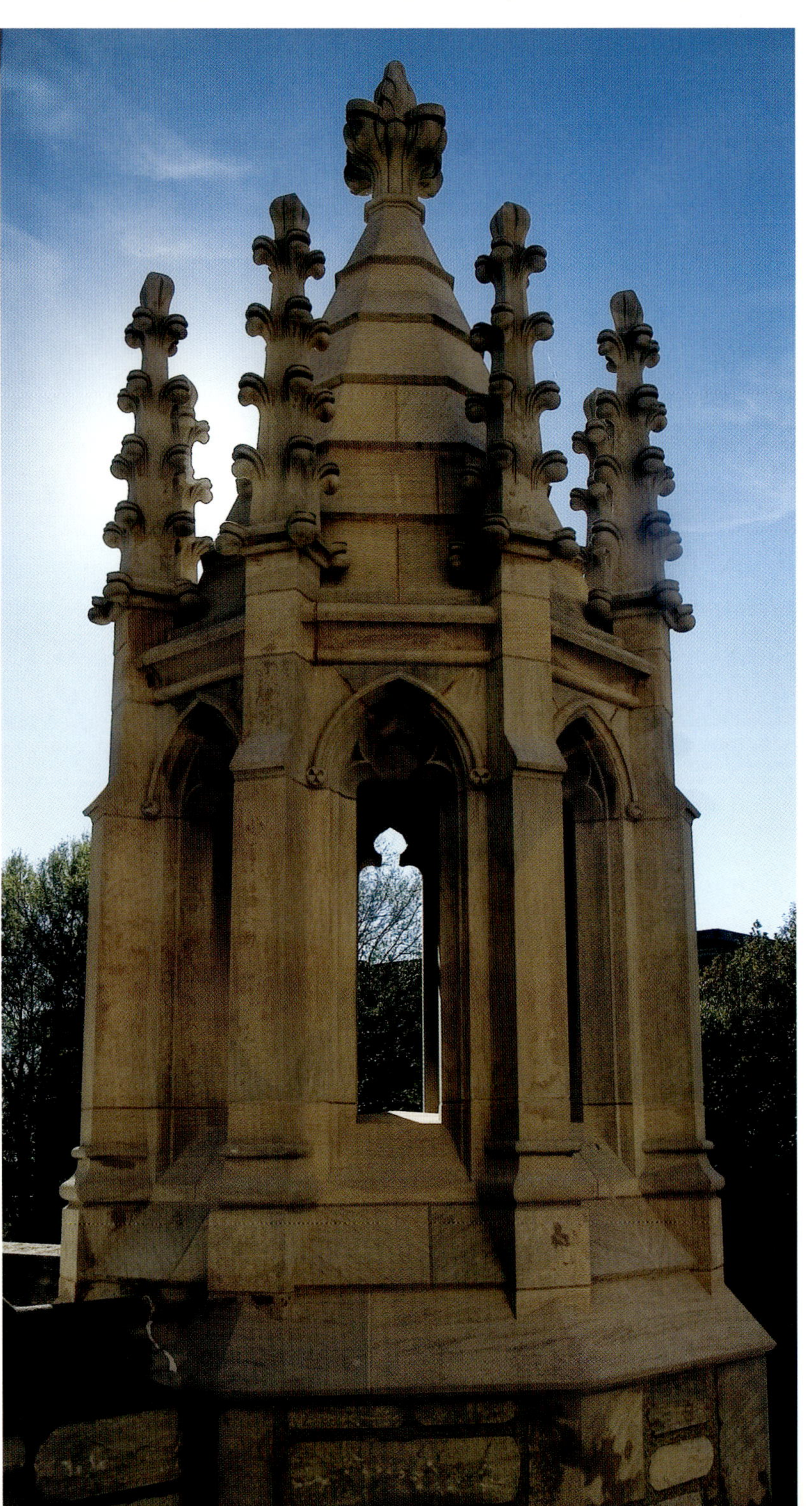

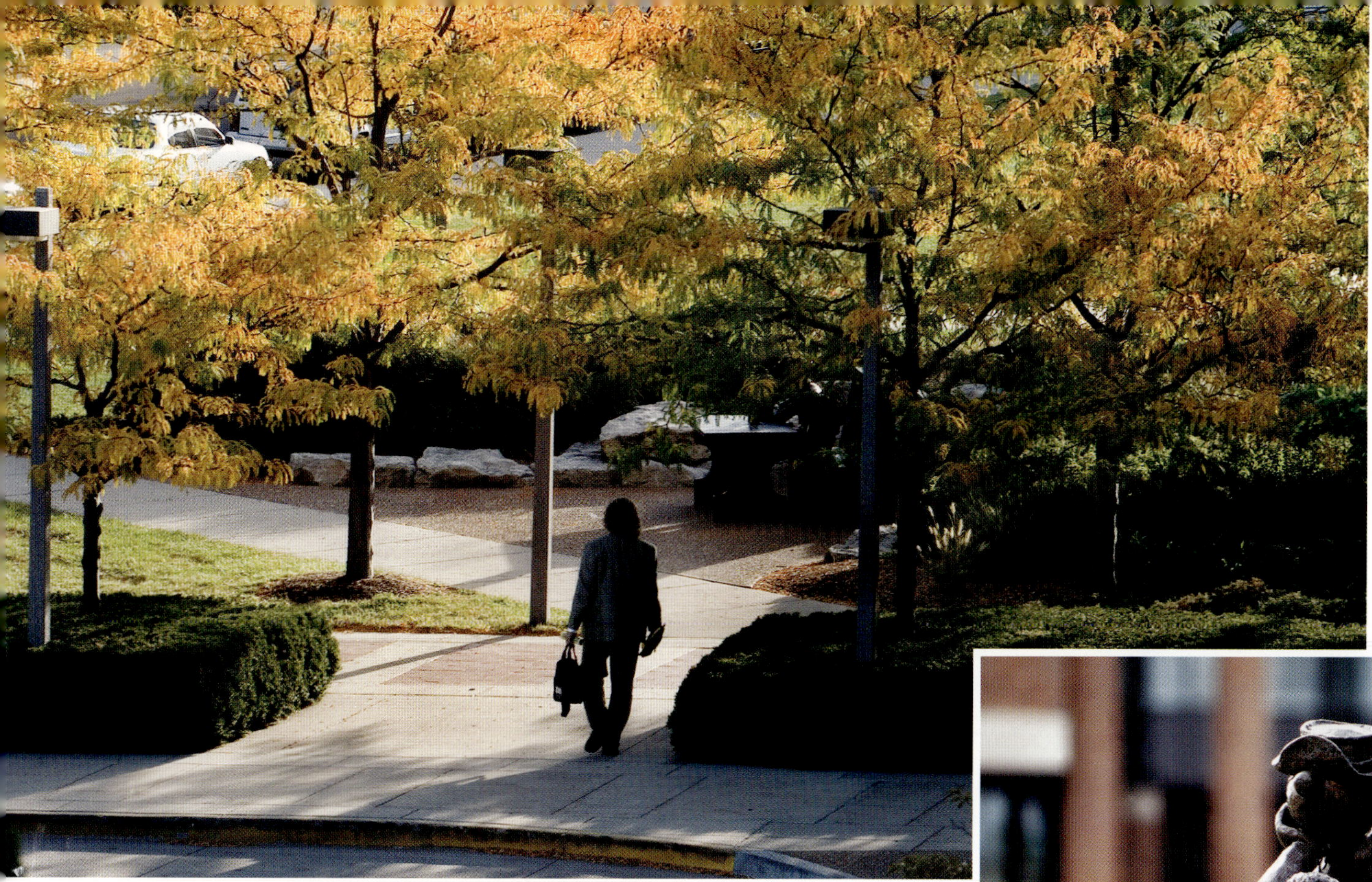

Thornless honey locust trees line the walk in front of Reynolds Alumni Center. The sidewalk is the site for the Mizzou Legacy Walk, a Mizzou Alumni Association project to endow a scholarship fund. The statue of Beetle Bailey can be seen under the trees.

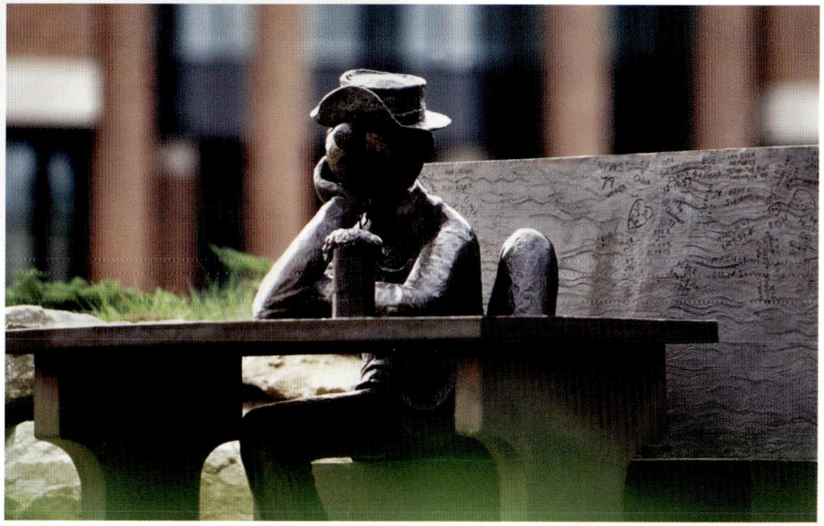

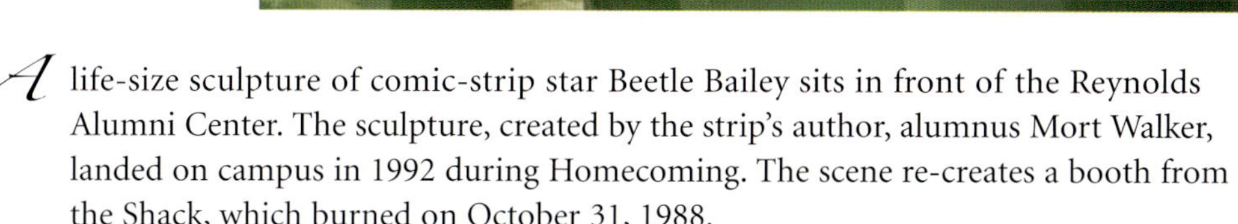

A life-size sculpture of comic-strip star Beetle Bailey sits in front of the Reynolds Alumni Center. The sculpture, created by the strip's author, alumnus Mort Walker, landed on campus in 1992 during Homecoming. The scene re-creates a booth from the Shack, which burned on October 31, 1988.

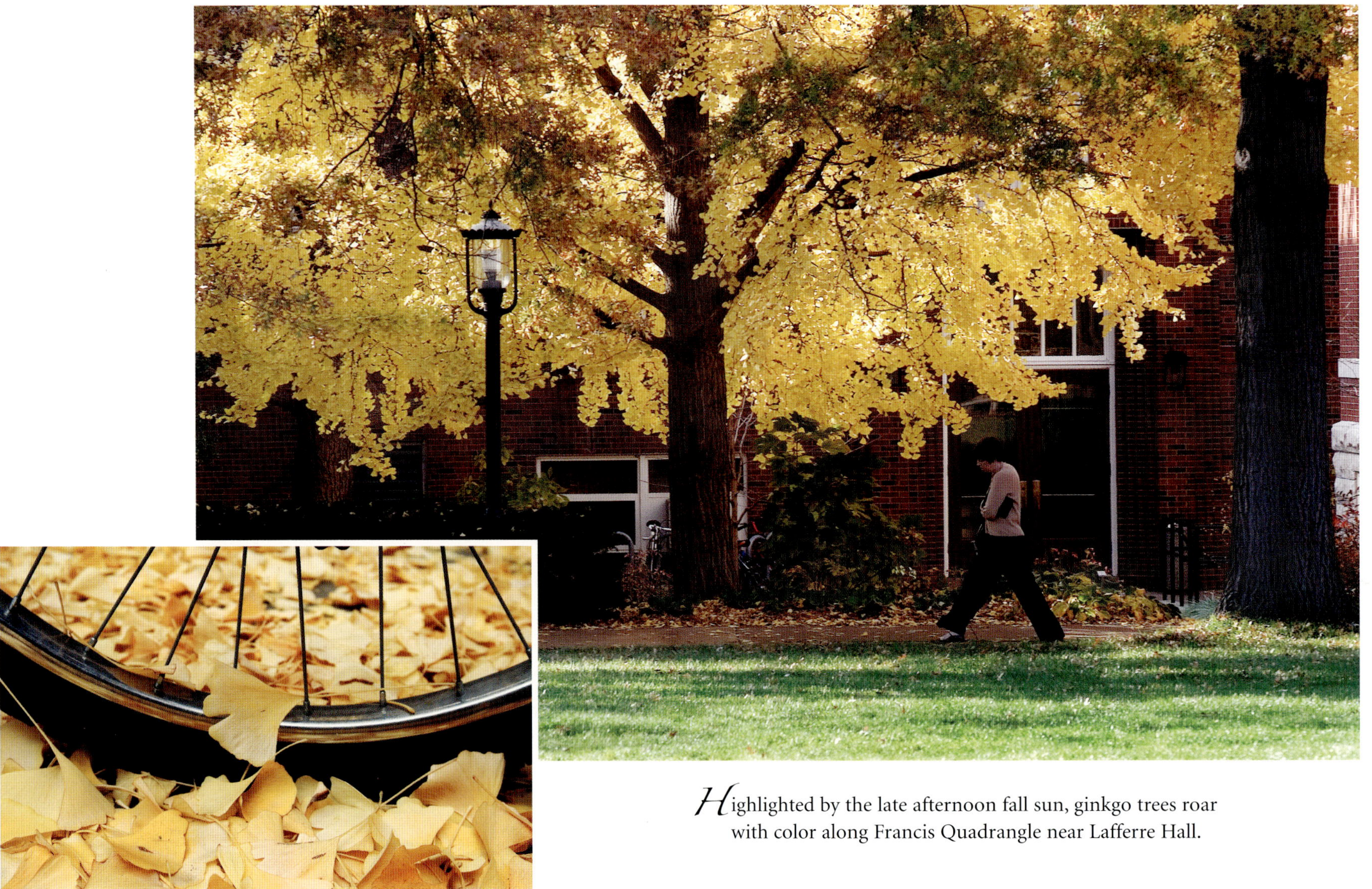

*H*ighlighted by the late afternoon fall sun, ginkgo trees roar with color along Francis Quadrangle near Lafferre Hall.

*G*inkgo leaves intertwine with the spokes of a bike.

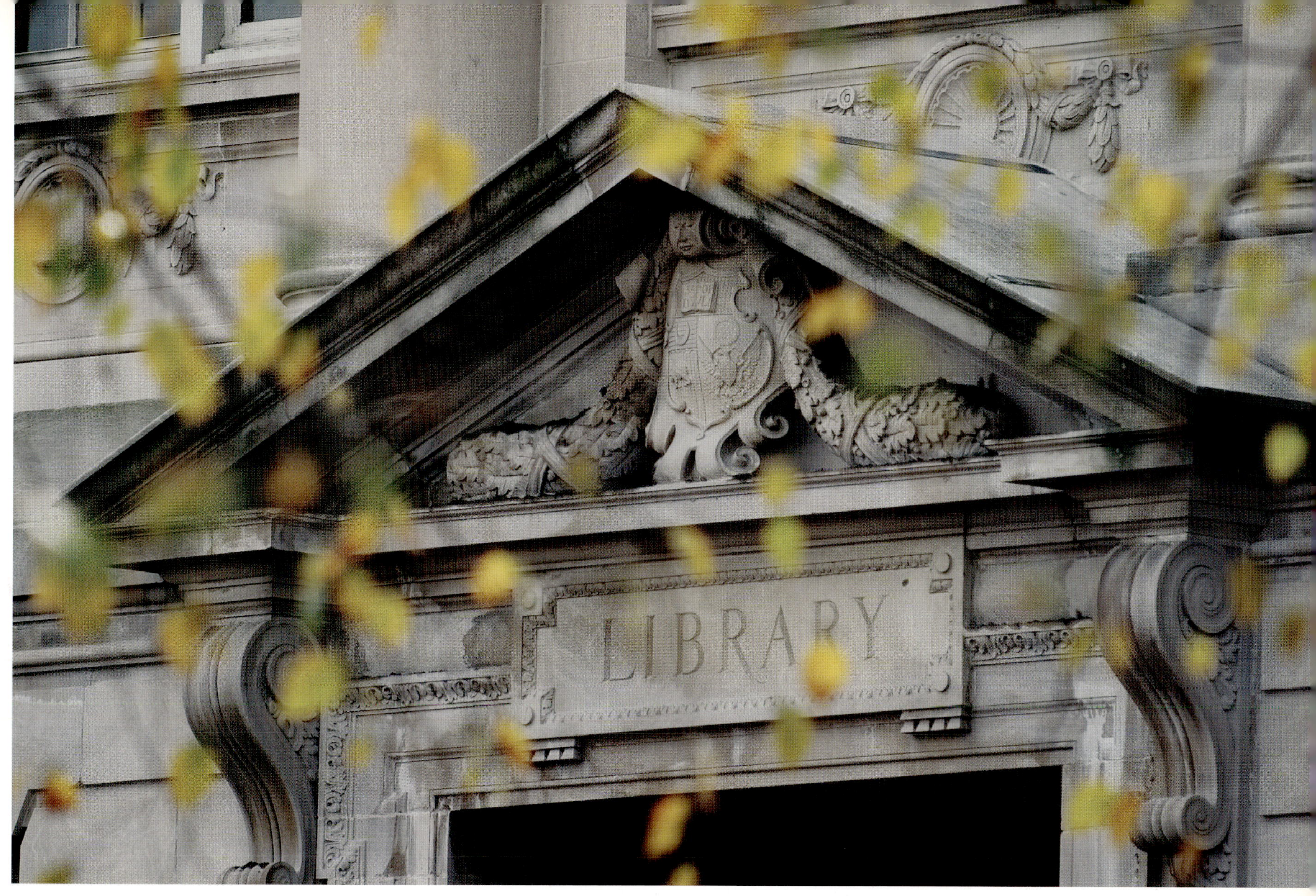

A sculpture of the University of Missouri seal sits above the pediment of the north door to Ellis Library in a triangular space called a tympanum. The seal displays the words *Salus Populi,* Latin for "the welfare of the people."

Two students walk past Thomas Jefferson's original tombstone, which rests on Francis Quadrangle. Jefferson left these handwritten instructions for its simple geometric design: "a plain die or cube of 3 f. without any mouldings, surmounted by an Obelisk 6 f. height, each of a single stone." He also asked for it to be made of coarse stone so "that no one might be tempted hereafter to destroy it for the value of the materials." Jefferson's heirs gave the tombstone to the University in 1883 after Congress decided in 1882 to place a fancier one on his grave at Monticello.

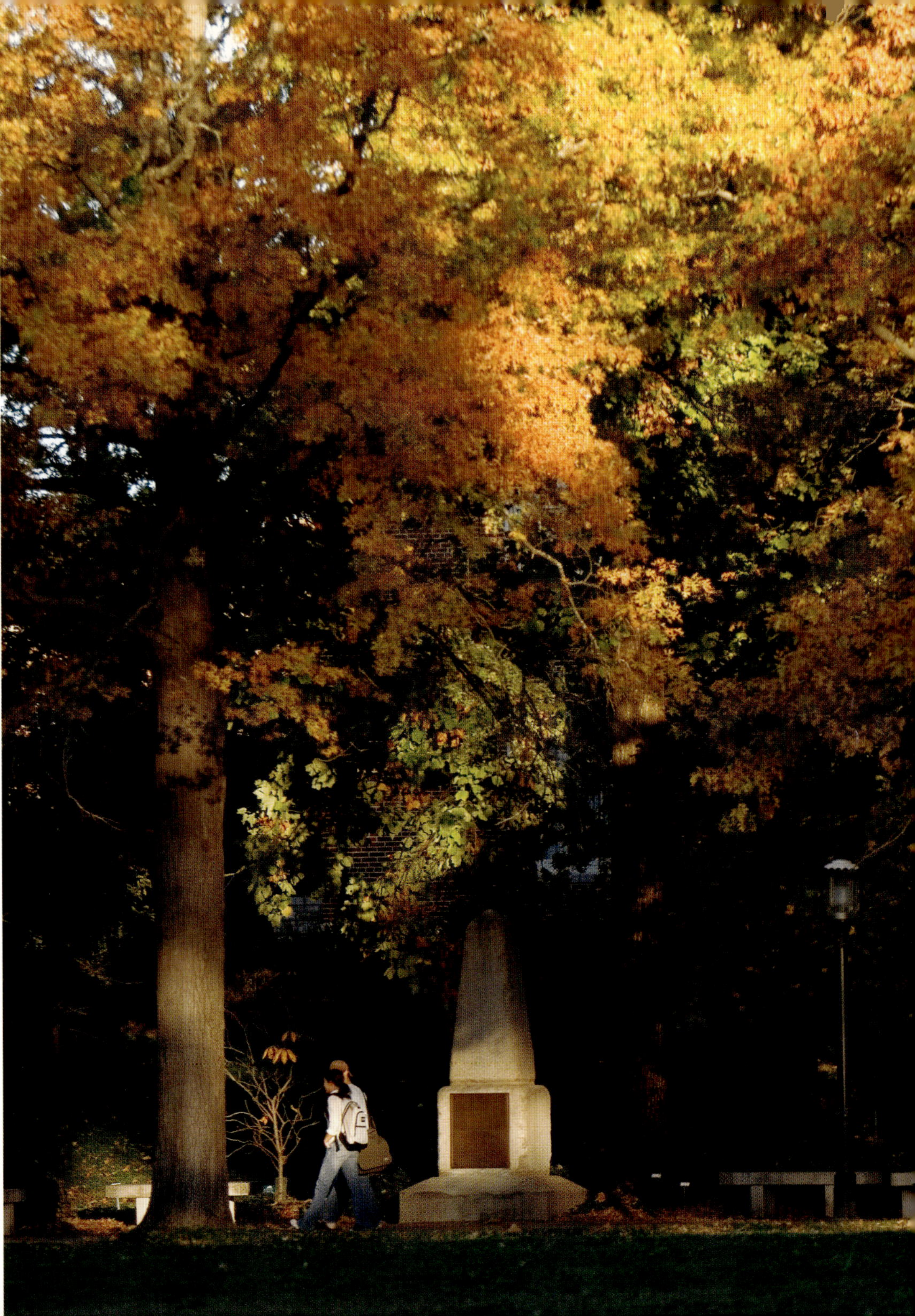

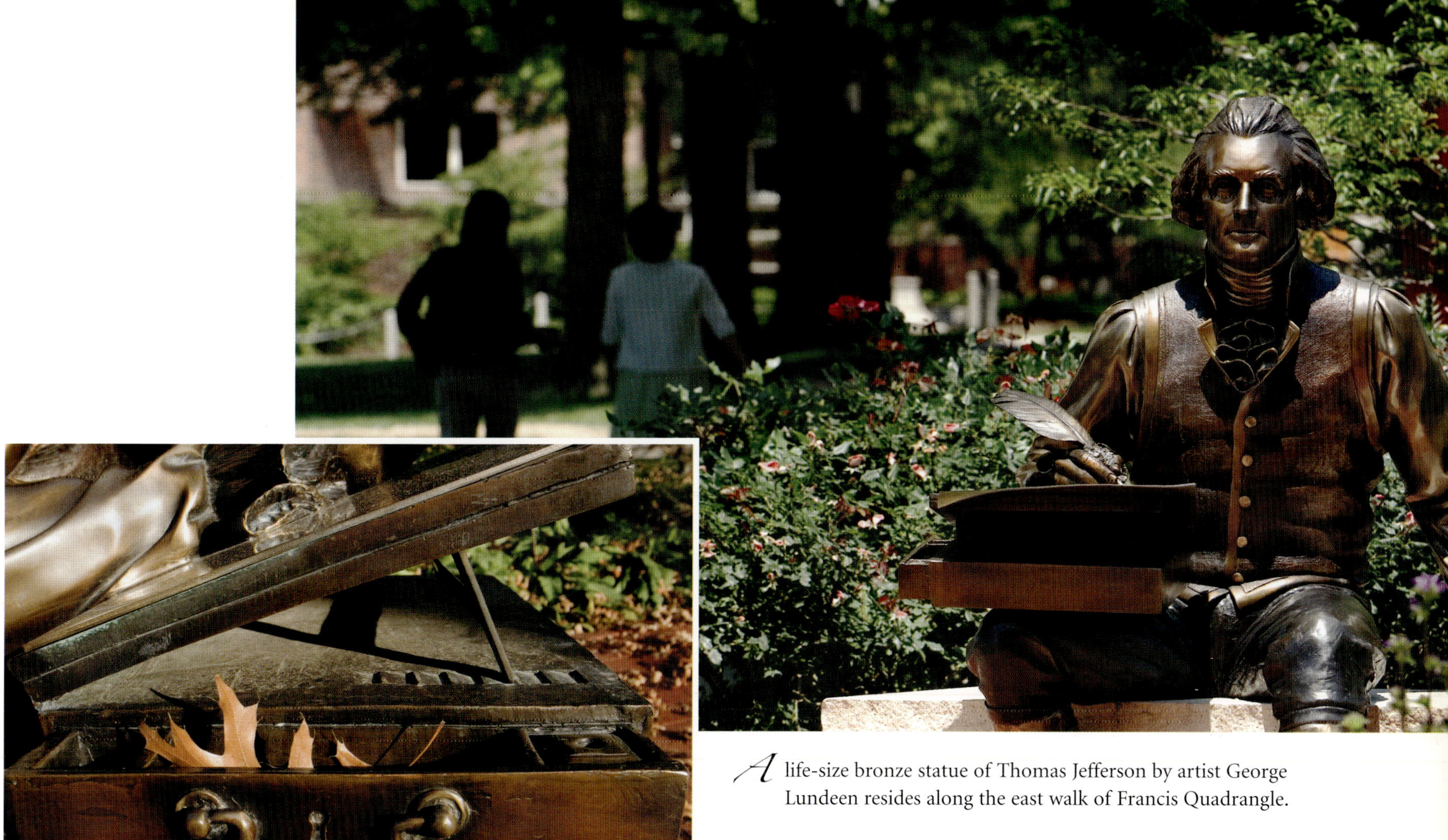

A life-size bronze statue of Thomas Jefferson by artist George Lundeen resides along the east walk of Francis Quadrangle.

An errant pin oak leaf finds its way into Thomas Jefferson's desk drawer. The Jefferson Club Trustees dedicated the monument, adjacent to the Jefferson tombstone, on September 29, 2001.

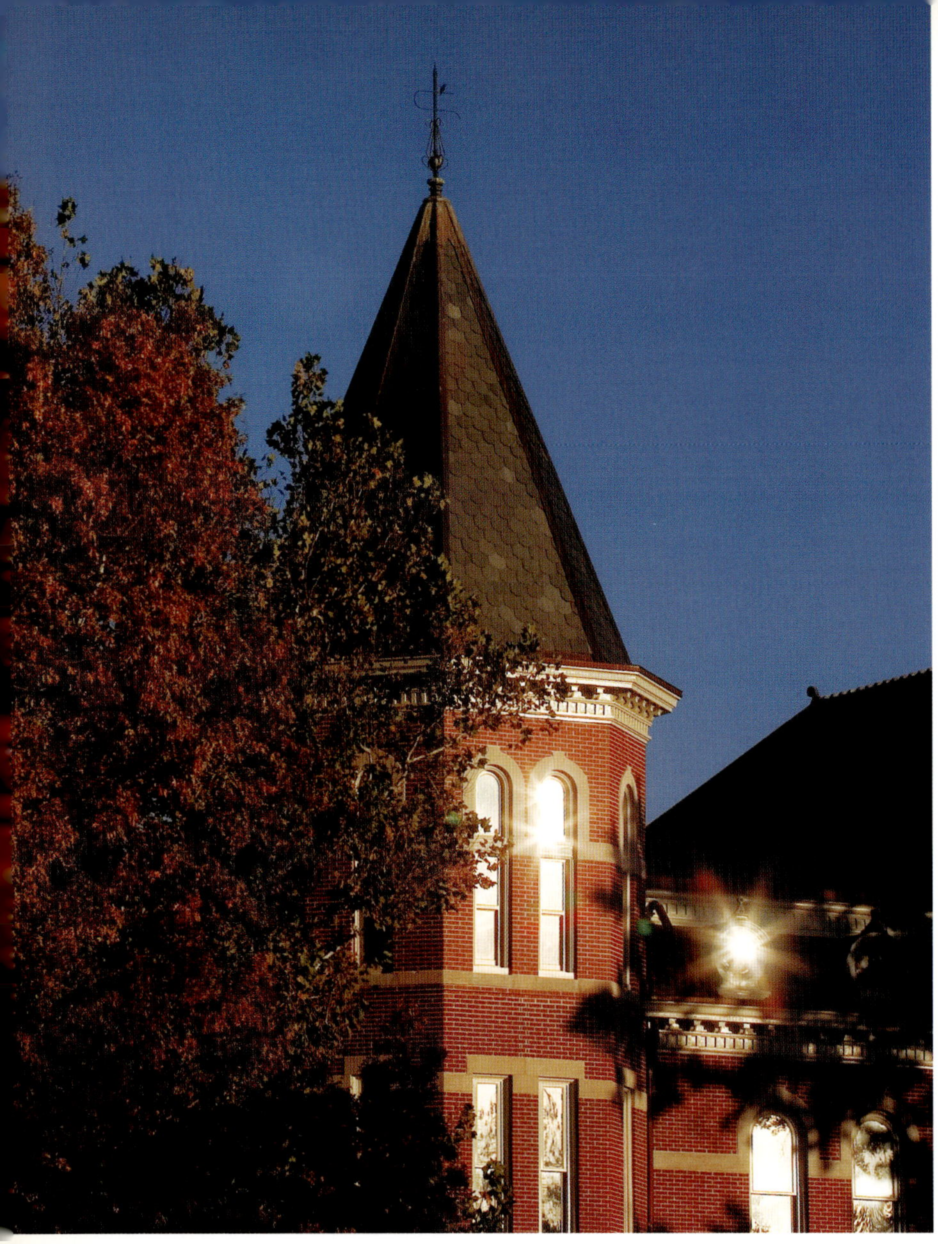

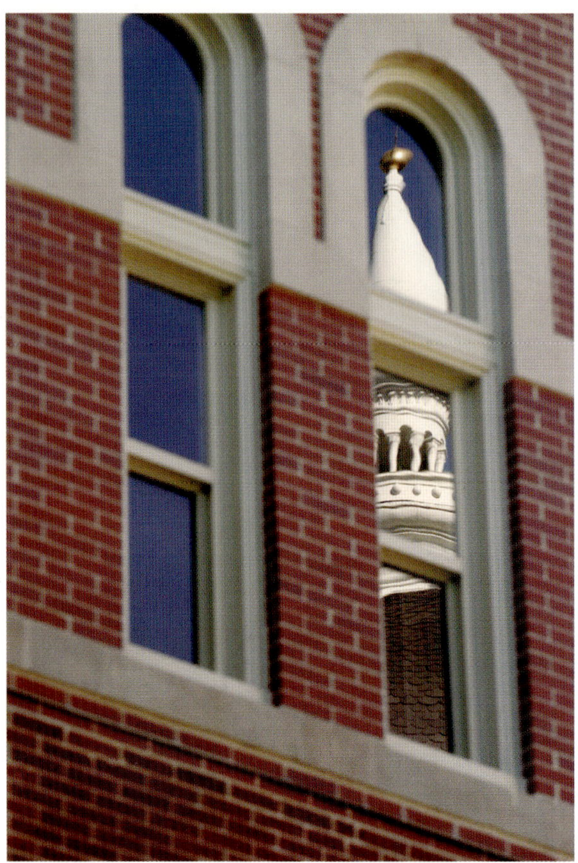

Arched windows of Swallow Hall reflect the Jesse Hall dome. The dome is supported with heavy timbers internally, and its outside cornices are mostly stamped sheet metal.

Late-afternoon sun reflects from the windows of Swallow Hall, built in 1893 from a design by architect M. F. Bell. After a tornado snatched one of the corner conical towers in 1931, the other was removed to maintain symmetry. Affectionately known as witch's hats, they were reproduced and replaced in 2001. The towers are secondary to the nearby Jesse Hall dome but animate the silhouette of Francis Quadrangle.

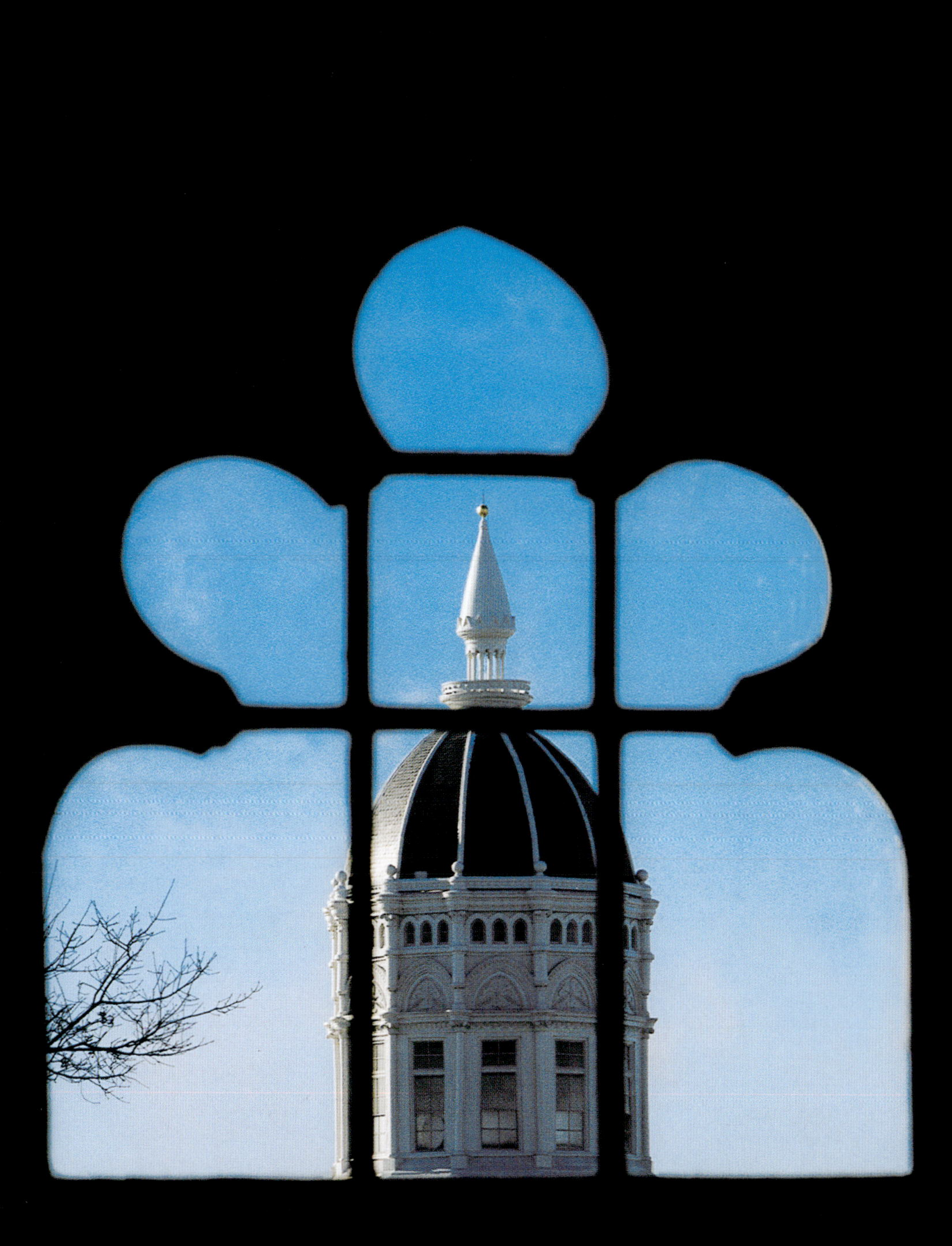

The silhouette of the University is punctuated by two much-loved towers, those of the Memorial Union and Jesse Hall. In this photo, one of the Union's Gothic second-floor windows provides a dramatic frame for the Jesse dome. Preserving a view of both towers is part of the campus's long-range master plan.

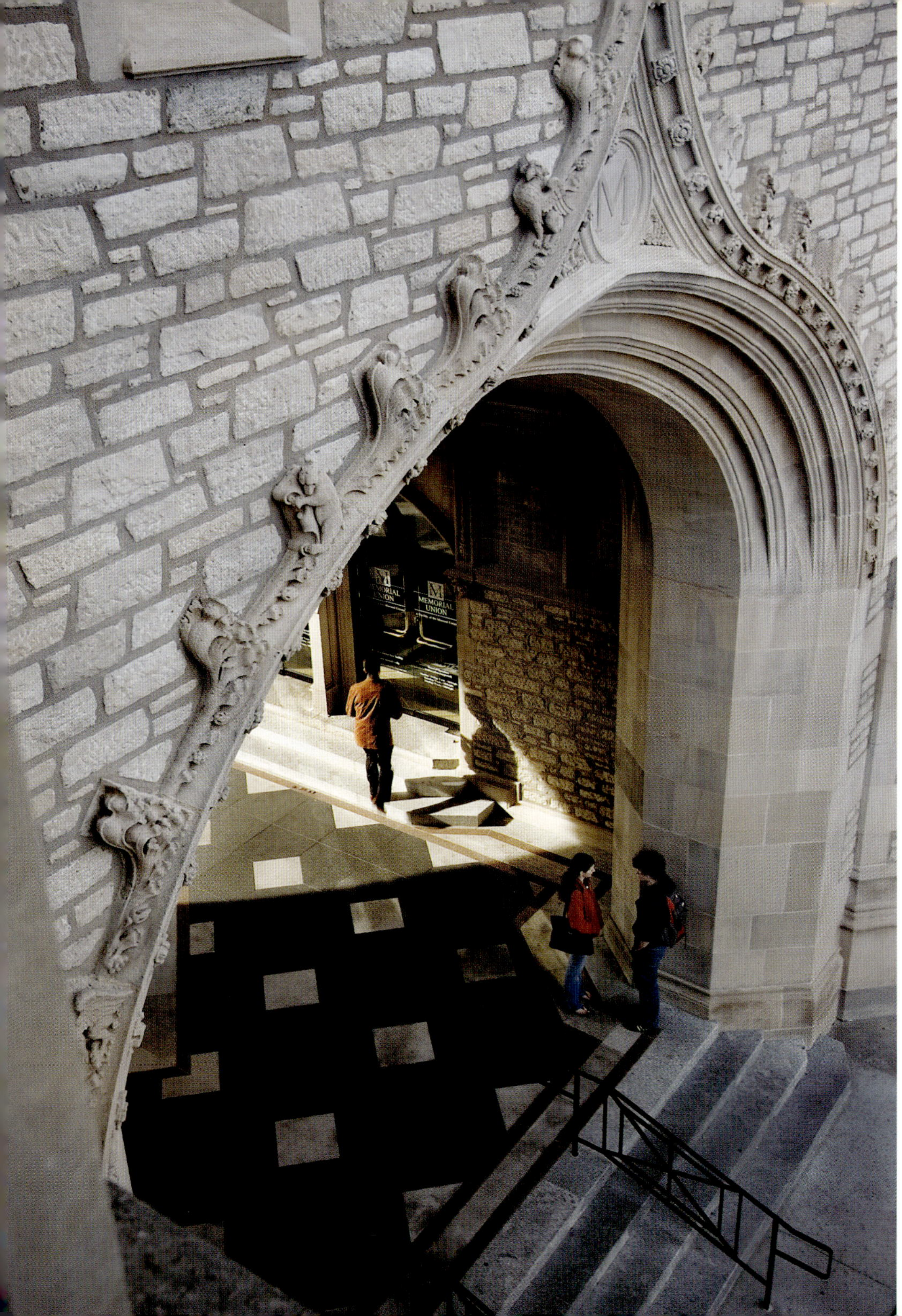

This ogee arch of Memorial Union includes humorous depictions about academic life. The little stone carvings on this and other White Campus buildings include soldiers, sailors, mythological beasts, and farm symbols such as plows. Today, the Gothic bell tower connects the north and south wings of Memorial Union. The tower, approximately 140 feet tall, stood alone from 1926 until 1952. It honors 117 Missouri sons who lost their lives in World War I.

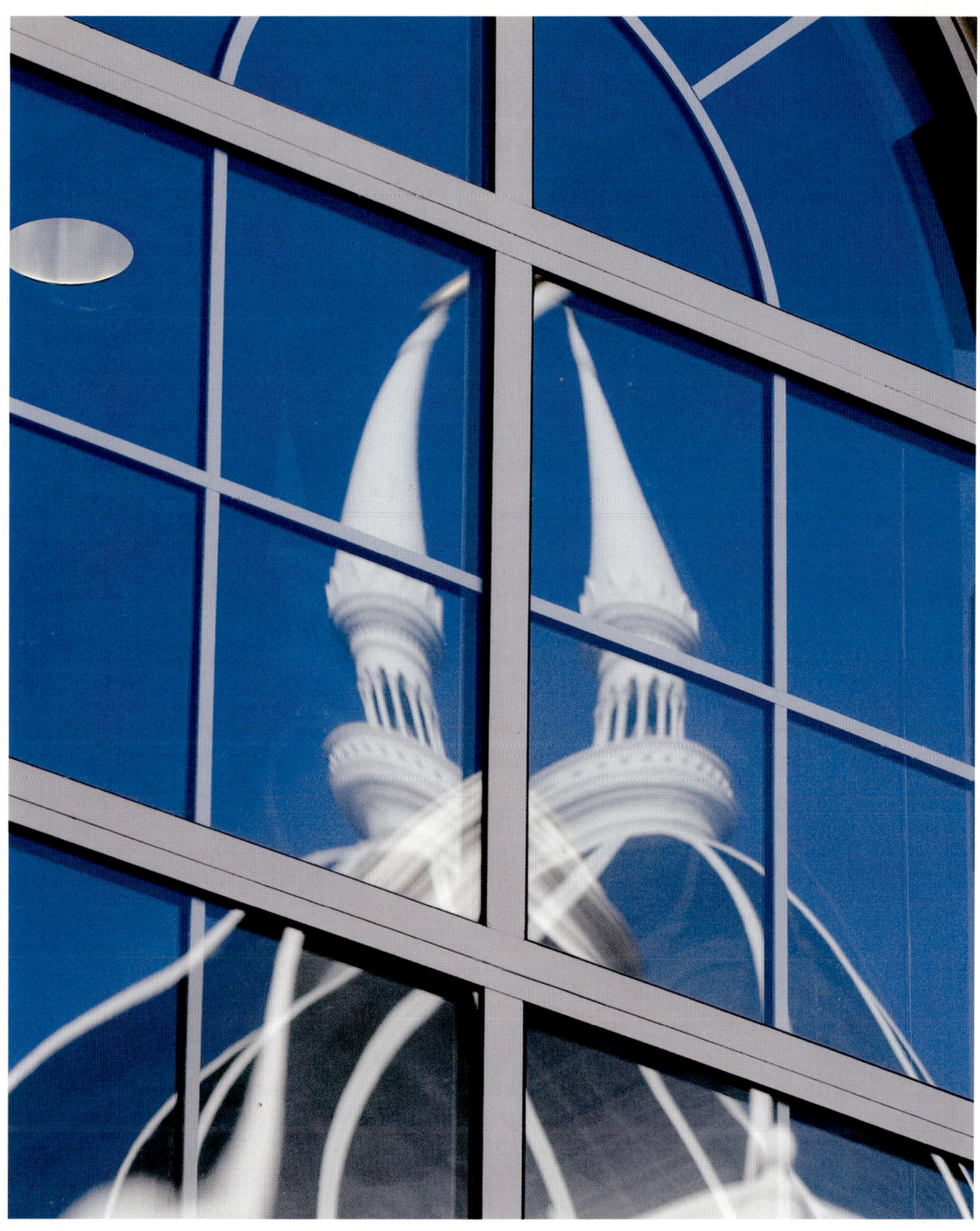

Through its reflective glass, Townsend Hall, renovated in 1998, pays a compliment to the historical and deorative building next door, Jesse Hall.

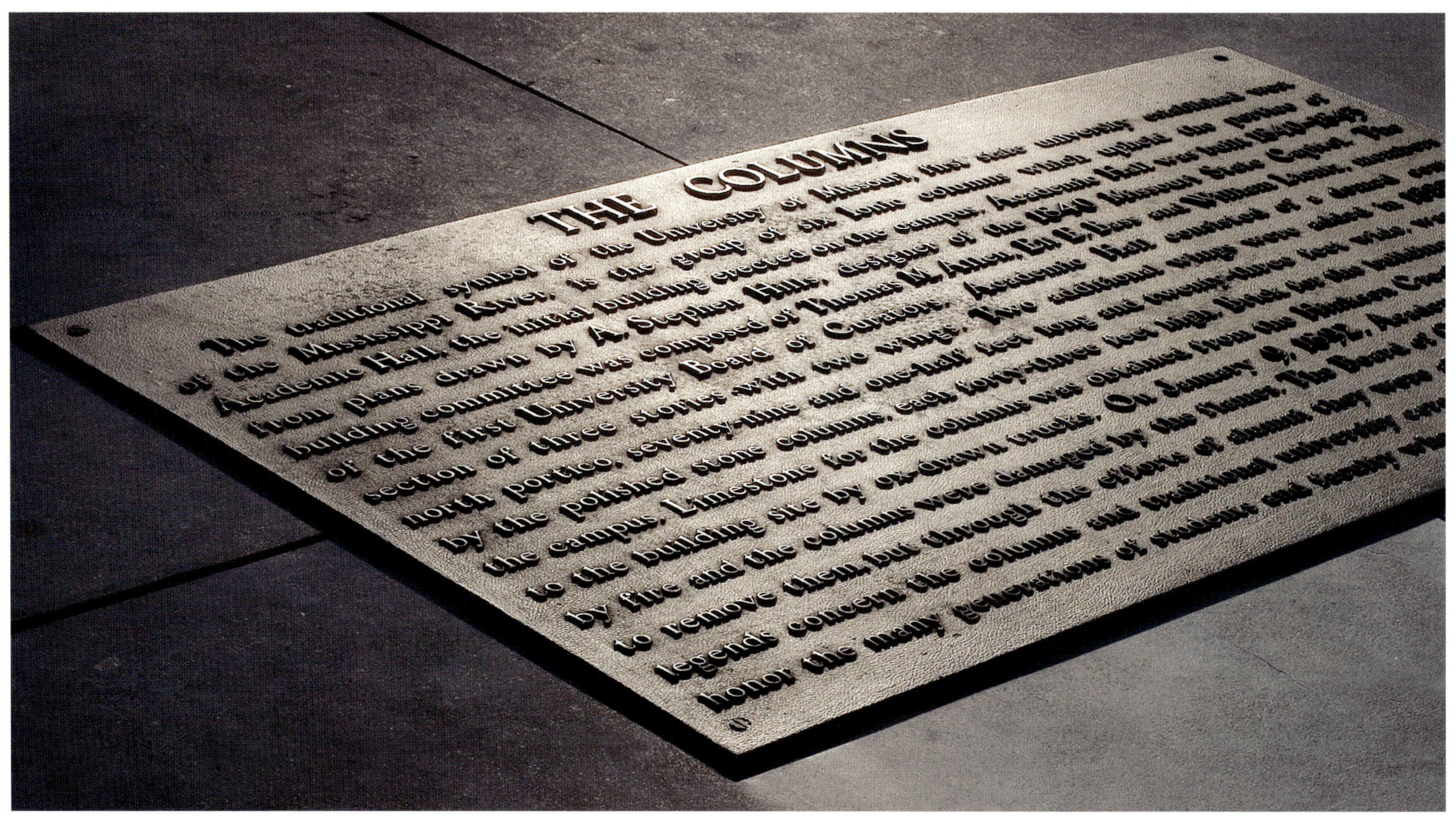

A tablet at Circle Drive details the history of the Columns. When a fire destroyed Academic Hall in 1892, story has it that the president of the Board of Curators ordered a pair of mule teams to tear down the still standing Columns. Alumni and townspeople got wind of it and persuaded the curators to cease and desist. The revered Columns stand as a symbol of the spirit of Mizzou.

In late summer, a half moon rises in a blue sky over the Columns on Francis Quadrangle. The Greek Ionic capitals sit on unfluted column shafts, a Neoclassical combination invented in the eighteenth century. The Columns stand an estimated forty-three to forty-six feet in height, including the pedestals.

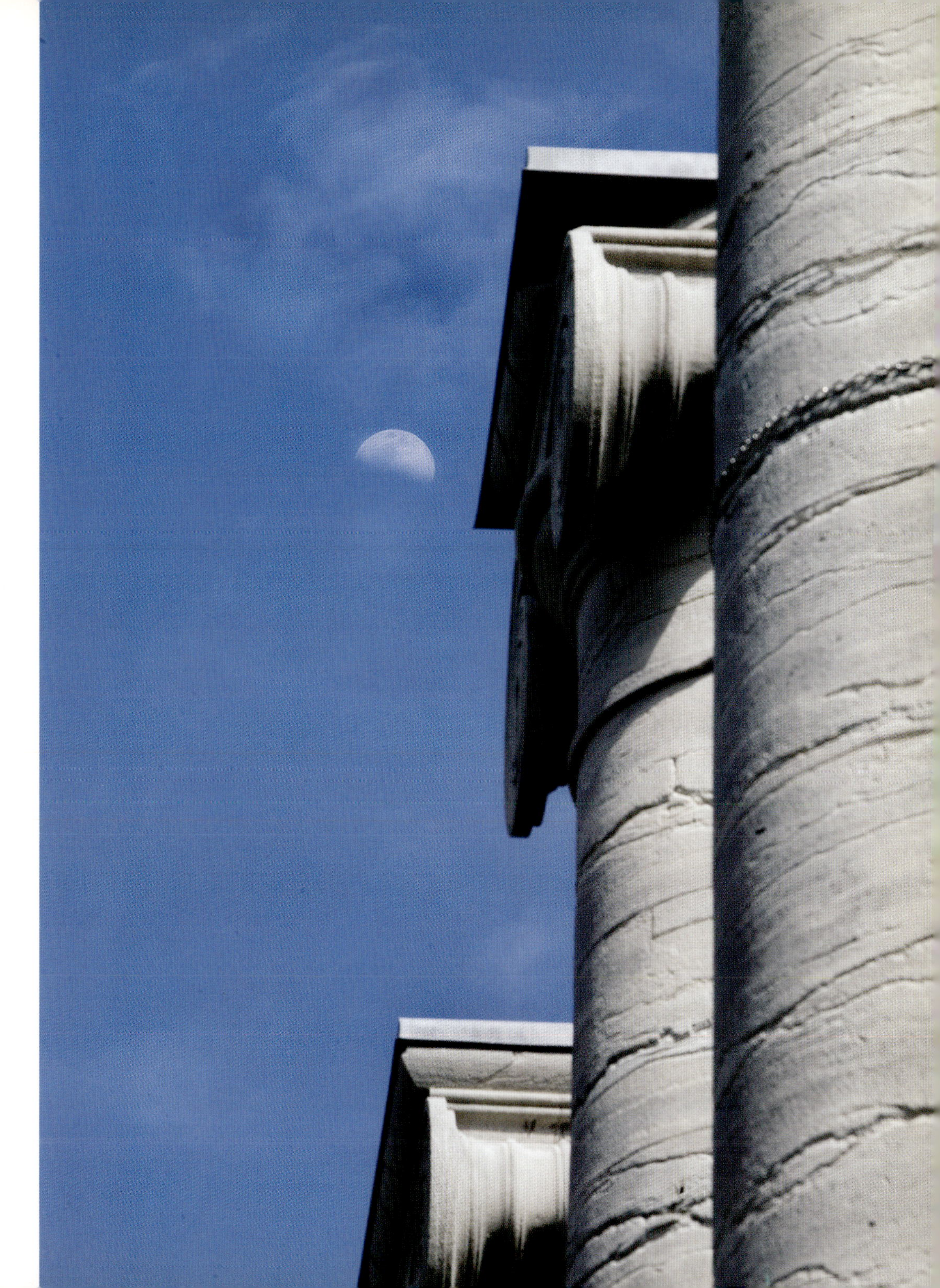

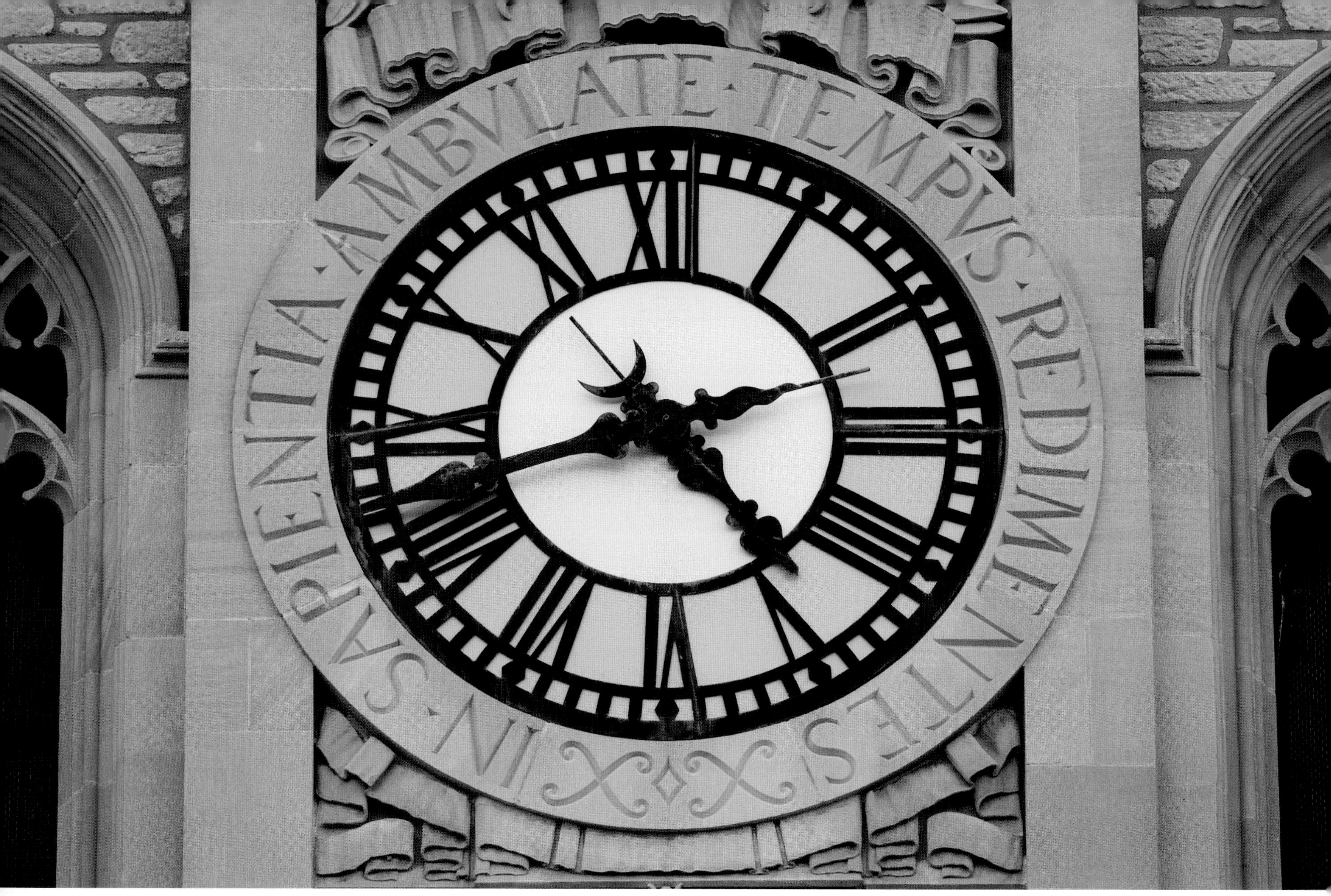

The Latin inscription on the Memorial Union tower clock reads, *In sapientia ambulate tempus redimentes.* Translated, it means, "Walk in wisdom, gaining time." Memorial Union was built in four parts—tower, north wing, chapel, and south wing—beginning in 1923 with the tower.

Students scurry past a flowering crab apple tree on Lowry Mall.

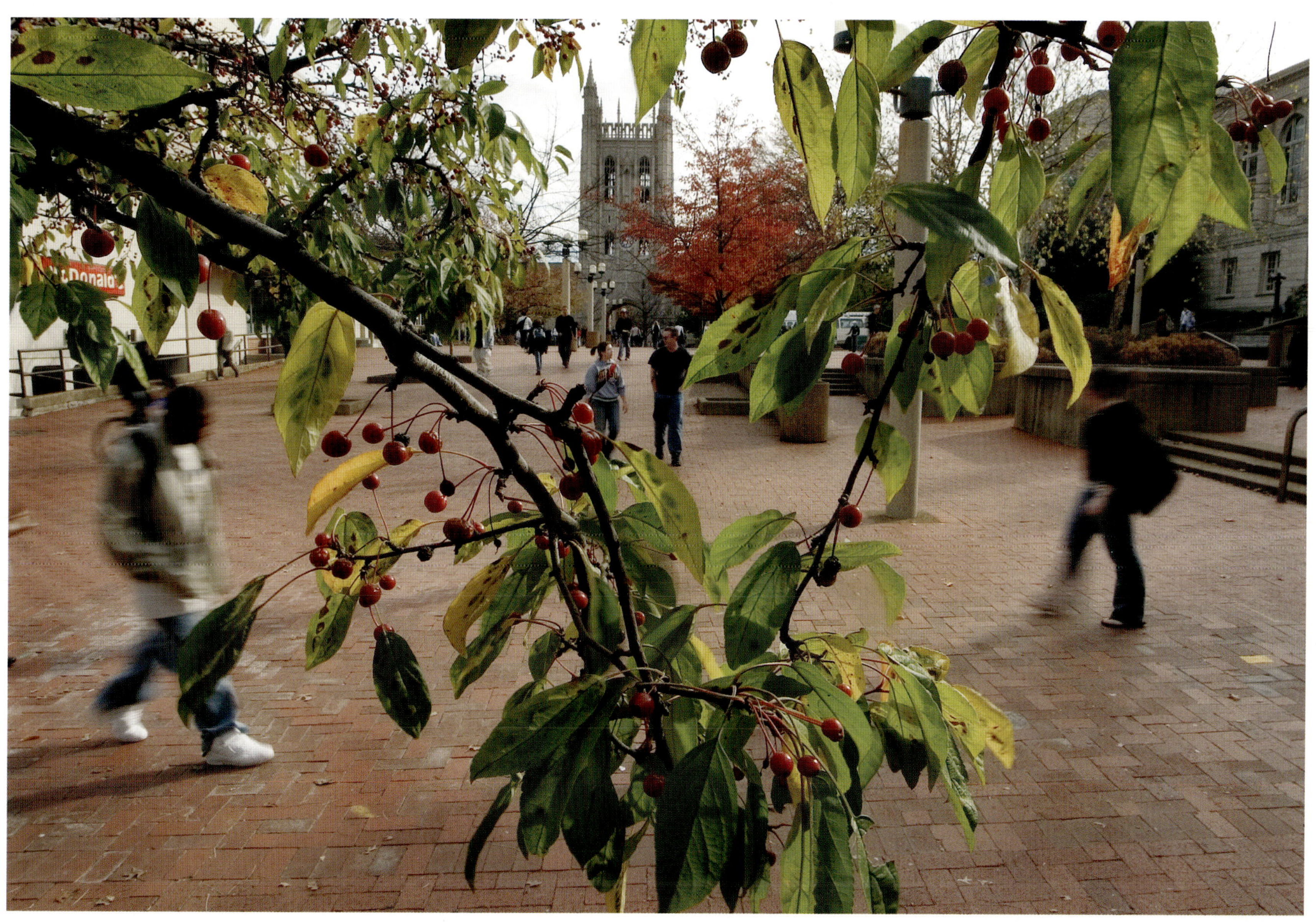

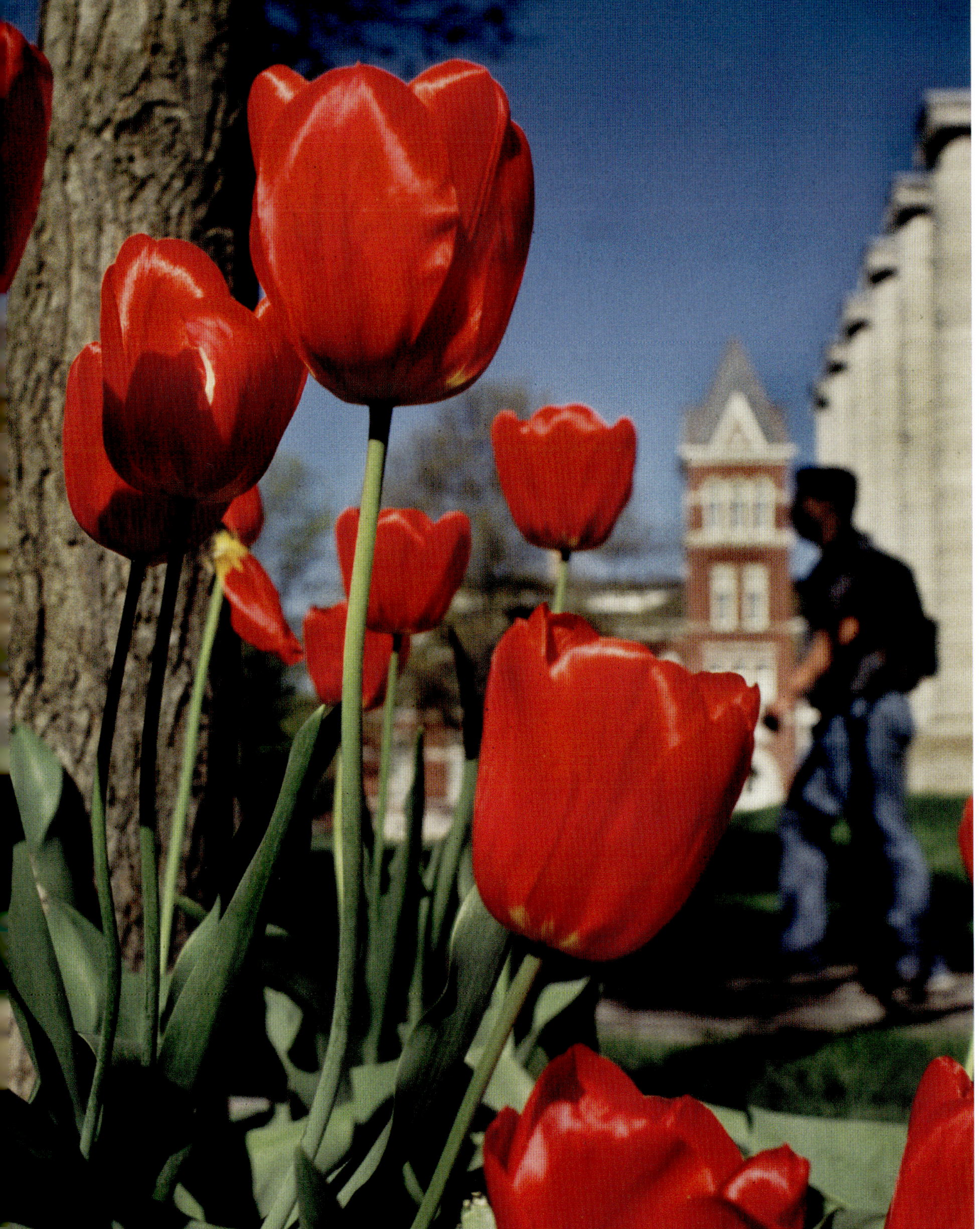

Red tulips bloom in spring beside the Thomas Jefferson tombstone. The simply designed monument was given to MU in 1883 by Jefferson's heirs. The Columns and Lafferre Hall are in the background.

The texture of stone and brick sparkles in the early morning sun. A decorative masonry arch of five wedge-shaped voussoirs outlines a semicircular stained-glass window in Jesse Hall.

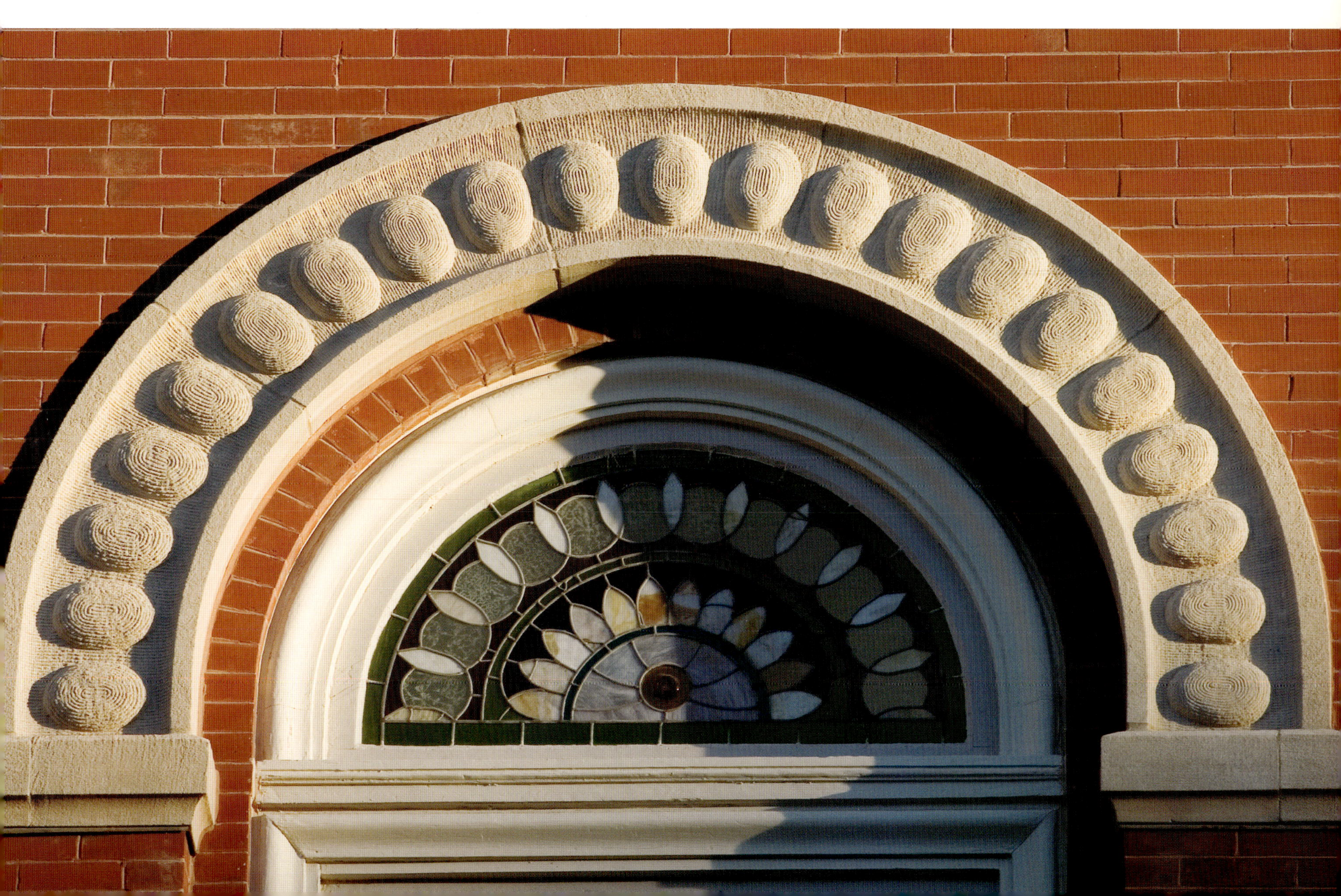

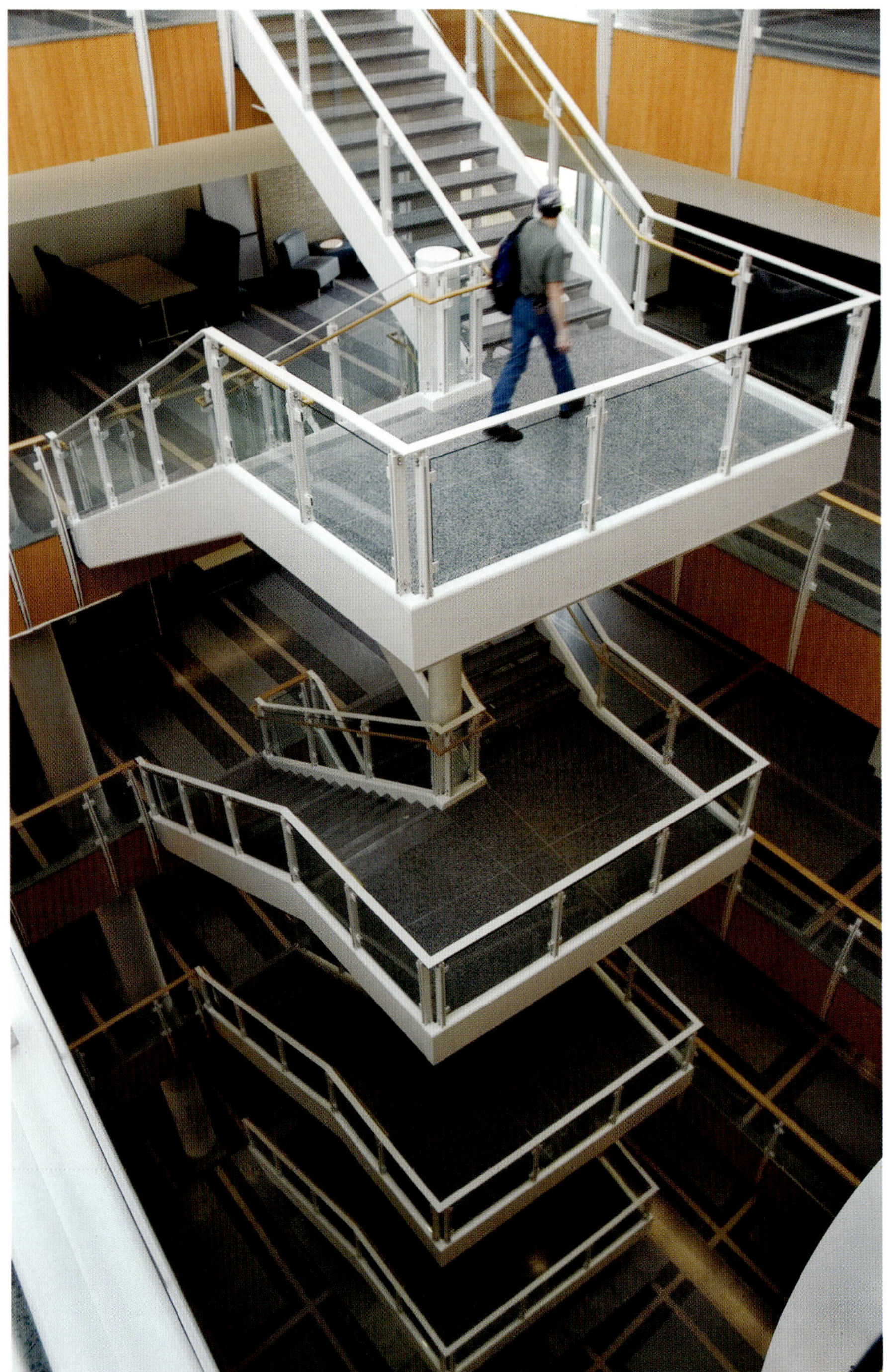

The Al and Mary Agnes McQuinn Atrium in the Christopher S. Bond Life Sciences Center, completed in 2004, fosters collaboration among scientists who work there. The building's upper levels offer spectacular views of campus.

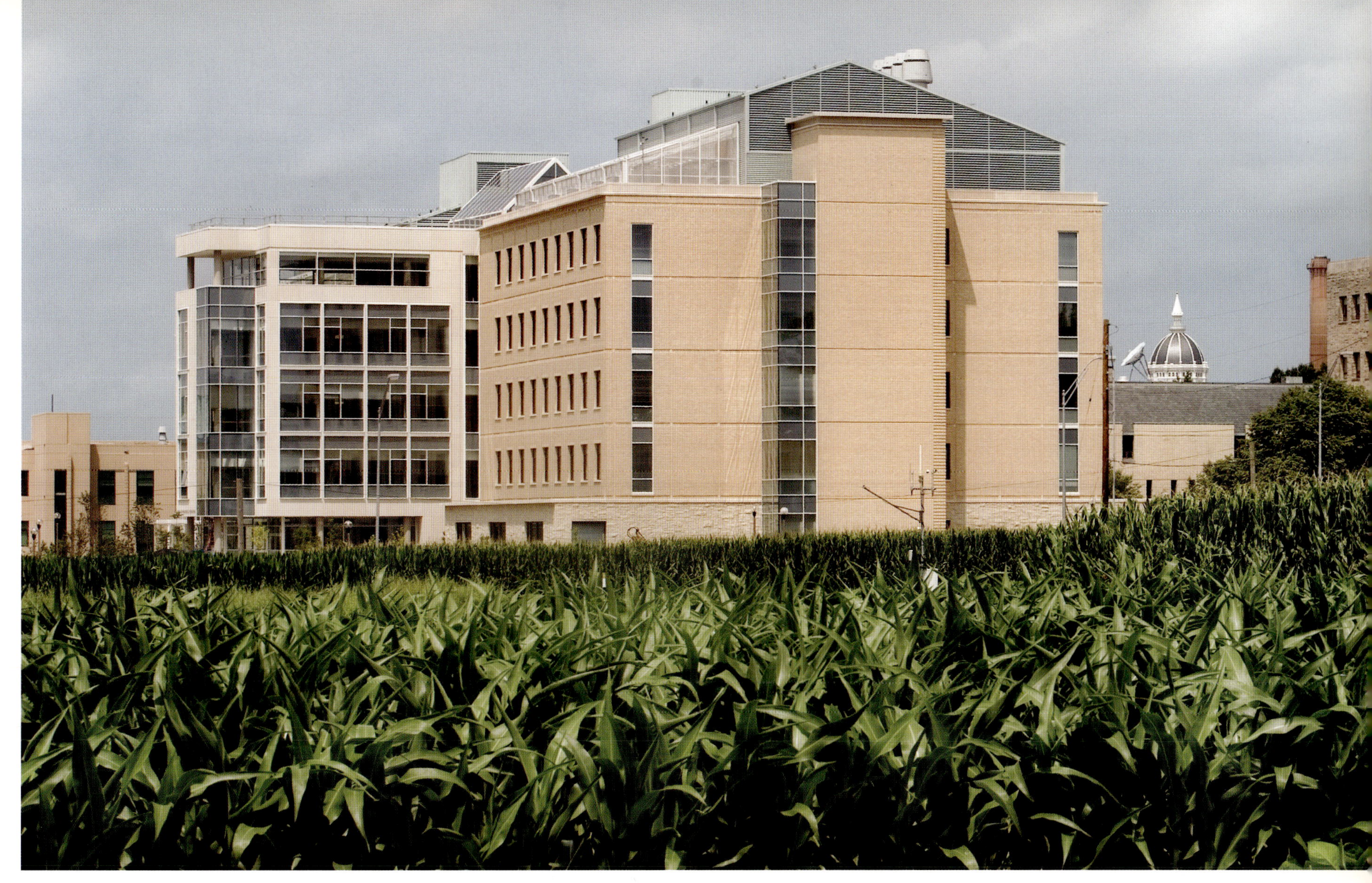

The Christopher S. Bond Life Sciences Center stands just west of the rows of corn in Sanborn Field. The field, begun in 1888, is the oldest agricultural experiment field west of the Mississippi River.

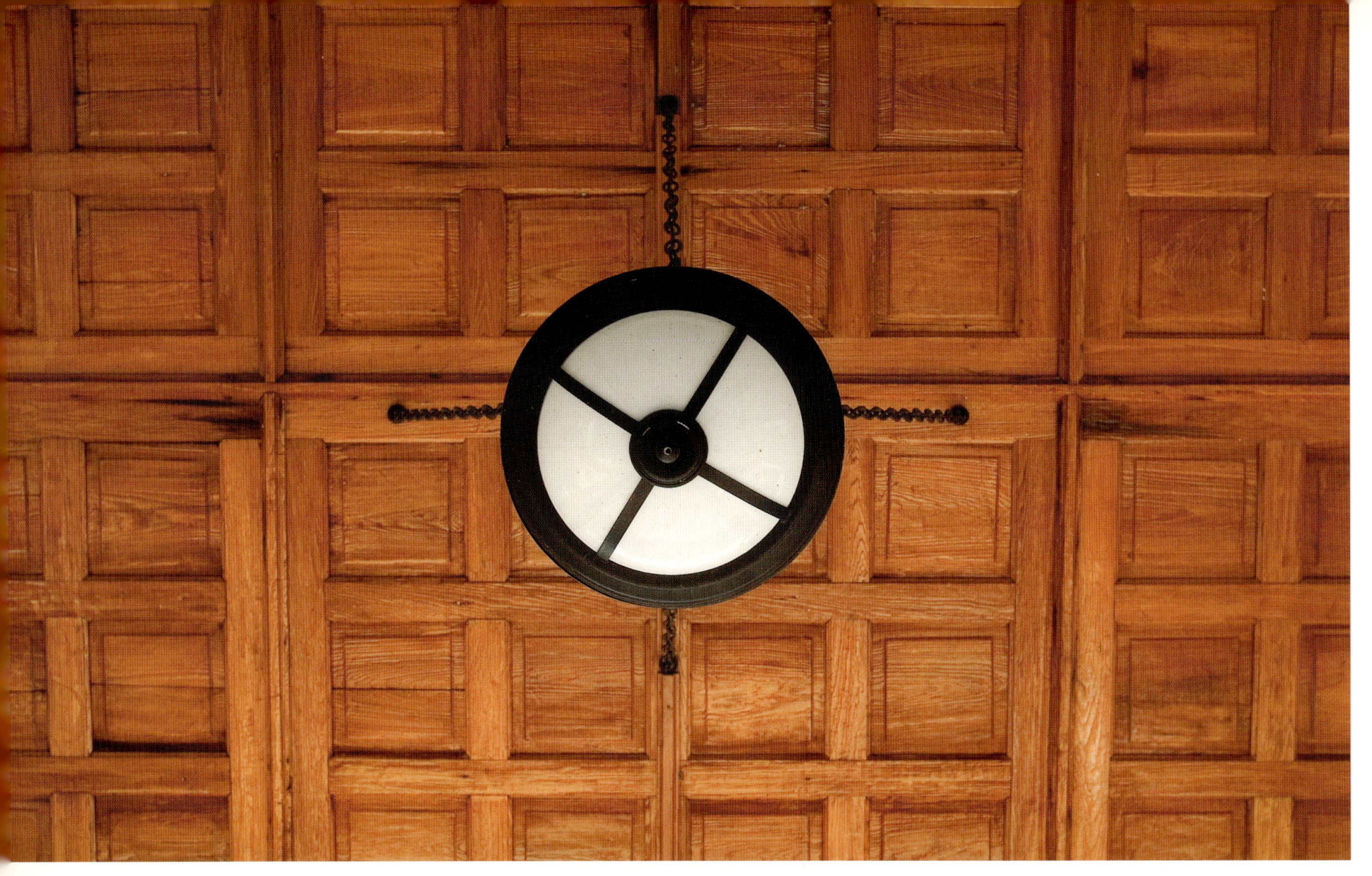

The wood-paneled ceiling on the south porch of Jesse Hall forms a geometric pattern.

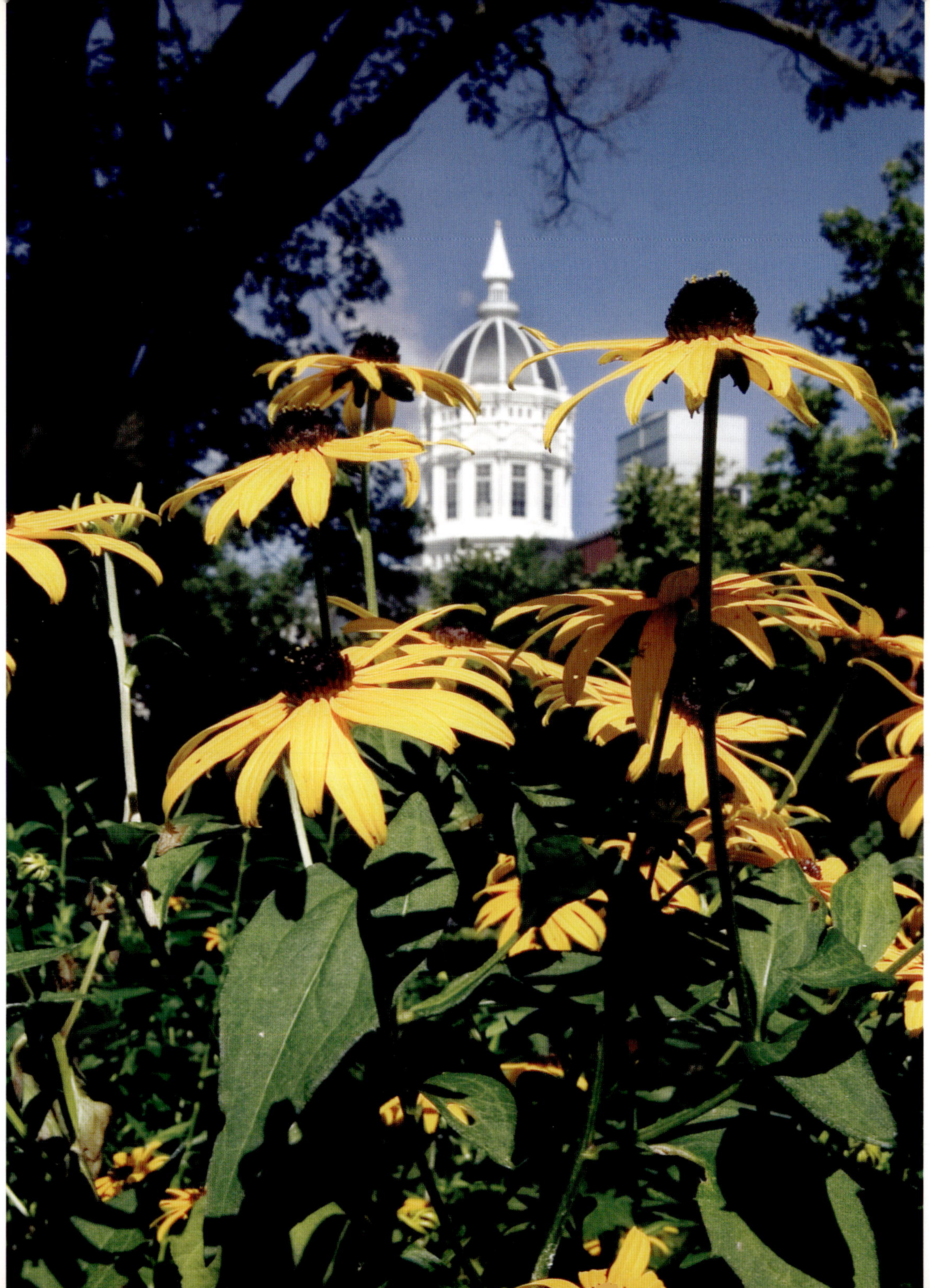

Black-eyed Susans stretch to the sun and frame the Jesse Hall dome as viewed from the west lawn of Ellis Library.

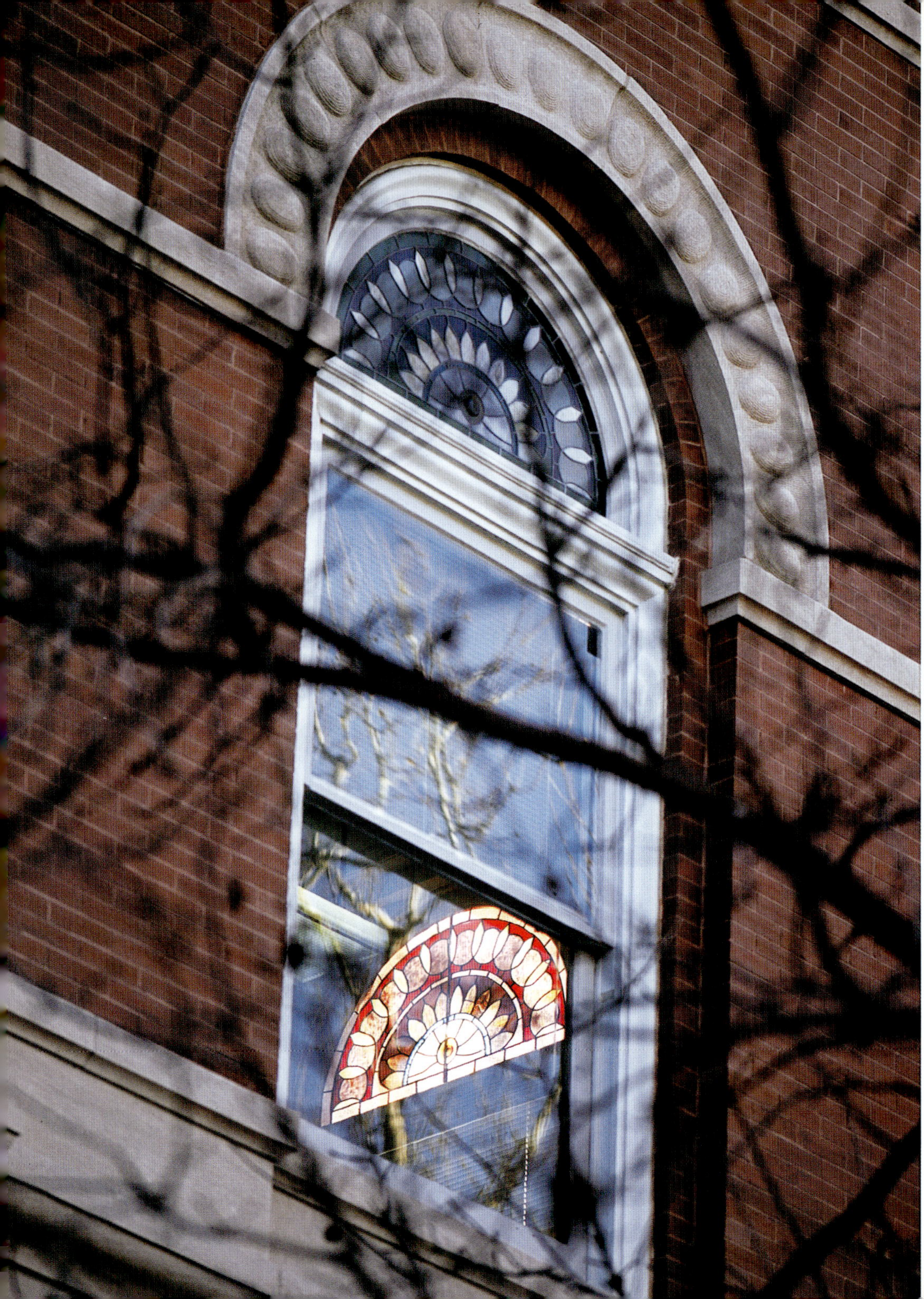

Stained-glass windows lit by the southern sun cast beautiful colors that extend outside Jesse Hall. Bare branches signal winter.

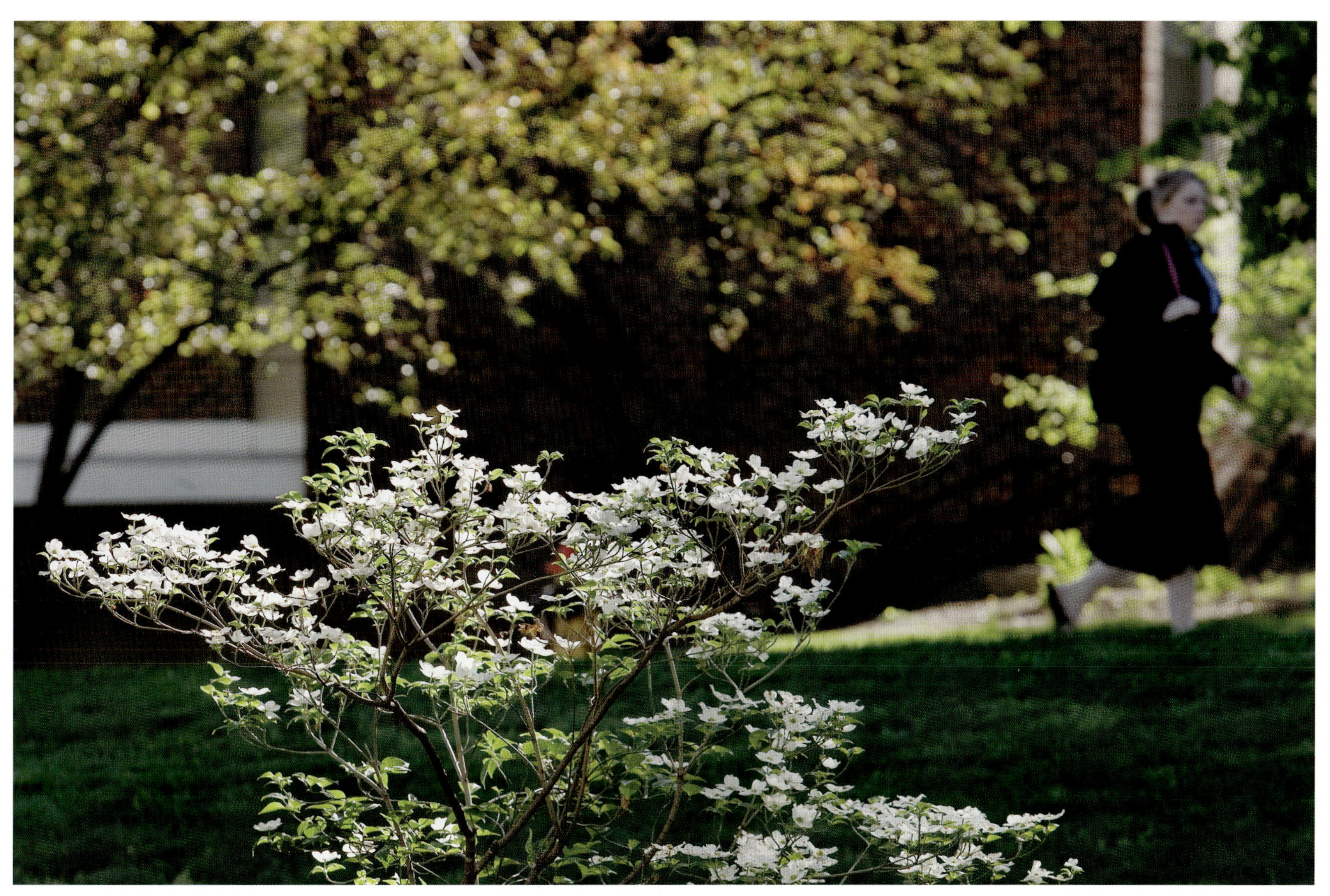

A student walks near Gannett Hall in this view from Peace Park. A dogwood flowers in the foreground.

Fall-planted Dutch bulbs explode with spring color in the beds along the Arts and Science Mall. Students with cell phones are ubiquitous as spring blooms on campus.

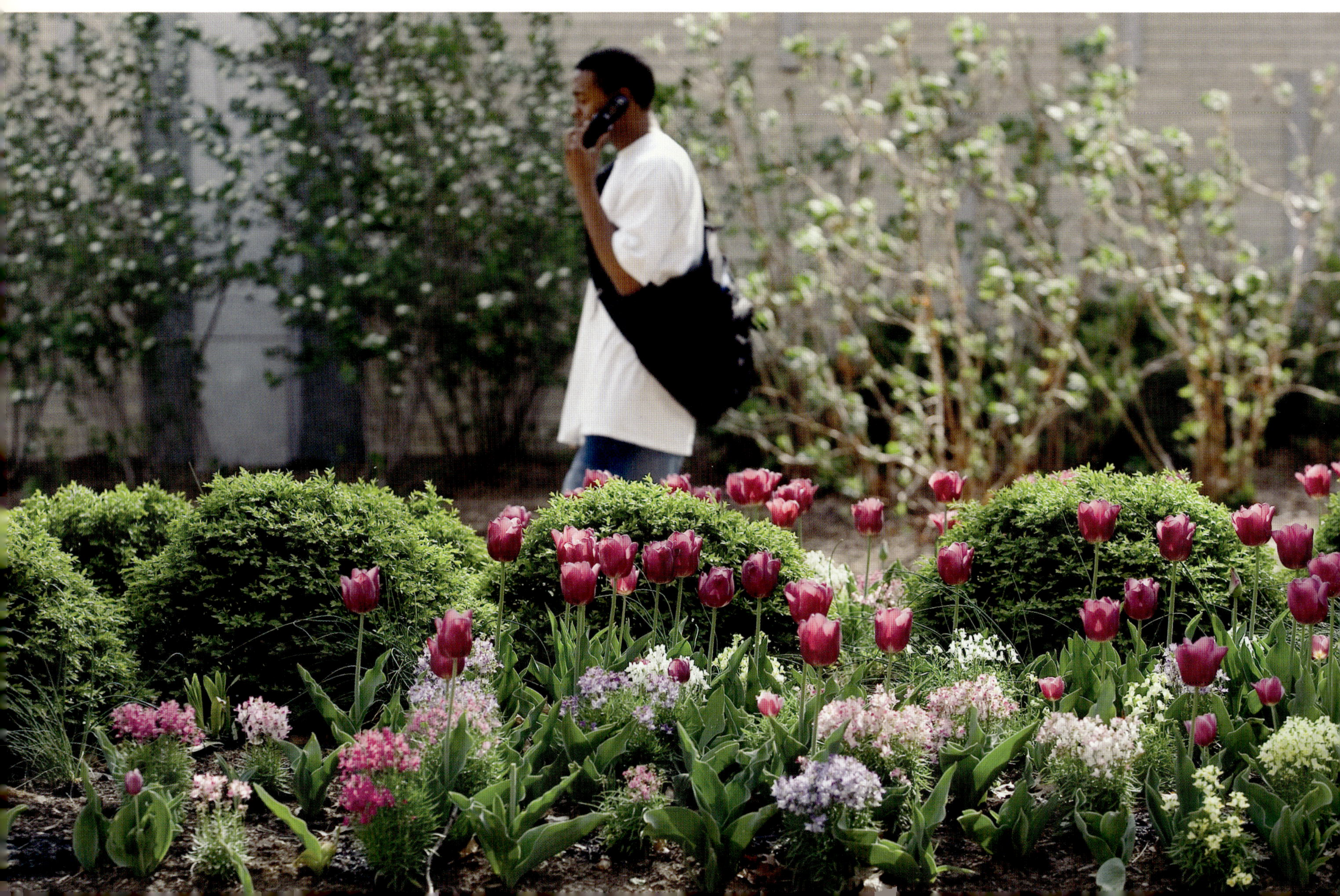

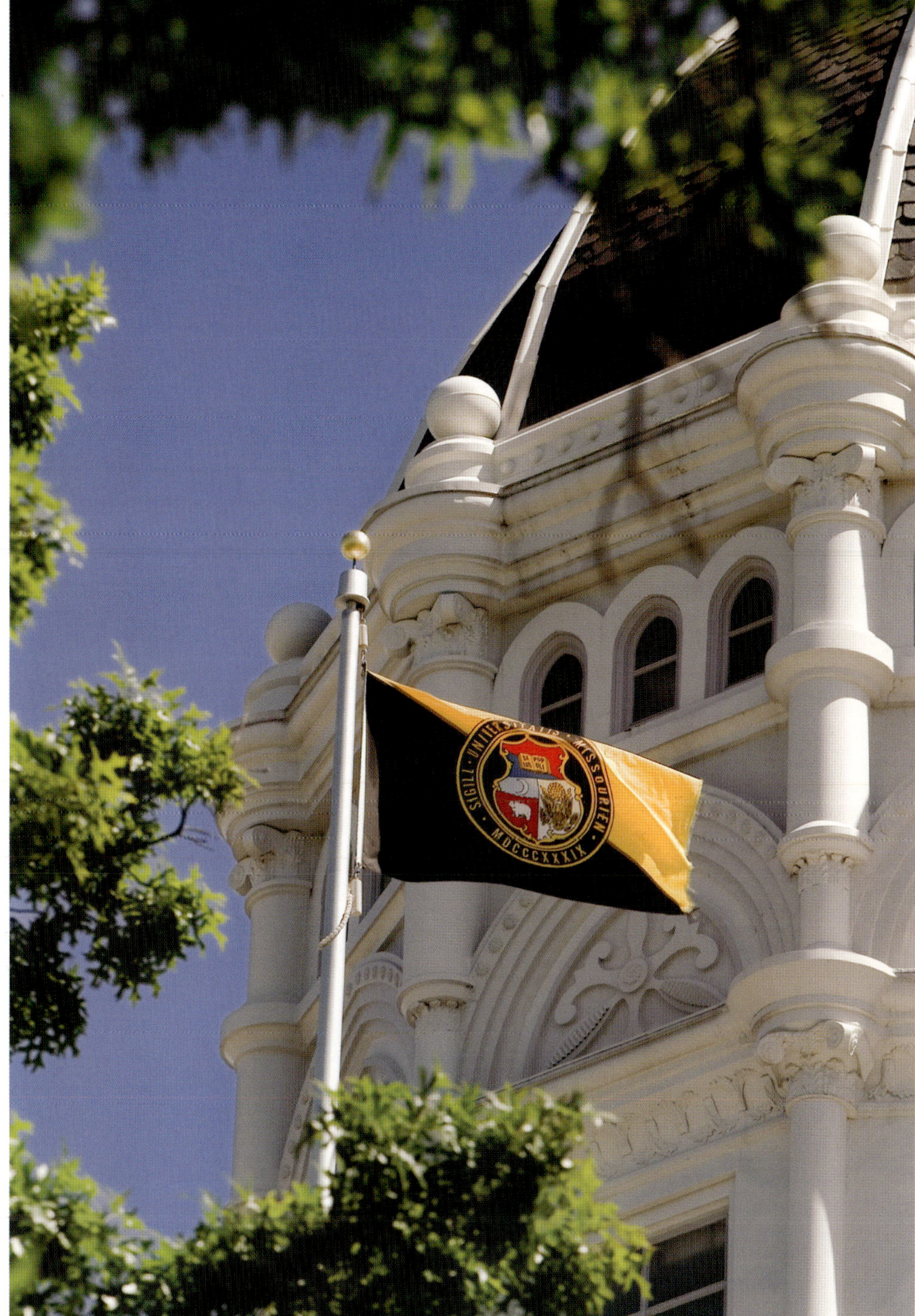

Framed with pin oak leaves from Francis Quadrangle, the University of Missouri flag in black and gold flies on the roof of Jesse Hall.

Morning sun backlights the fronds of a Christmas fern on the northwest lawn of Ellis Library.

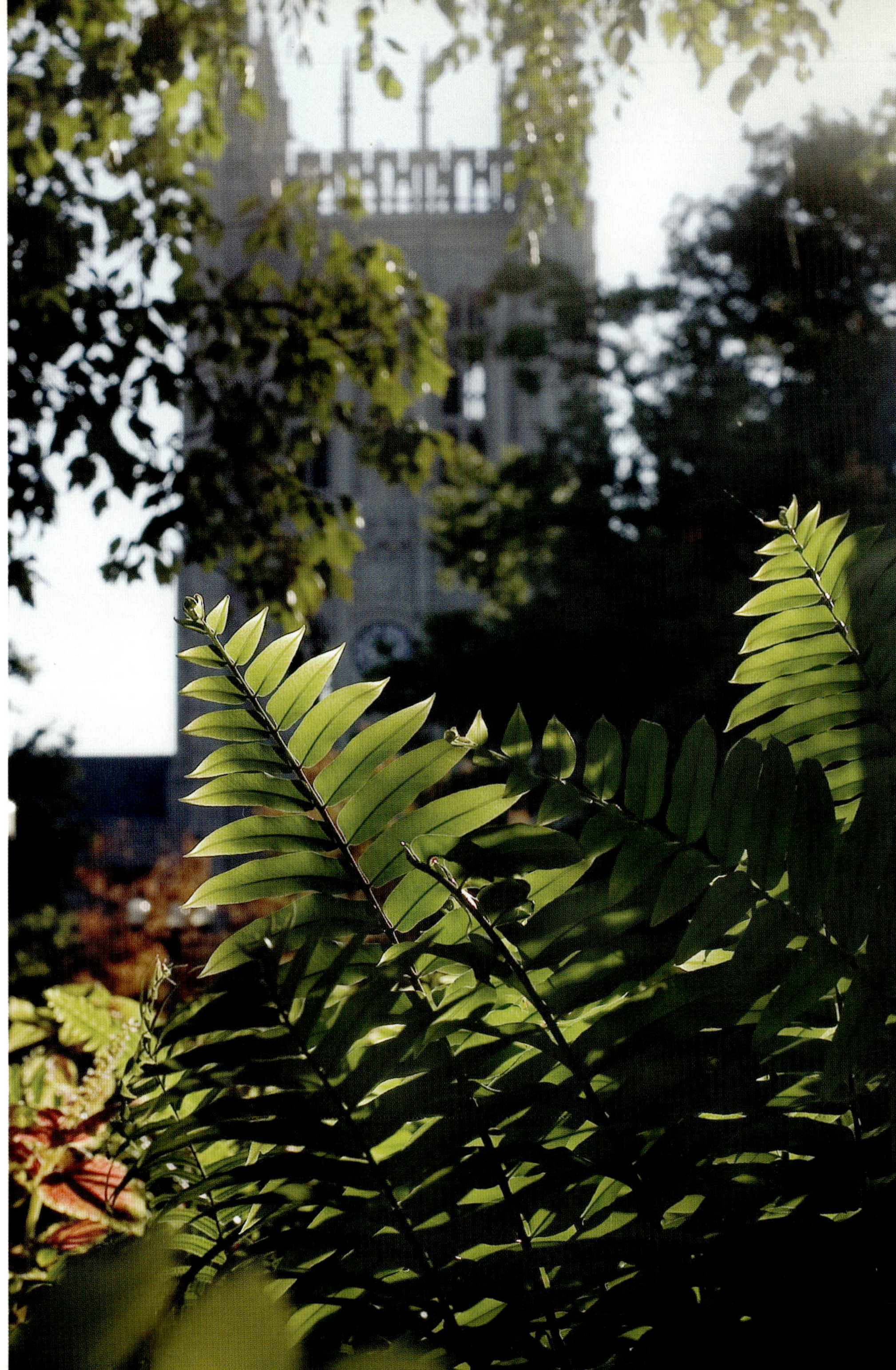

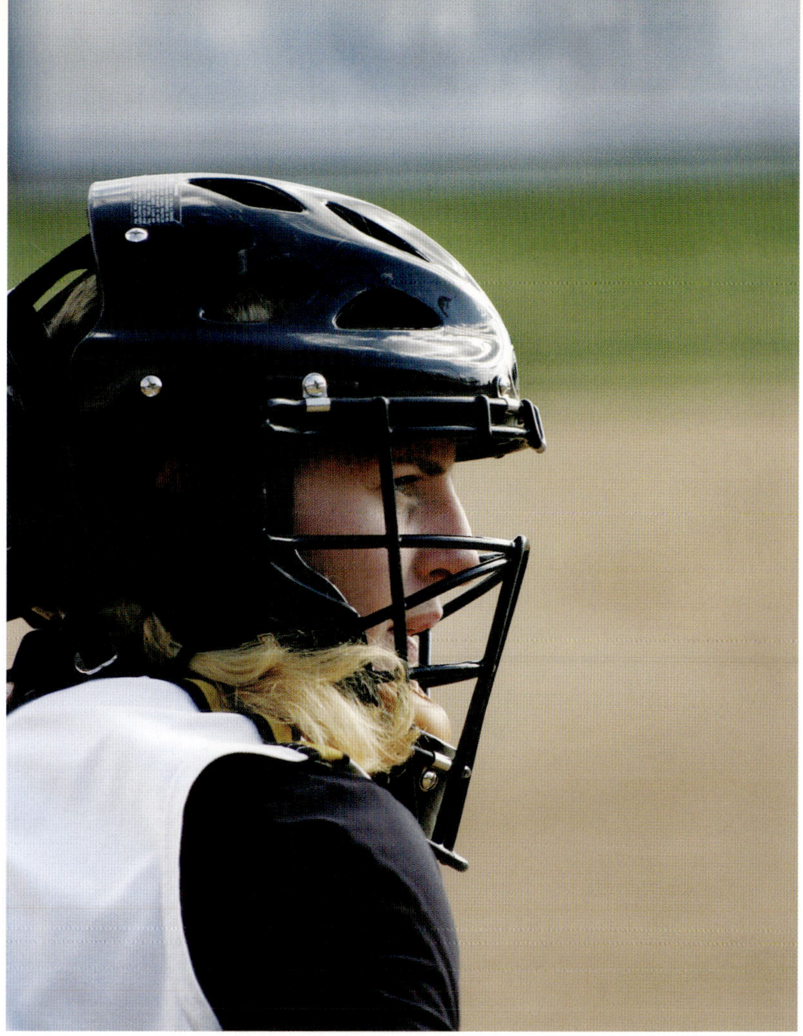

Catcher Kathy Masterson looks to the dugout for pitching signs during a softball game against Iowa State, April 2005.

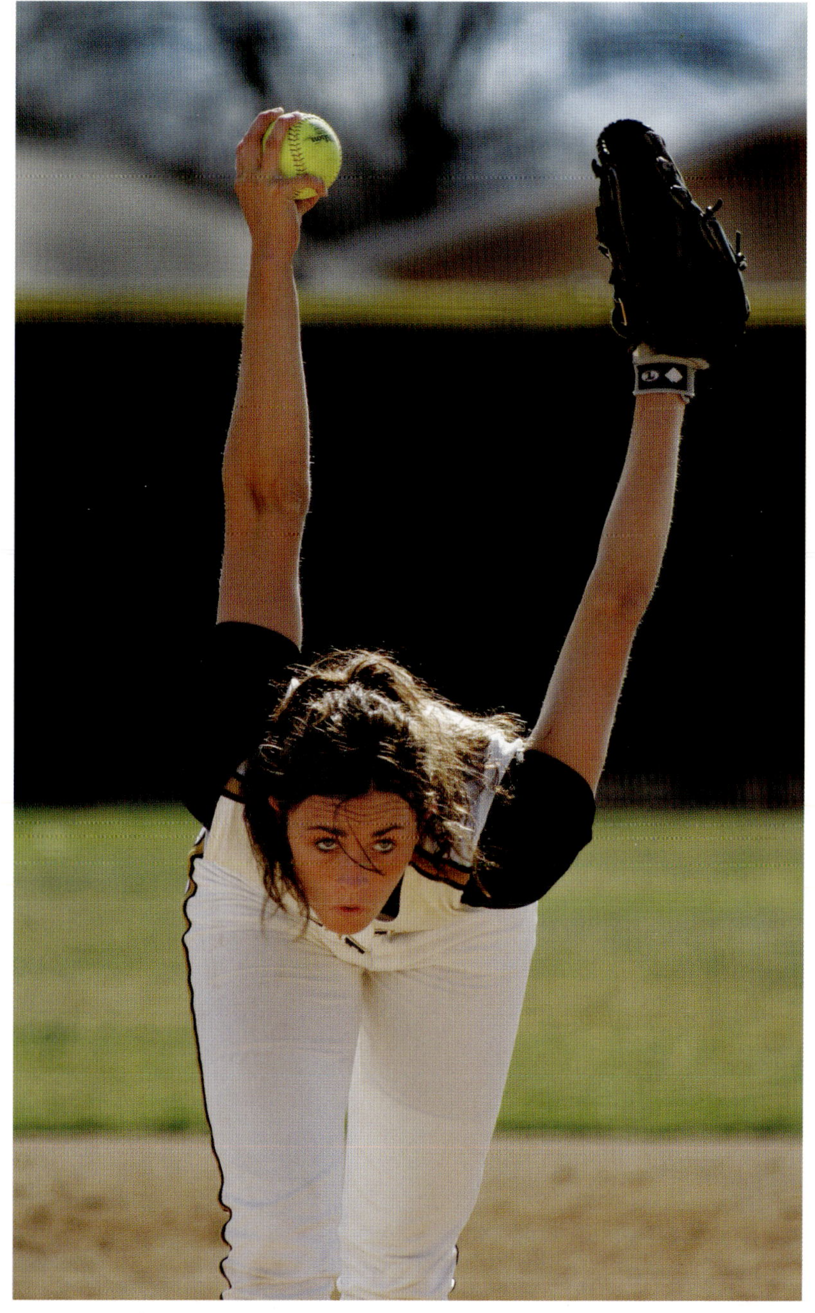

Jen Bruck delivers a pitch in a softball game at University Field, April 2005.

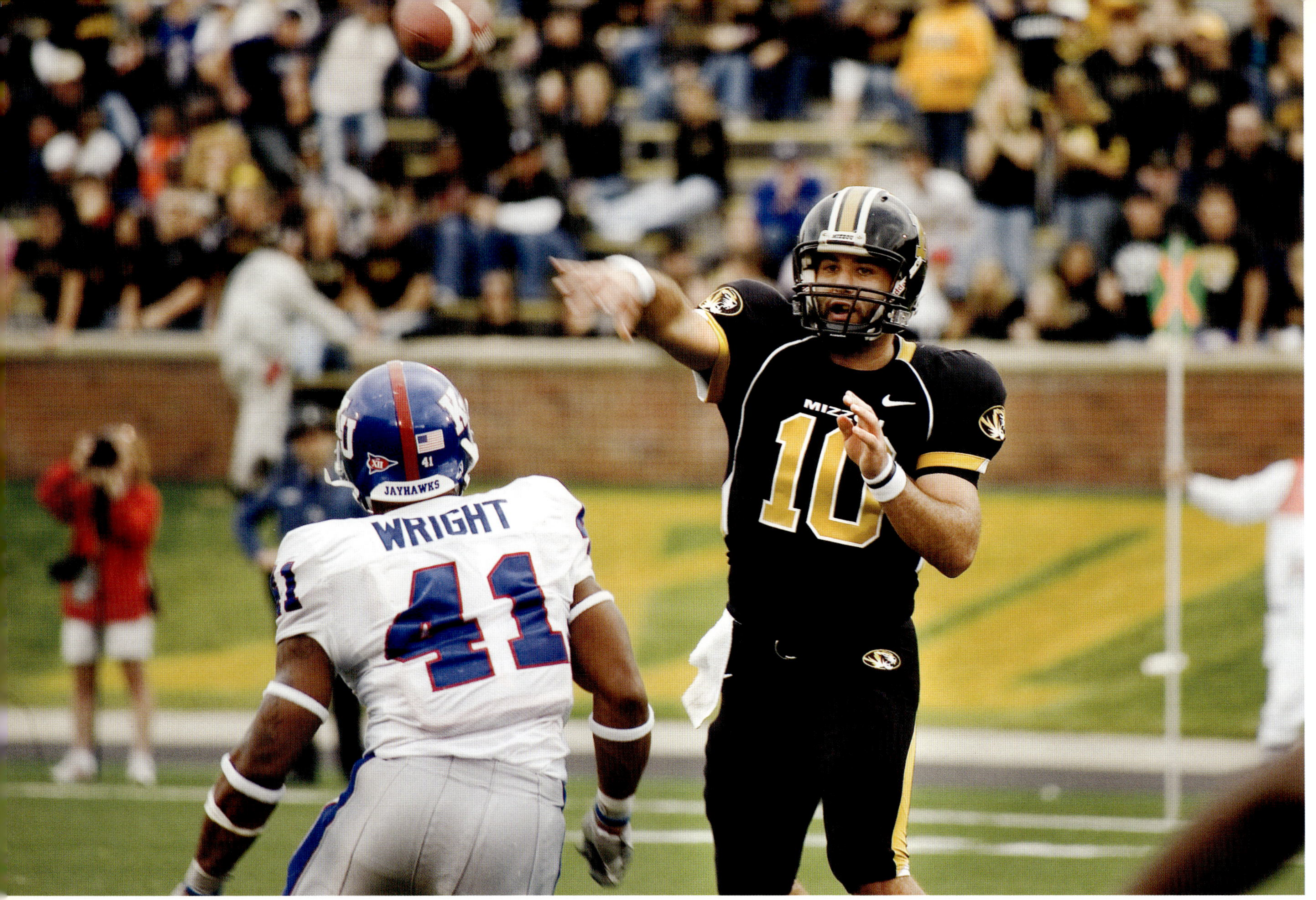

In the November 25, 2006, game versus the Kansas Jayhawks, quarterback Chase Daniel passes the ball to a Missouri receiver. In 2006, he leads Mizzou to an 8–5 record and an appearance in the Sun Bowl.

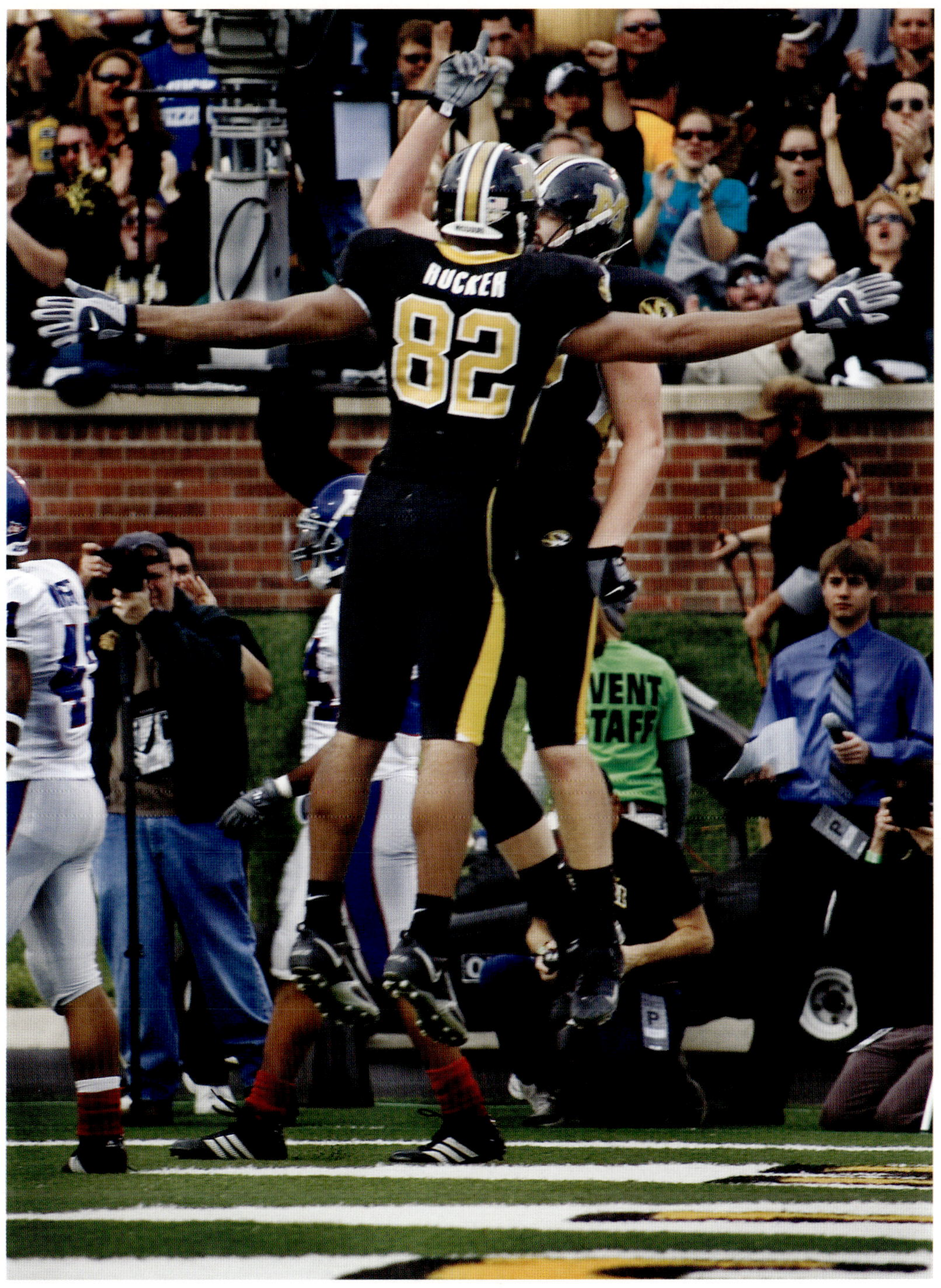

Martin Rucker and a teammate celebrate a touchdown against archrivals the Kansas Jayhawks, November 25, 2006. The Tigers win big, 42–17.

With much fanfare, the Tigers take to Faurot Field for the opening game of the season, September 2, 2006, versus Murray State. The Tigers win, 47–7.

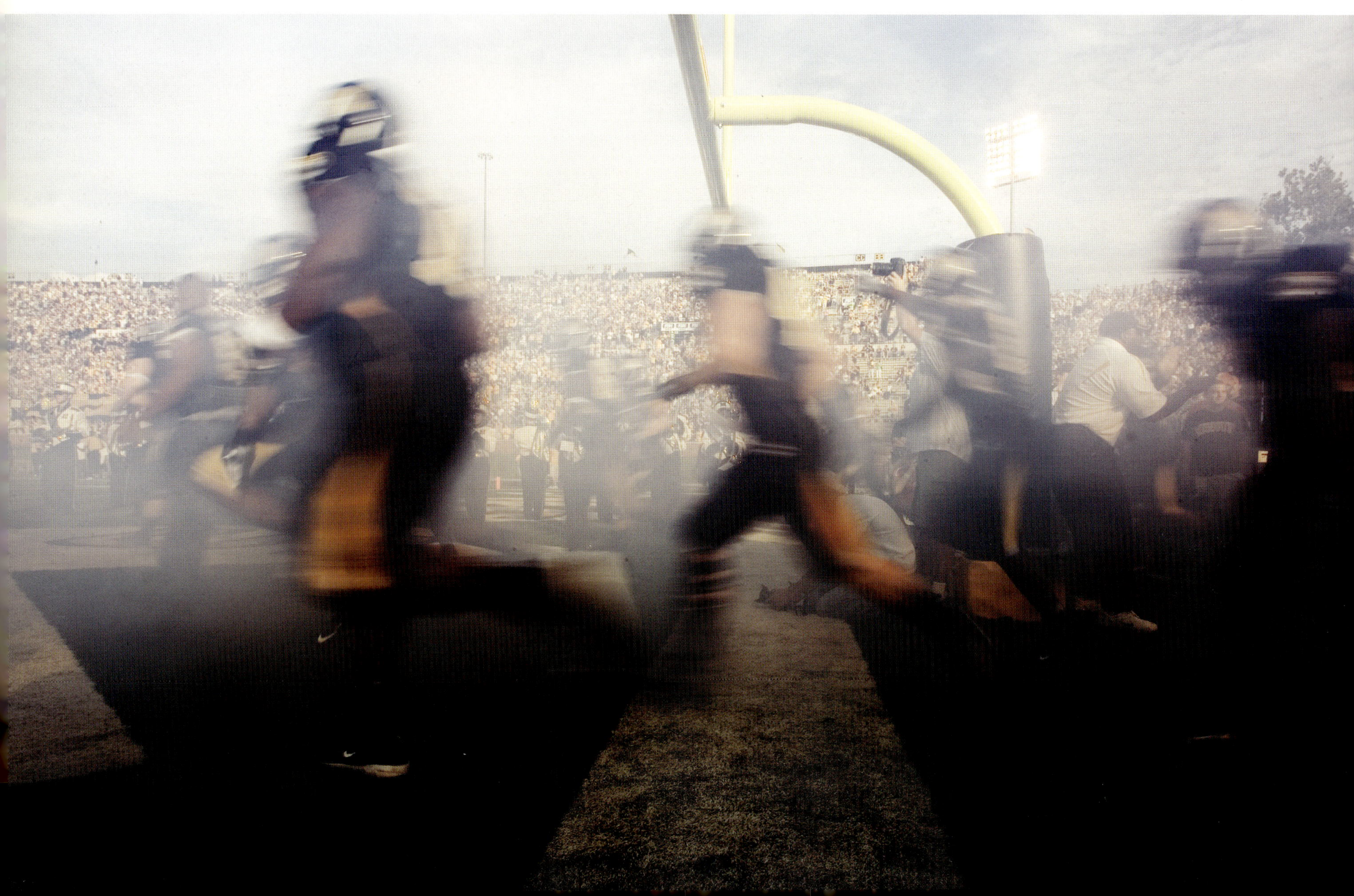

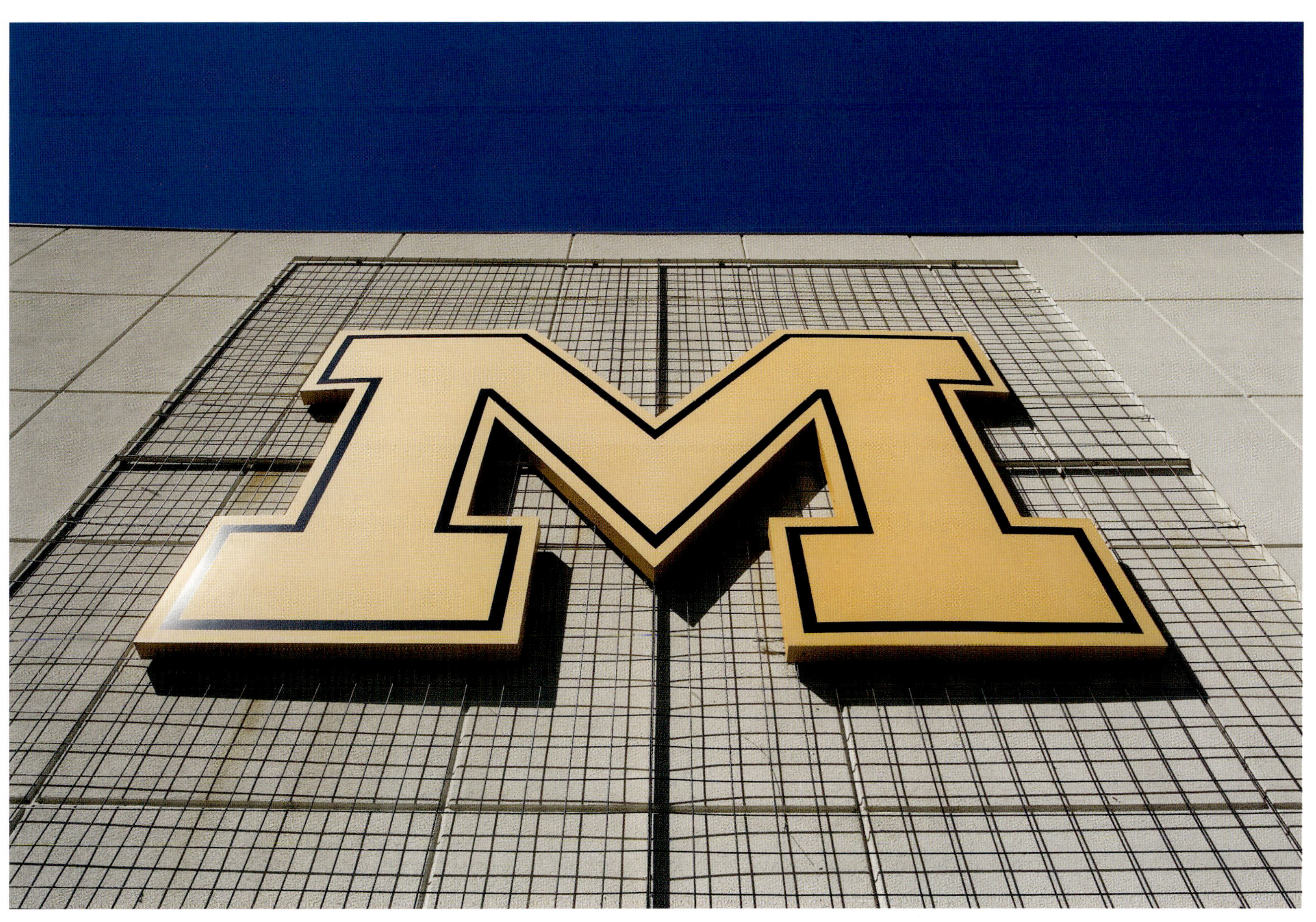

A golden block M proudly adorns the Daniel J. Devine Pavilion, an indoor practice facility of the Department of Intercollegiate Athletics, located along Providence Road south of Stadium Boulevard.

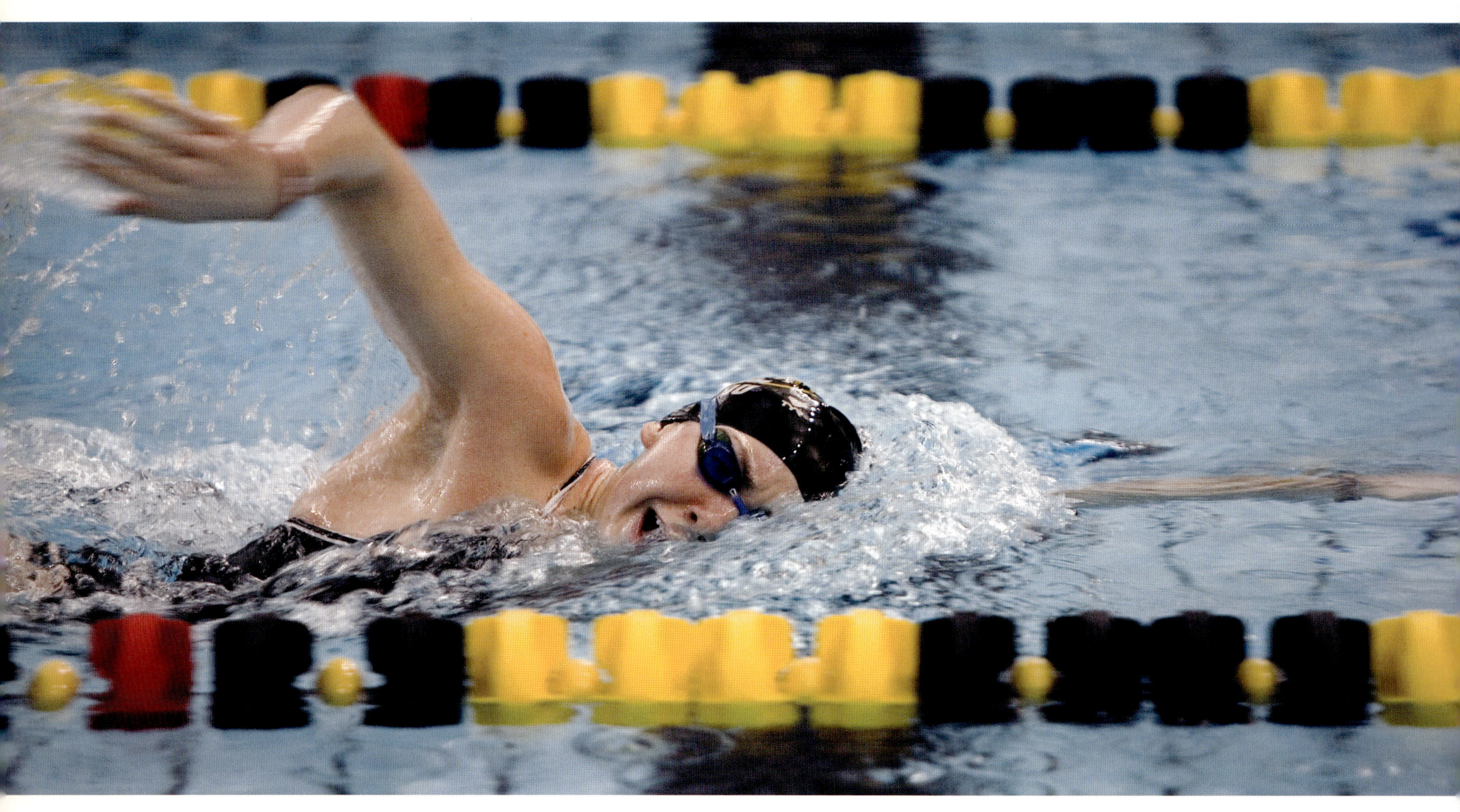

Lori Halvorson trains for the 2008 Olympic Team Trials in the 200-meter freestyle in December 2006 at the Mizzou Aquatic Center, part of the Student Recreation Complex

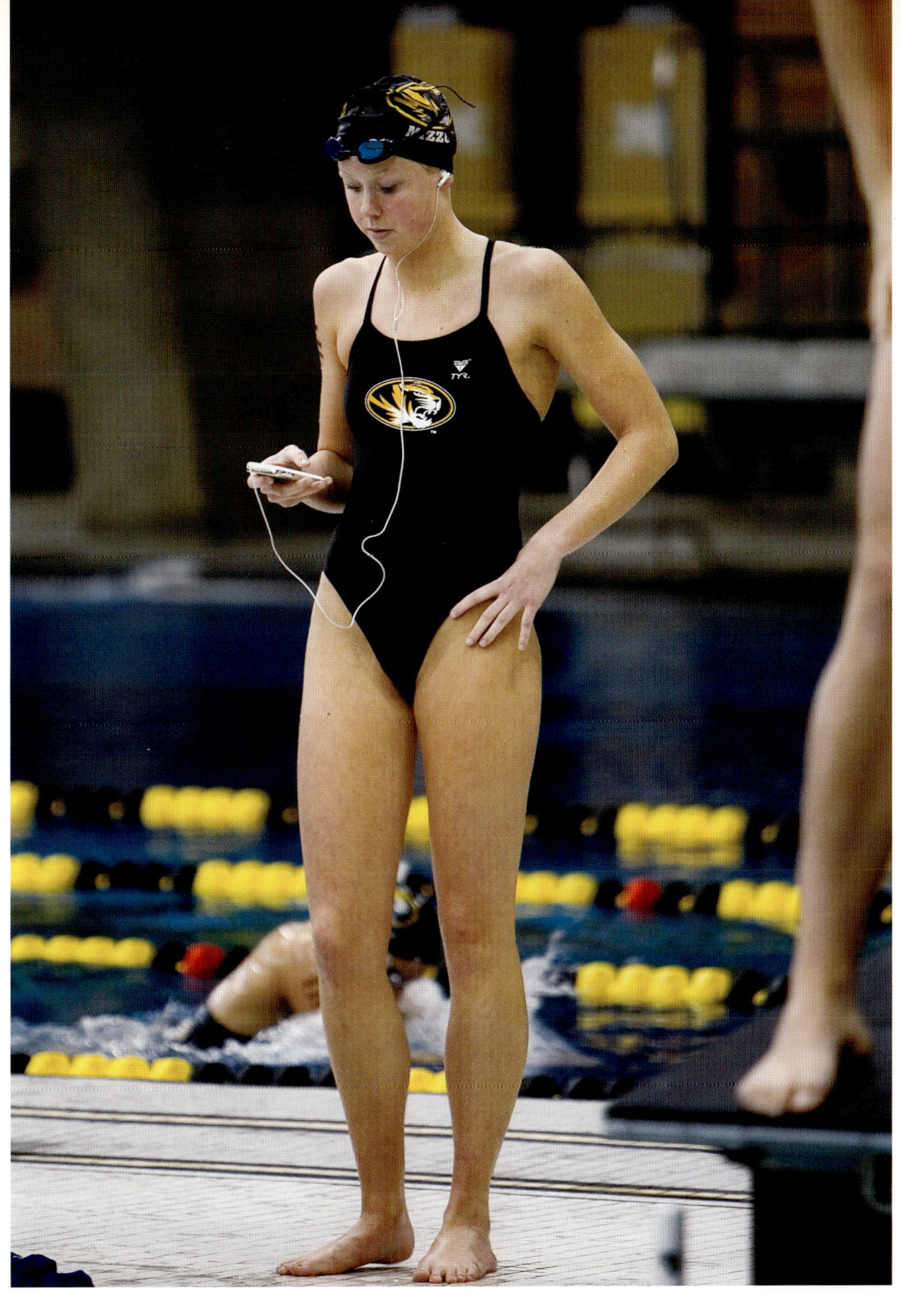

Sarah Menefee listens to music on her iPod between swim events at the Mizzou Aquatic Center, on Senior Day, February 4, 2006. In the meet with Nebraska, the Tigers win, 170–129.

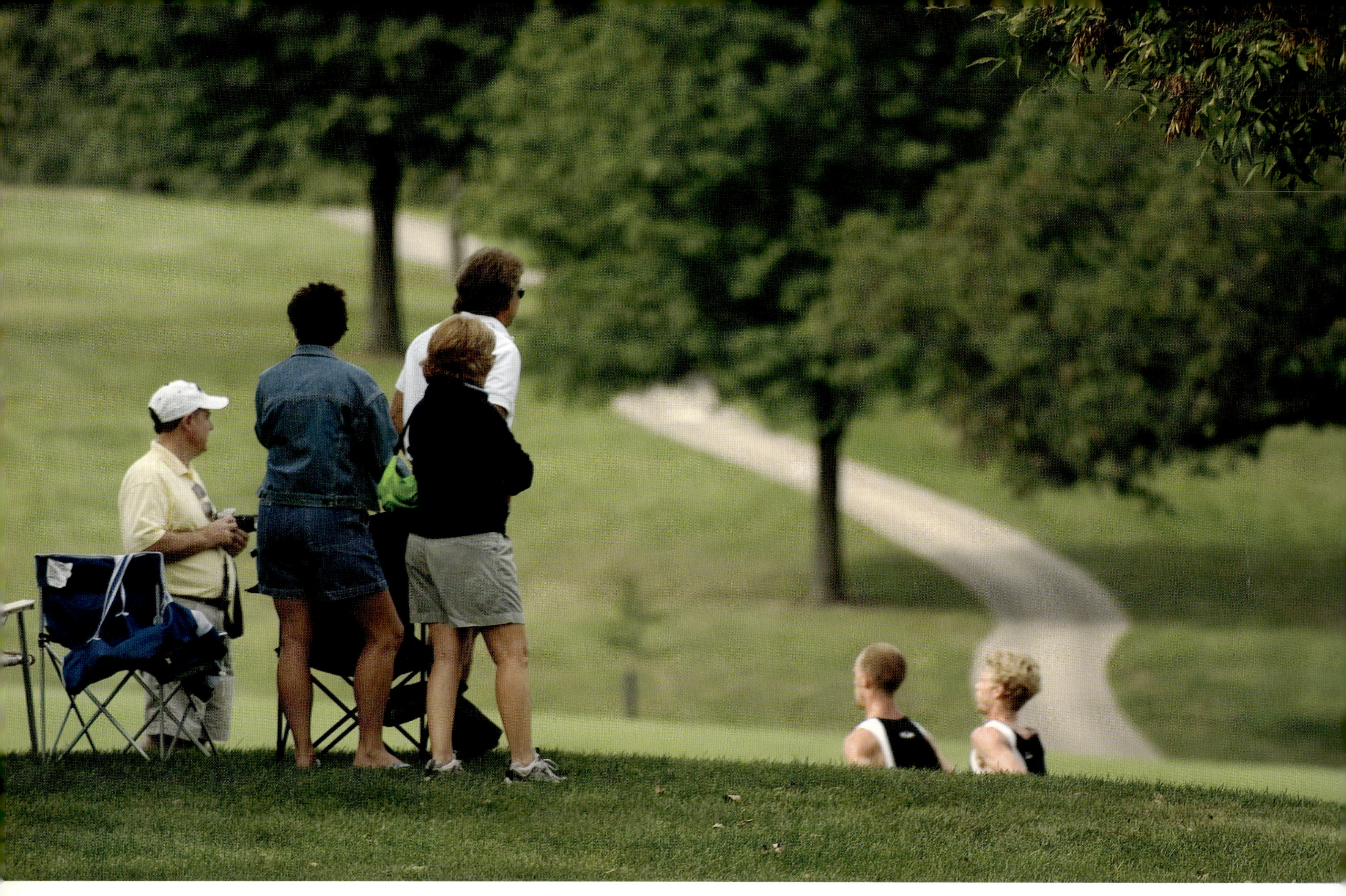

Spectators watch Missouri cross-country runners from the undulating landscape of A. L. Gustin Golf Course along Stadium Boulevard.

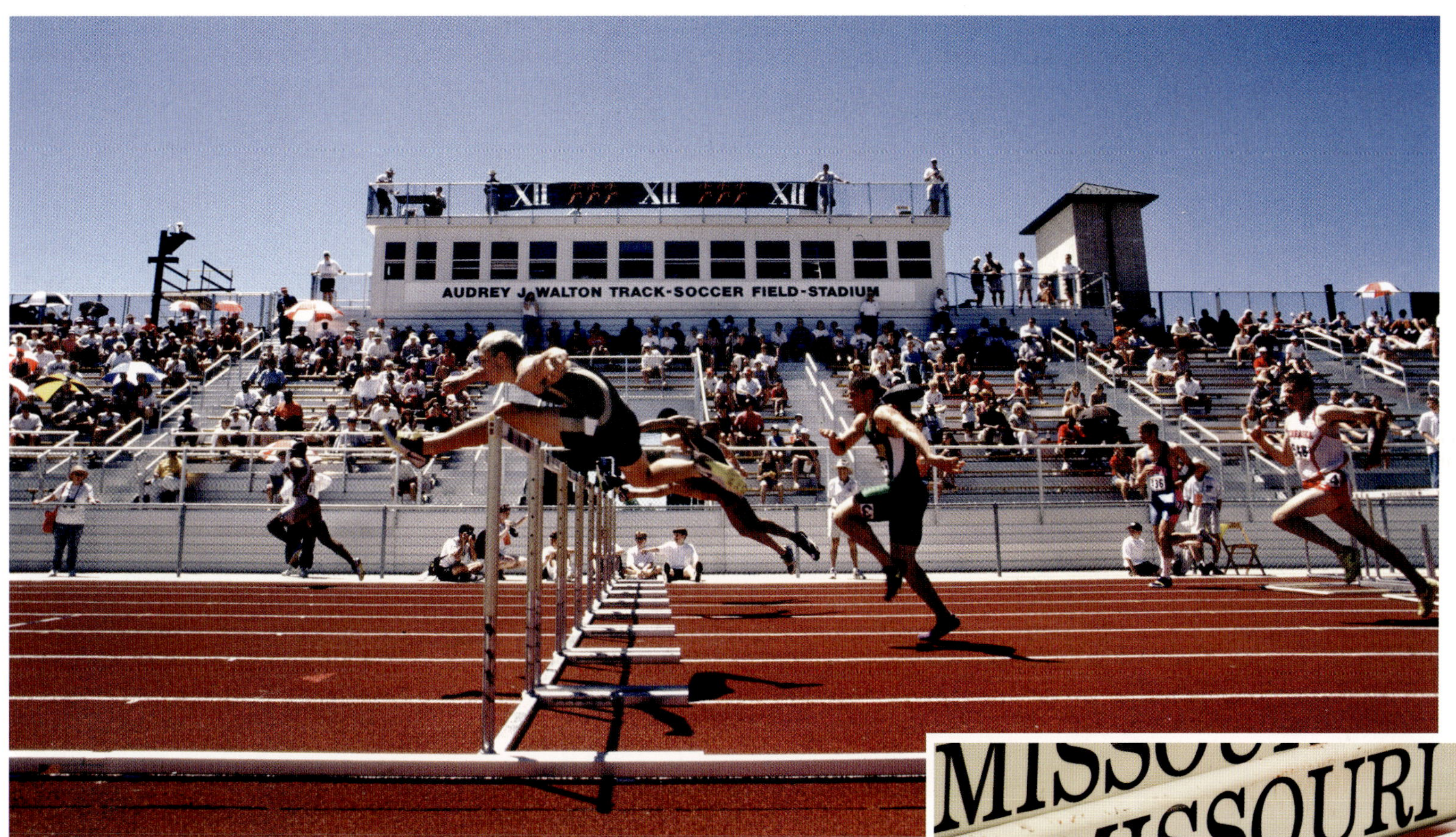

A Mizzou athlete leads the group running the hurdles at a spring outdoor Big 12 track meet at Audrey J. Walton Track–Soccer Field–Stadium. The stadium is one of several in the MU Sports Park.

Hurdles stand branded and ready for the runners of the Missouri track program.

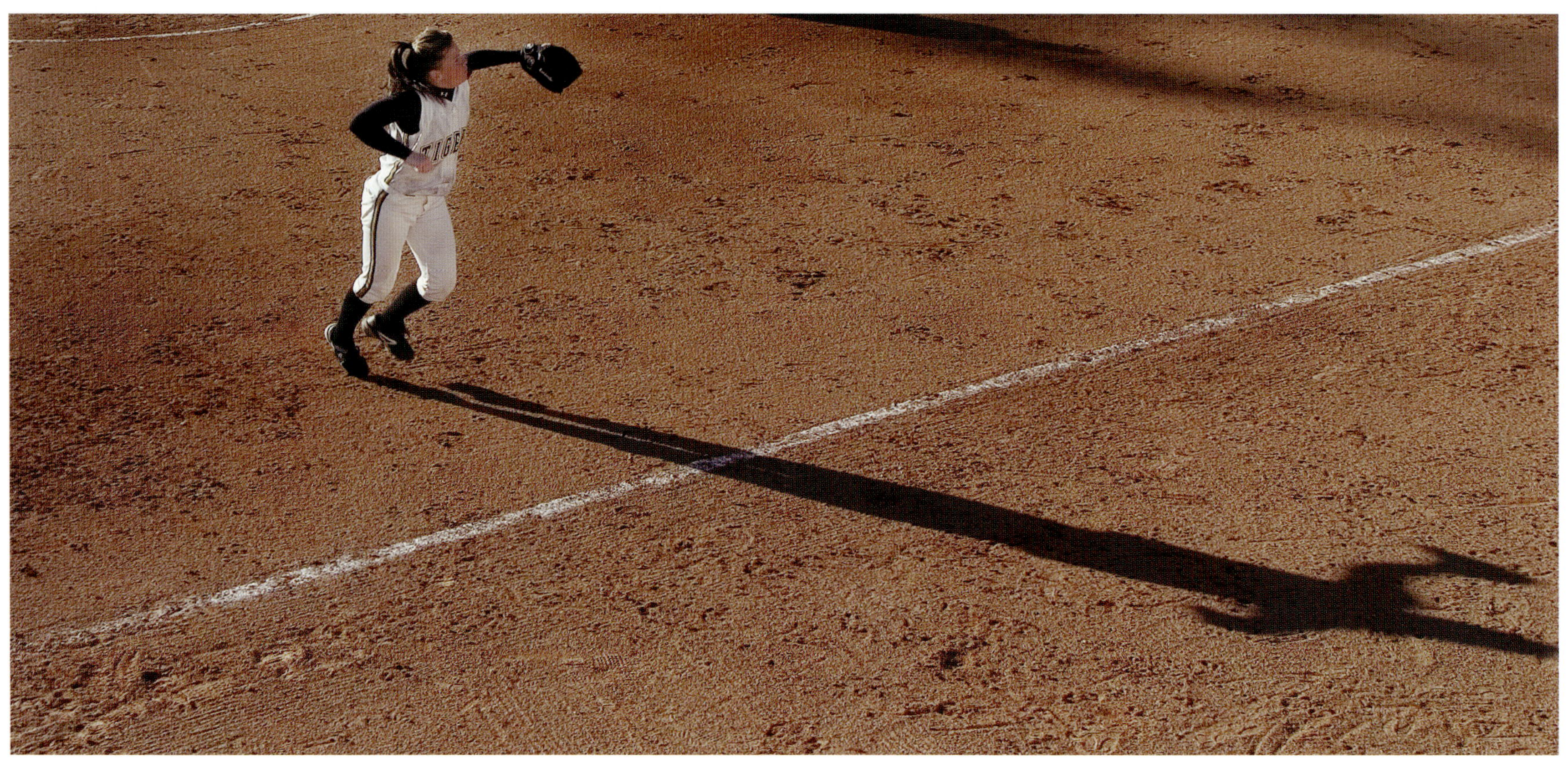

Early spring sunlight accents the play at third base during the women's 2005 home opener at University Field.

The renovated Taylor Stadium, named for Ralph and Debbie Taylor, opened for the 2000 baseball season. The stadium's design puts fans close to the action on Simmons Field, named for John "Hi" Simmons, legendary MU baseball coach for thirty-four years.

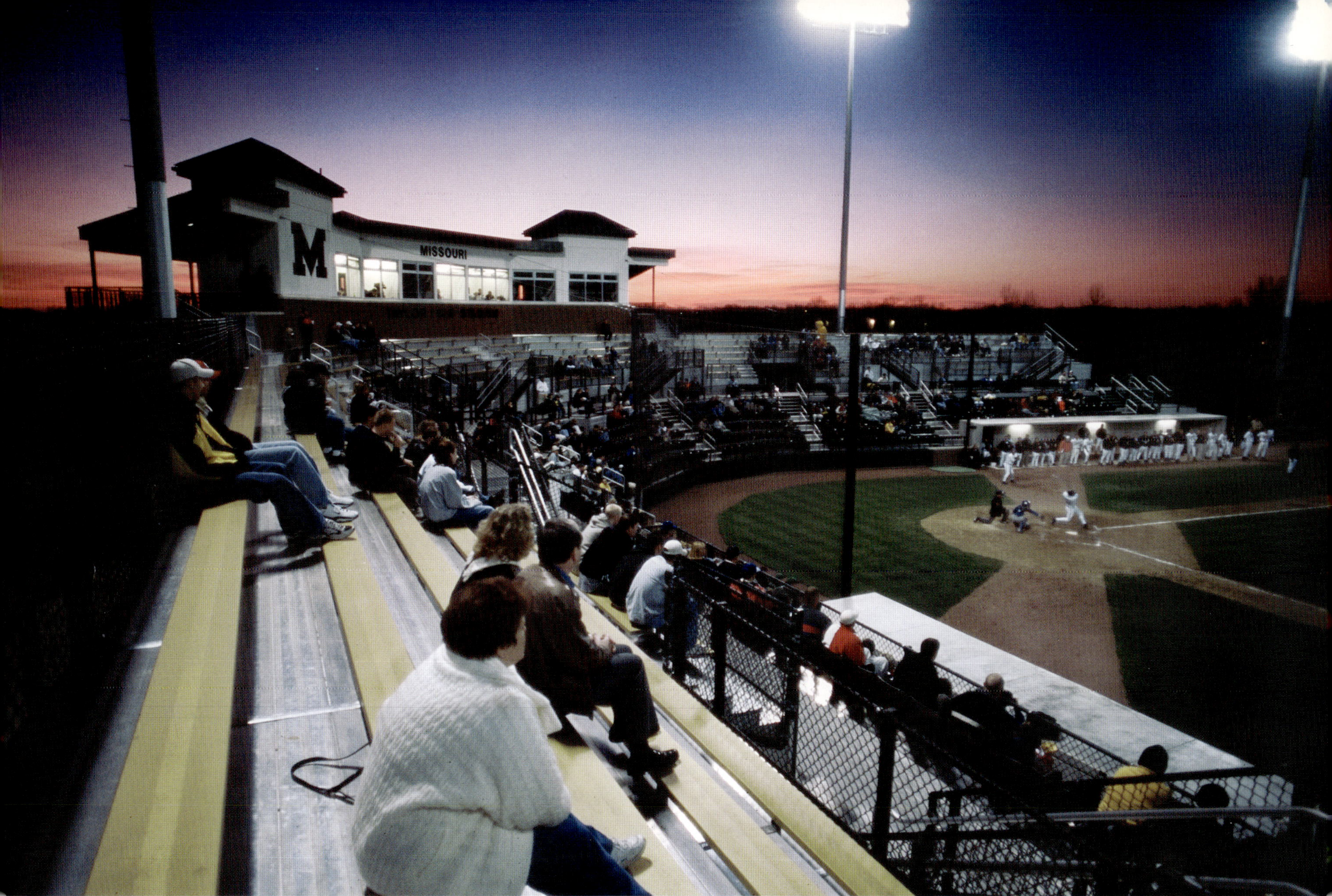
M
MISSOURI

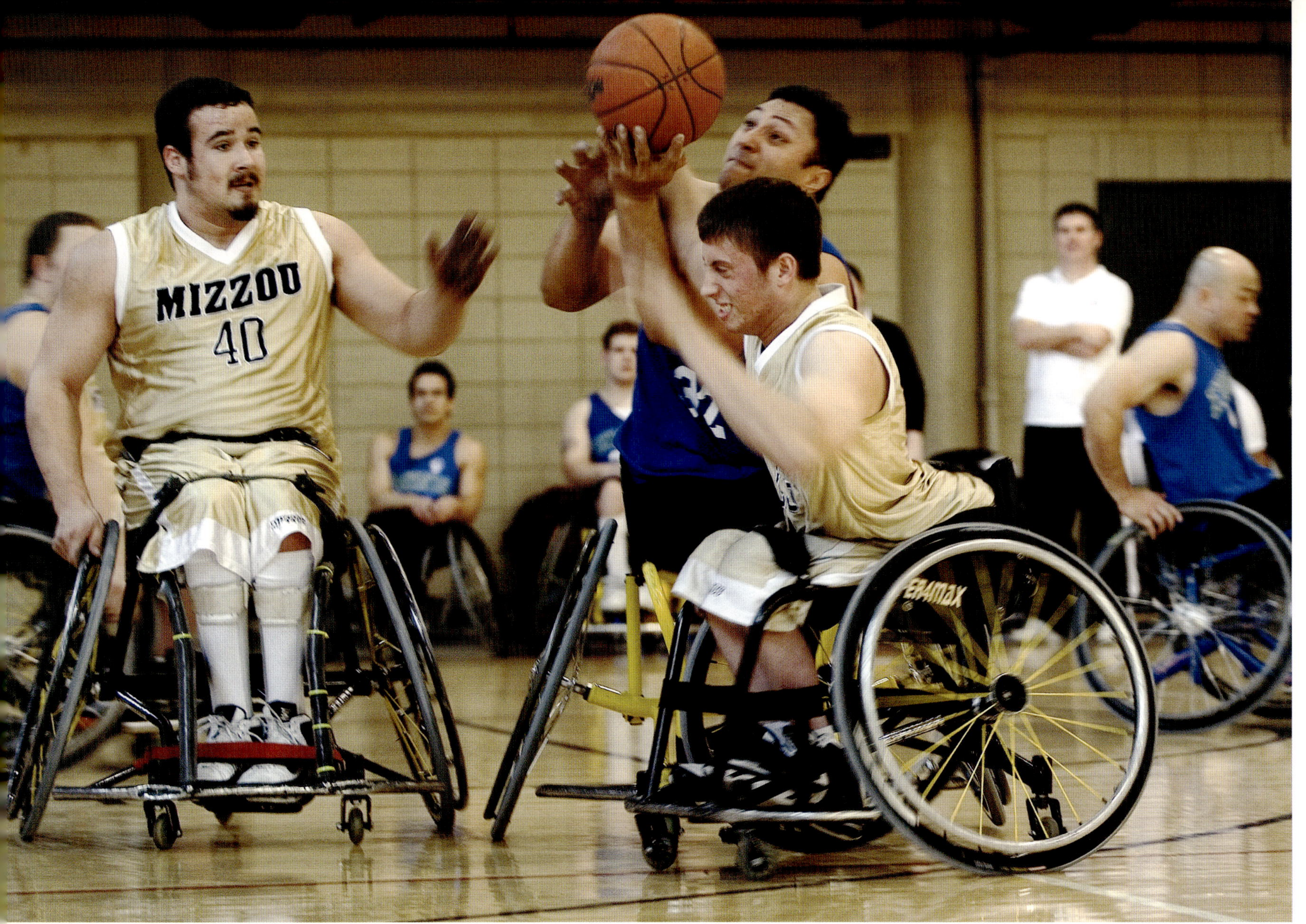

*T*iger teammates John Gilbert and Garrett French (No. 40) scramble for a loose ball in a game against the Edmonds (Washington) Community College Rolling Tritons. The Tiger Wheelchair Basketball Classic was held March 10, 2007, at the Student Recreation Complex.

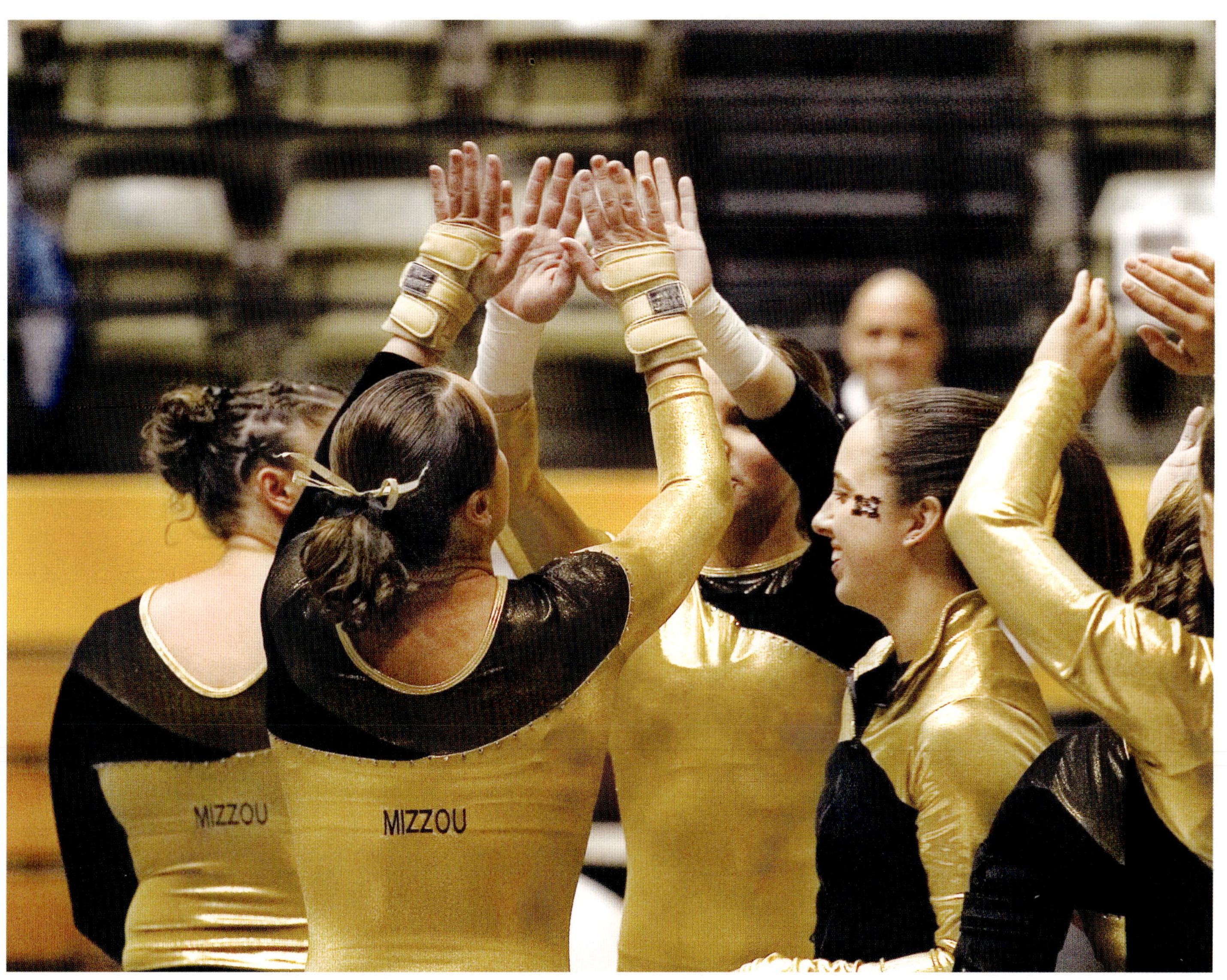

*G*ymnastics teammates celebrate after a good score.

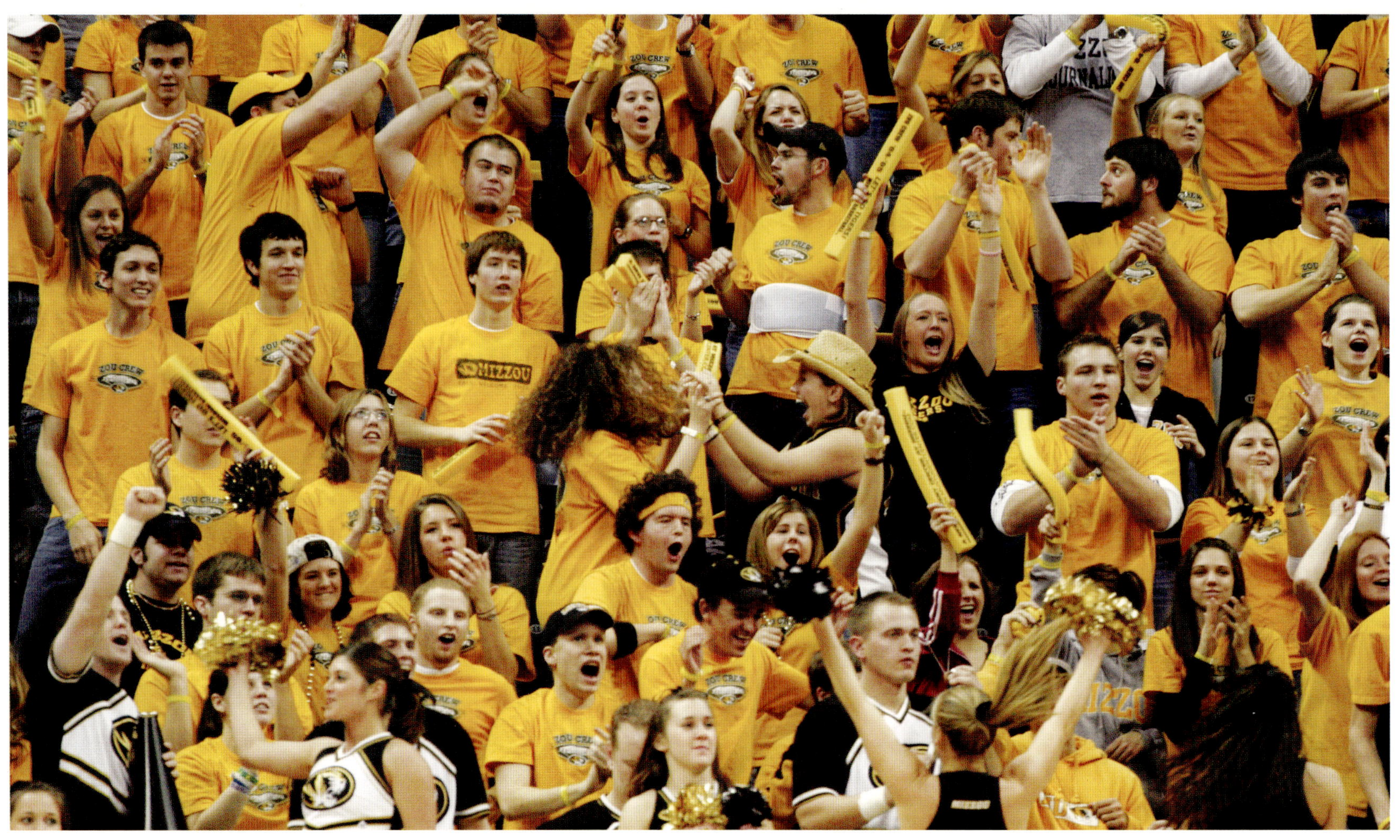

The student section offers loud support for the Tigers during basketball games in Mizzou Arena.

As he drives for a layup, No. 23 Marcus Watkins gets fouled by Colorado players, February 28, 2007. The Tigers win, 91–82, in a home game played in Mizzou Arena.

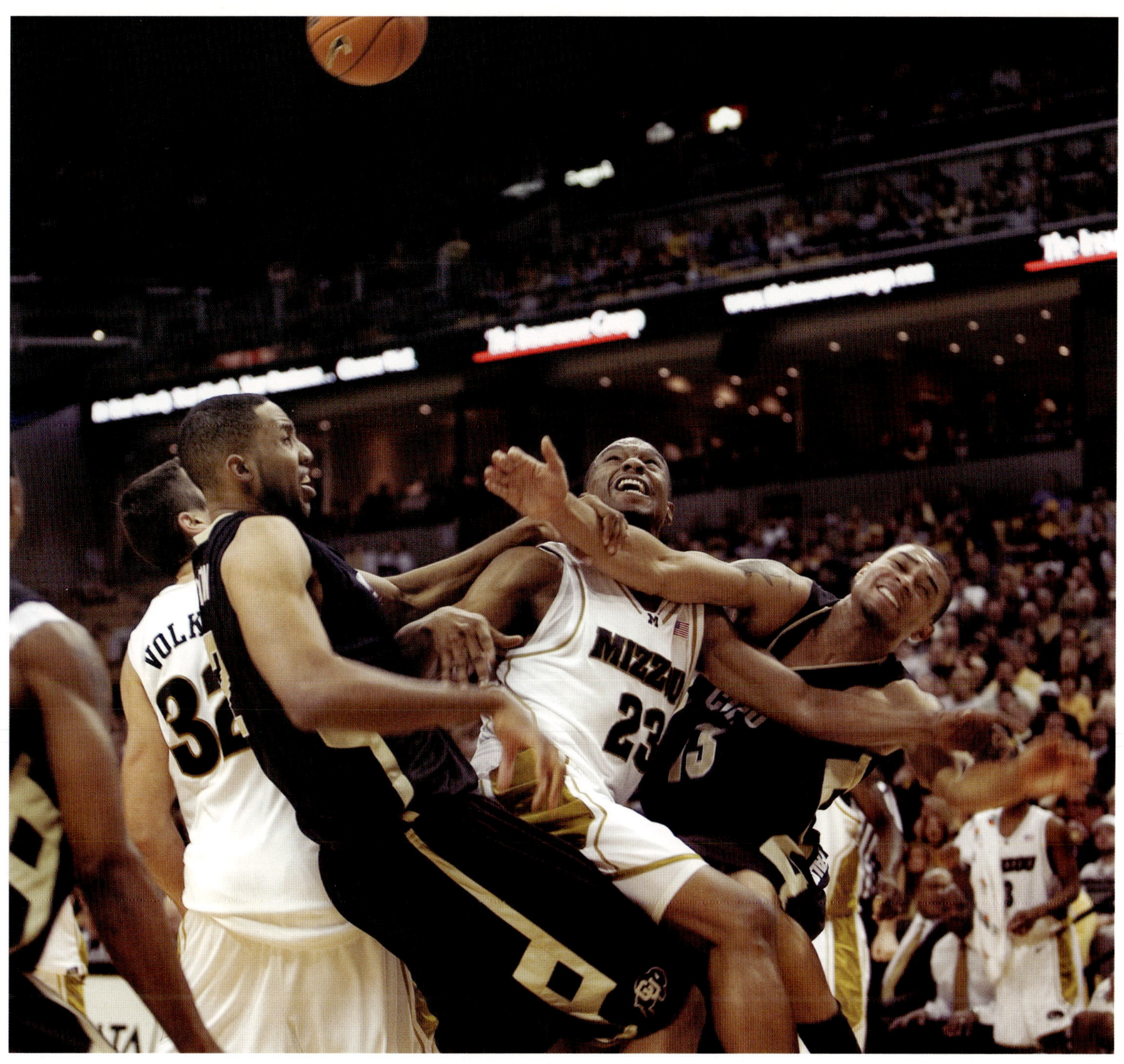
MIZZOU
23
32

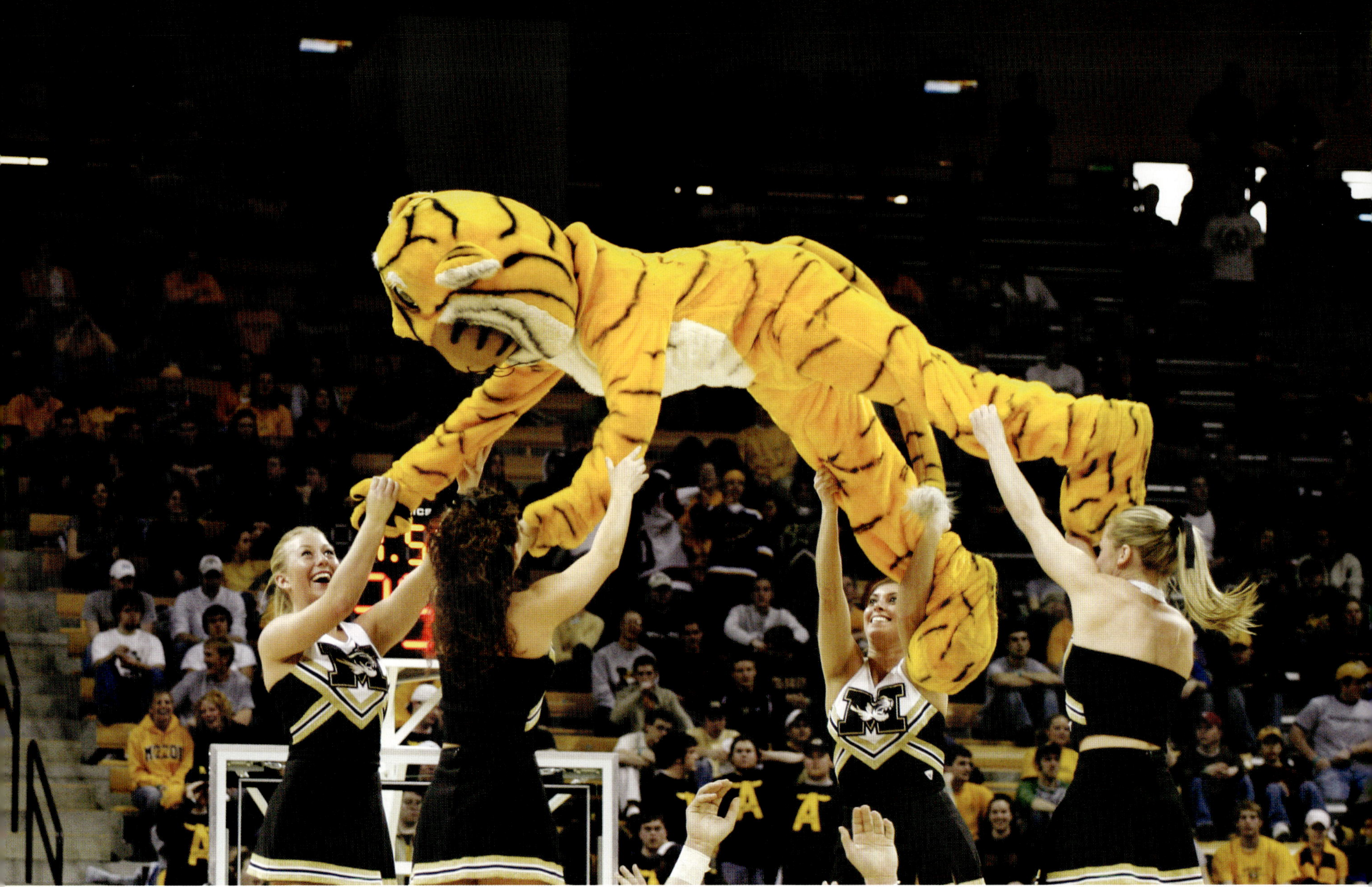

Four cheerleaders literally sweep Truman off his feet on Norm Stewart Court in Mizzou Arena.

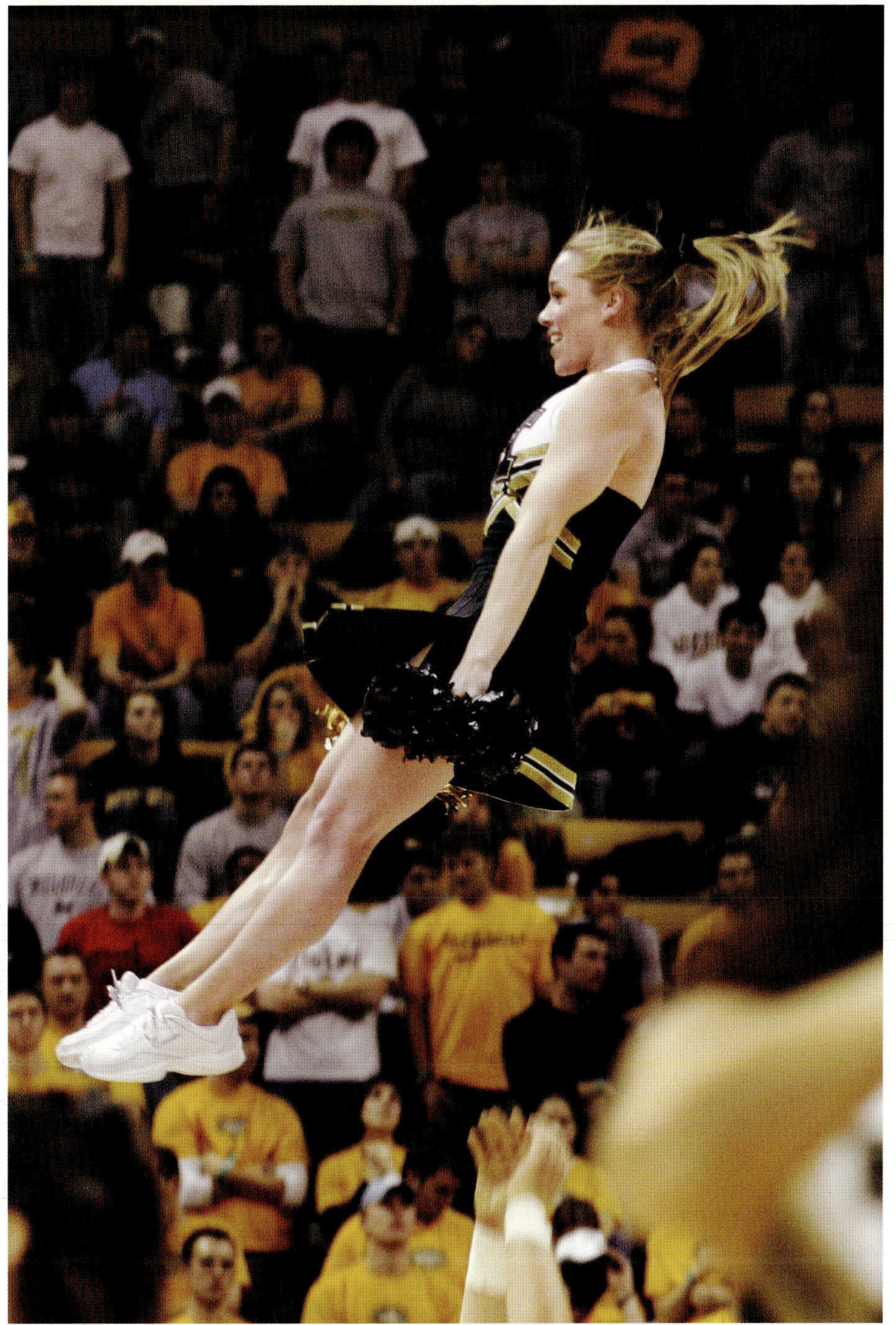

A cheerleader floats in the air during a timeout of a Tiger basketball game in Mizzou Arena.

When Missouri scores, Big MO bangs into action. Since 1993, local chapters of Kappa Kappa Psi and Tau Beta Sigma have maintained and played Big MO, reportedly the third largest bass drum in the world.

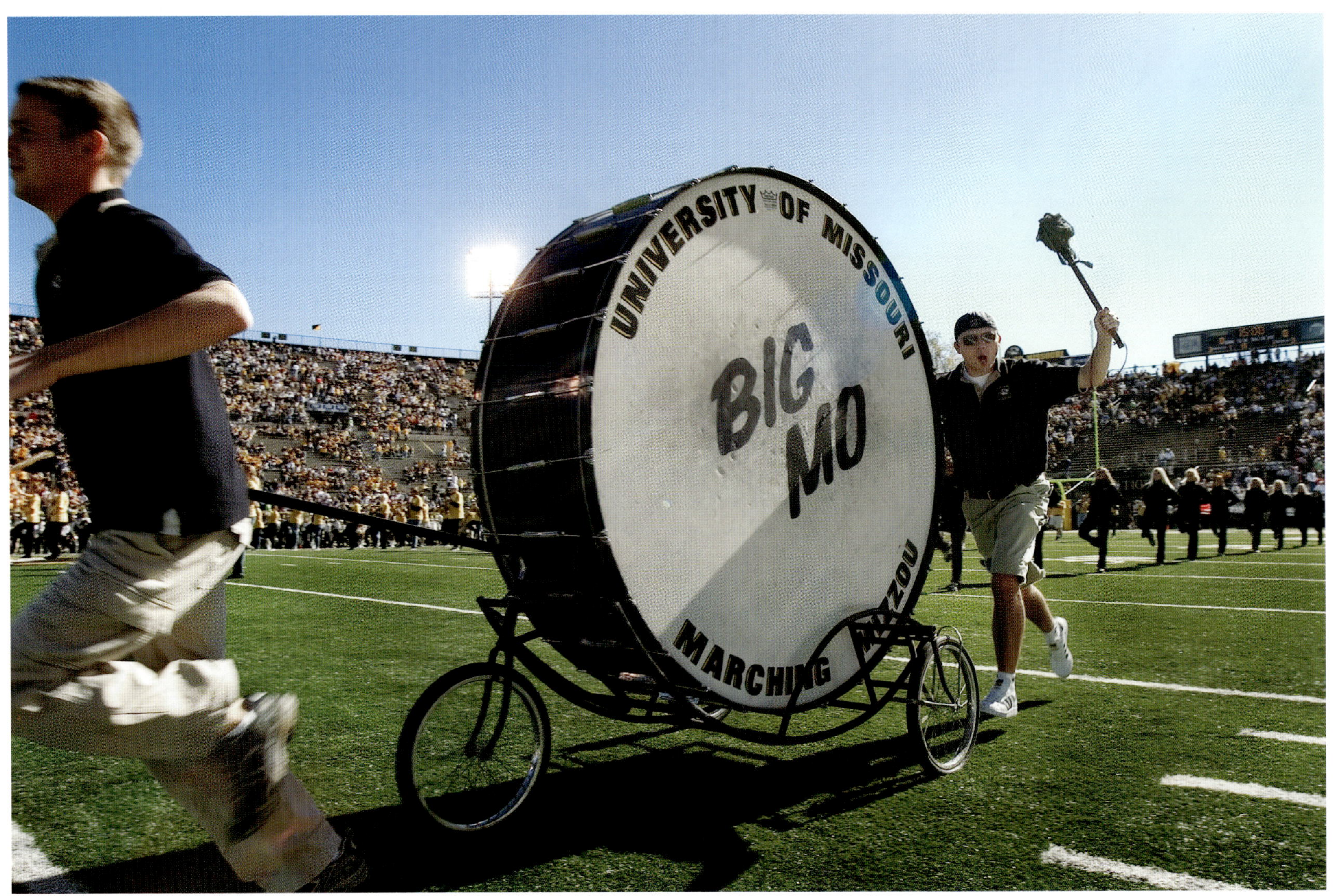

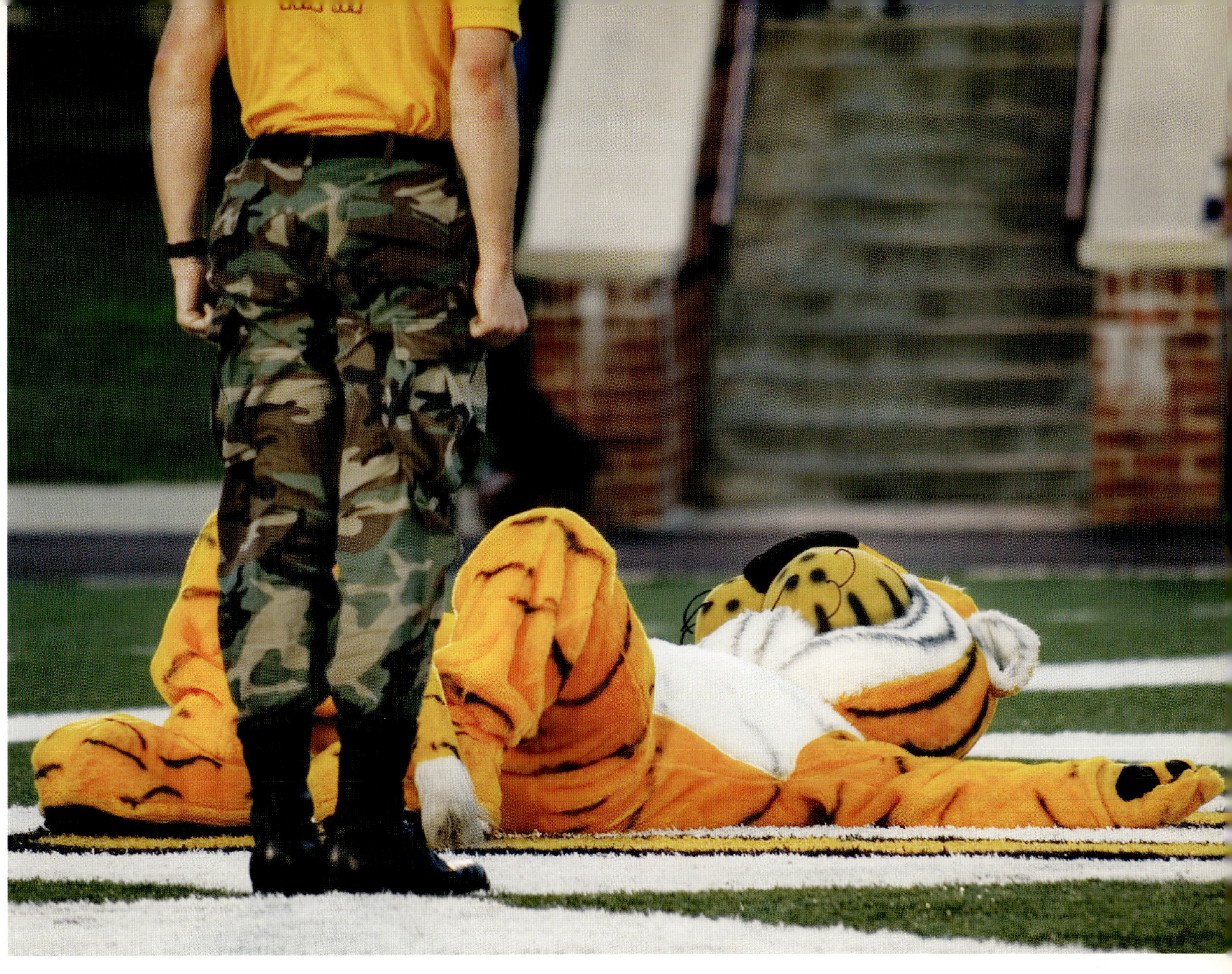

The mascot feigns exhaustion after joining ROTC cadets for touchdown pushups.

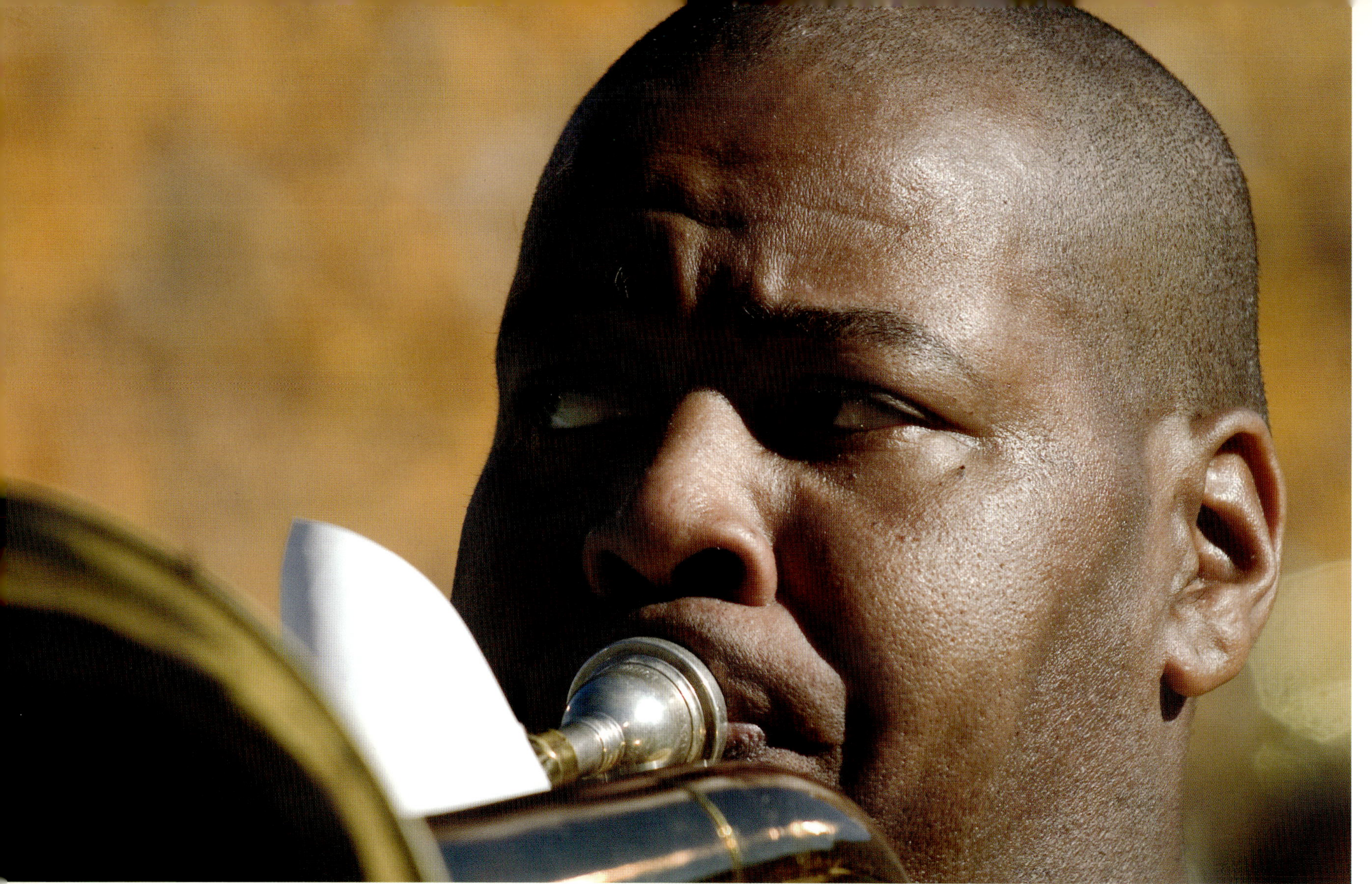

A member of the alumni band takes his cue from the band director during the pregame show at Homecoming.

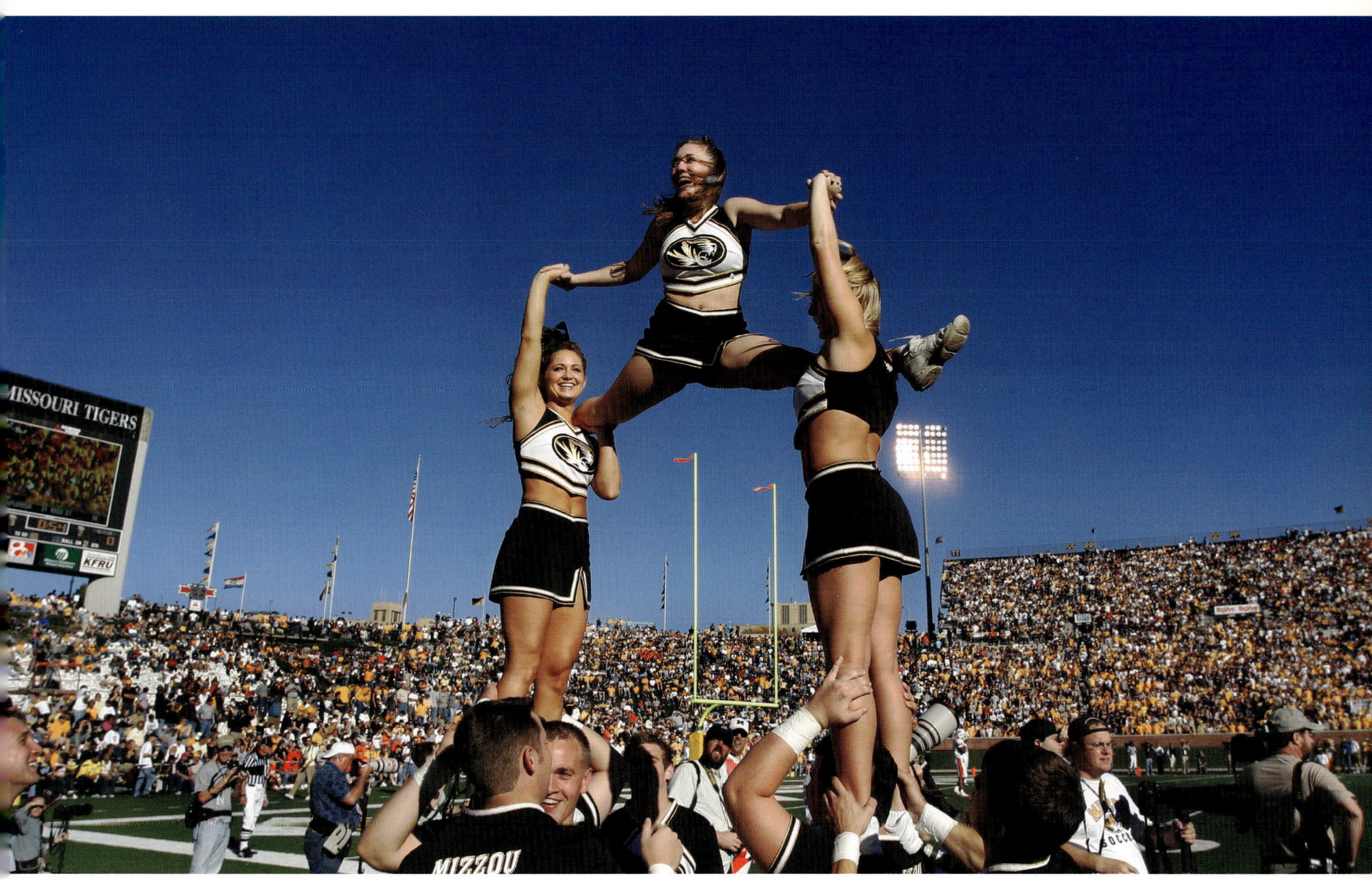

*C*rowd-pleasing cheerleaders build a pyramid.

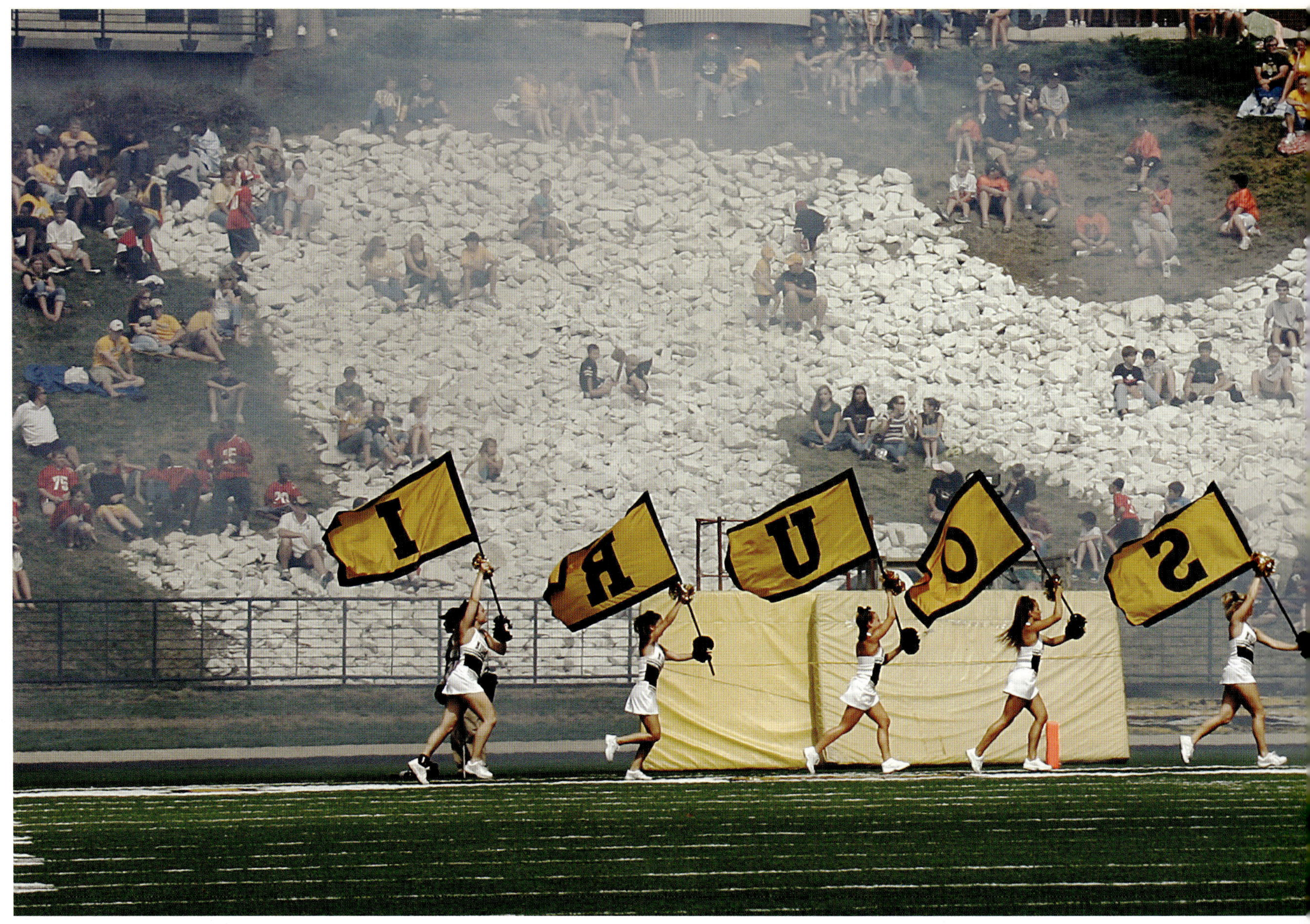

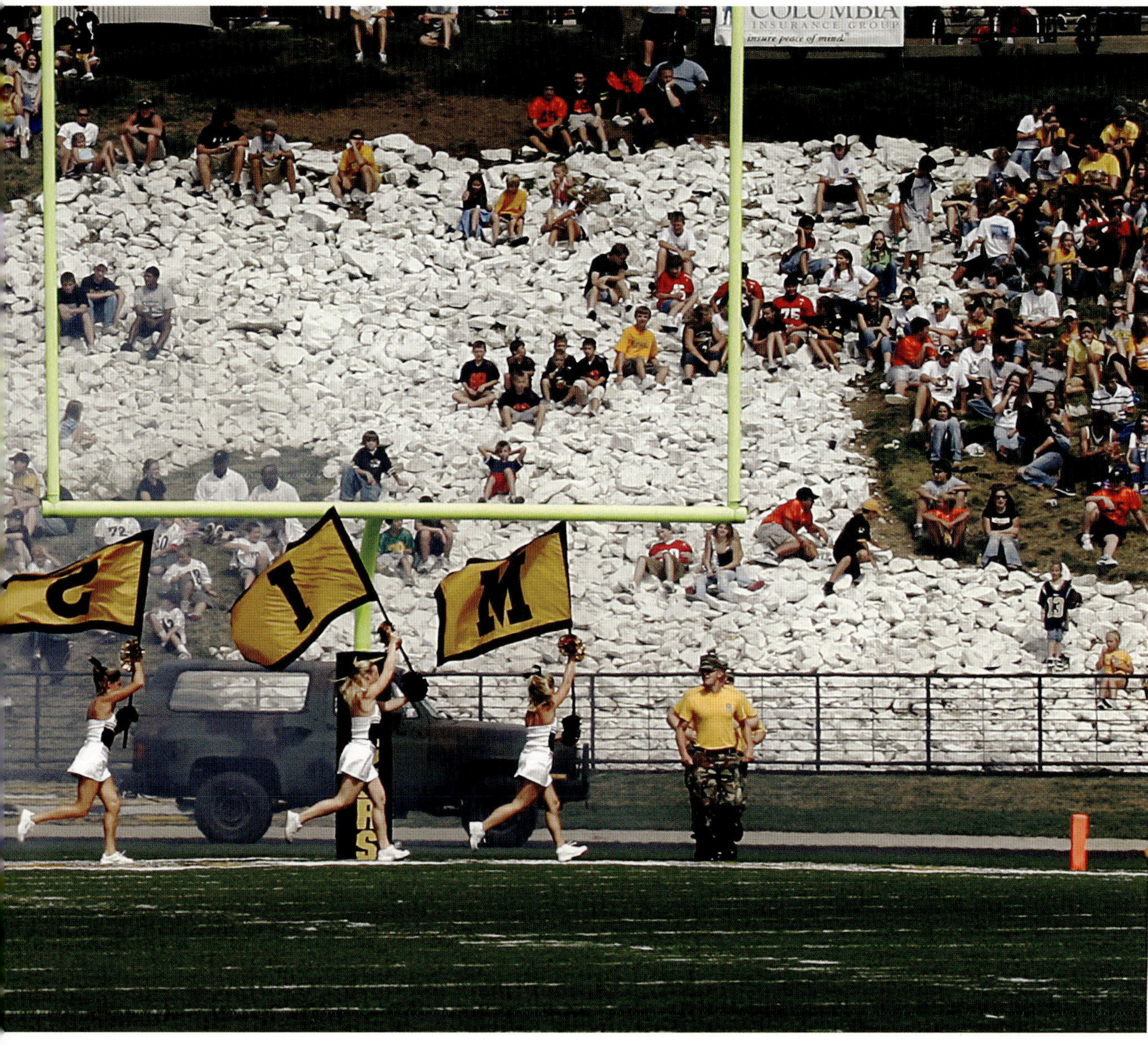

Touchdown Missouri! The cannon booms and the cheerleaders unfurl golden flags as they run across the field. Memorial Stadium, dedicated in 1926, honors Missouri residents who lost their lives in World War I. Faurot Field is named in honor of the legendary Don Faurot, the winningest football coach in Mizzou history and the inventor of the split-T formation. Seating capacity is 68,349.

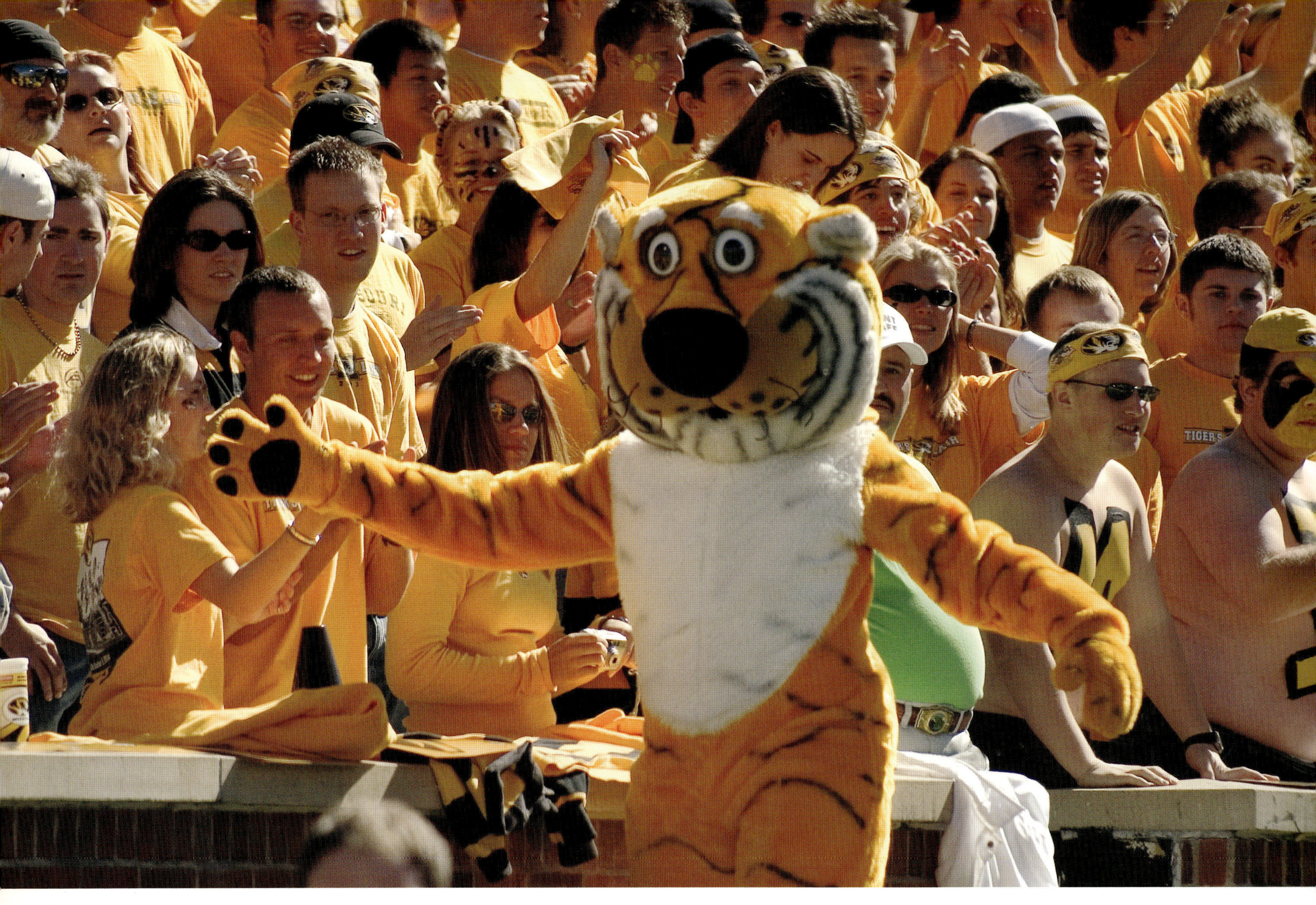

A wide-eyed Truman the Tiger high-fives students in the front row during a football game.

Cheerleaders and members of Marching Mizzou celebrate the relighting of the Tiger Hotel sign atop the nine-story downtown landmark, September 16, 2004. Except for a test run, the occasion marked the first time in fifty years that the word *Tiger* has graced Columbia's skyline.

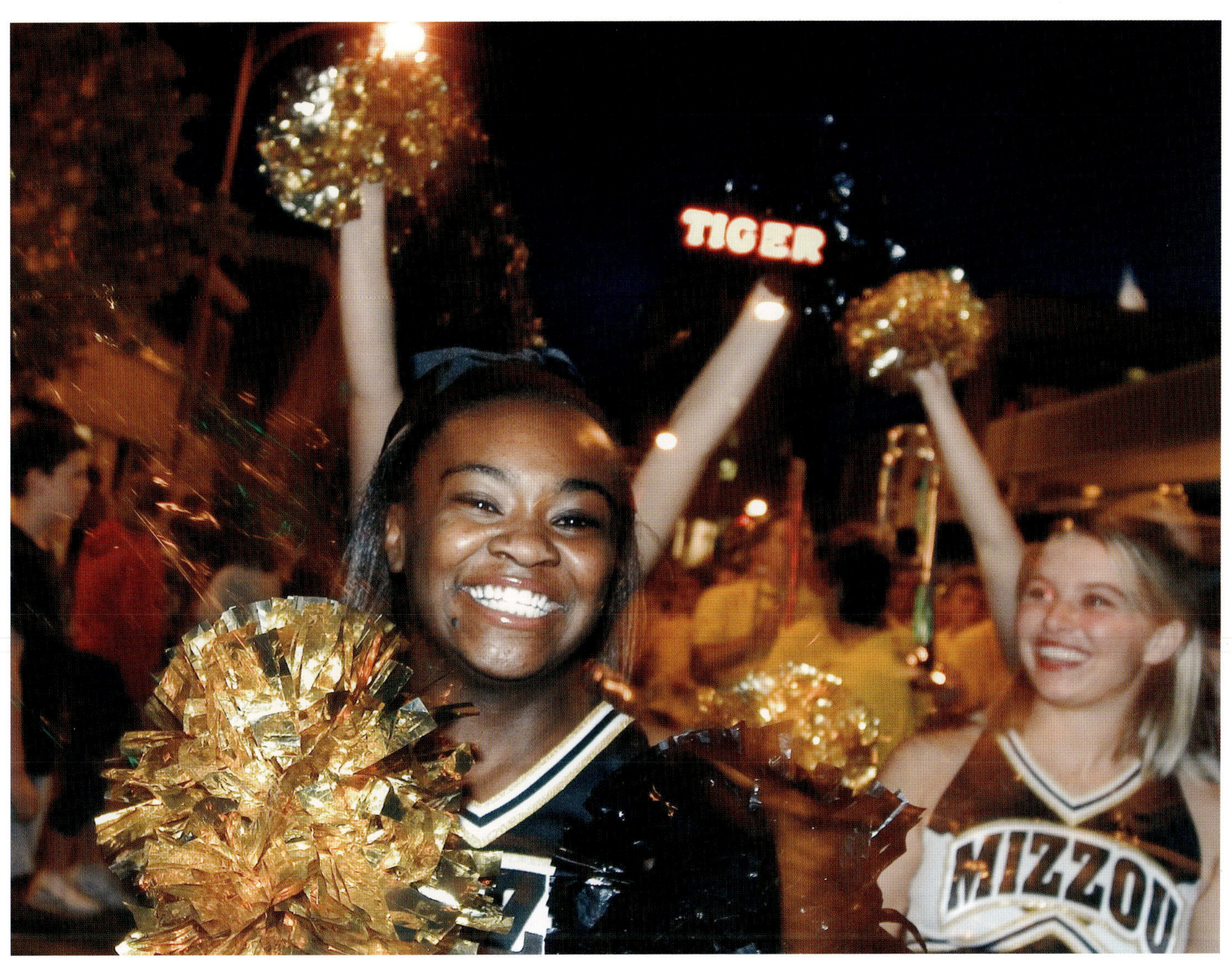

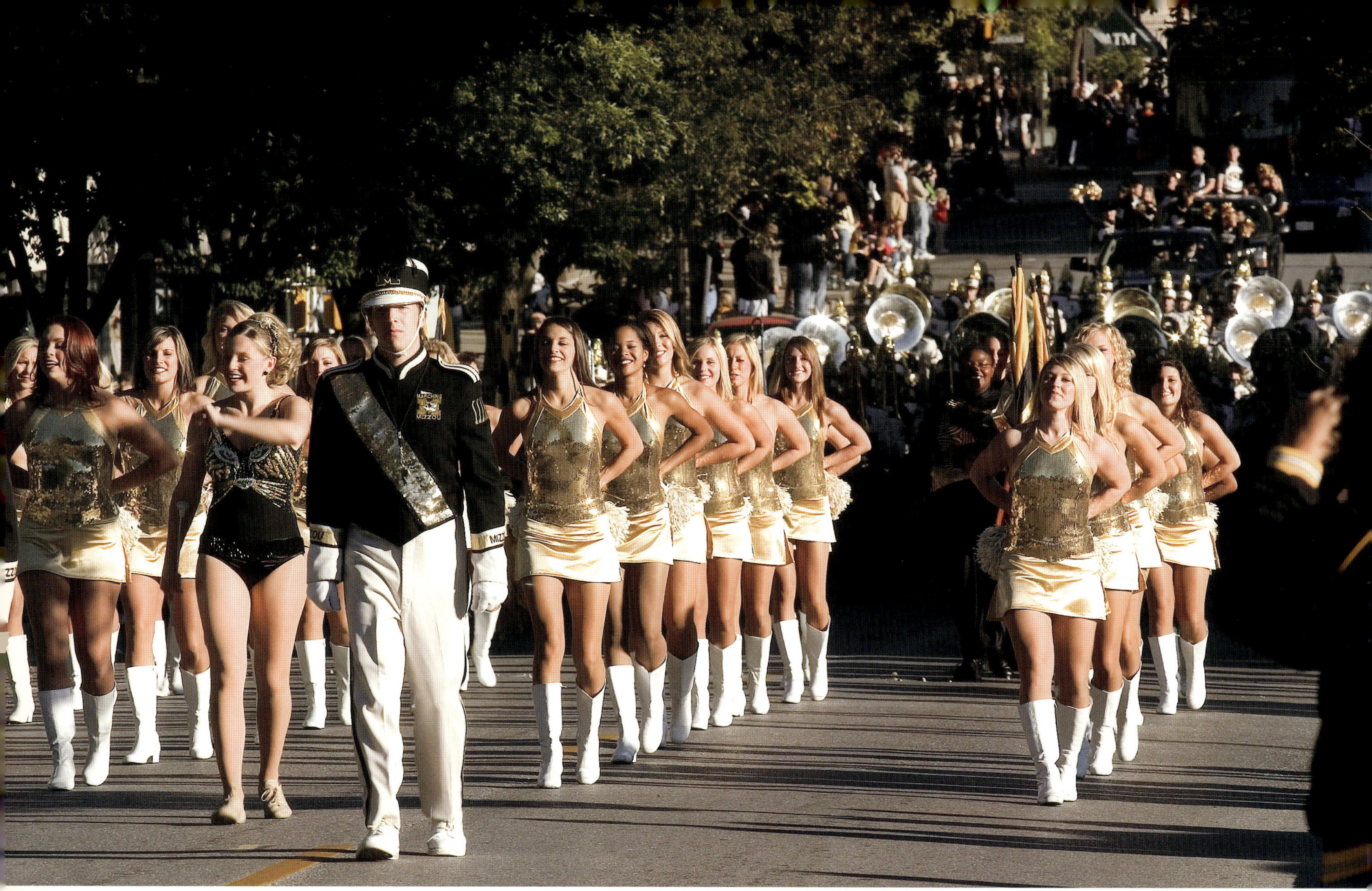

*D*rum major, baton twirler, Golden Girls, and flag corps members lead Marching Mizzou in the Homecoming parade along Ninth Street.

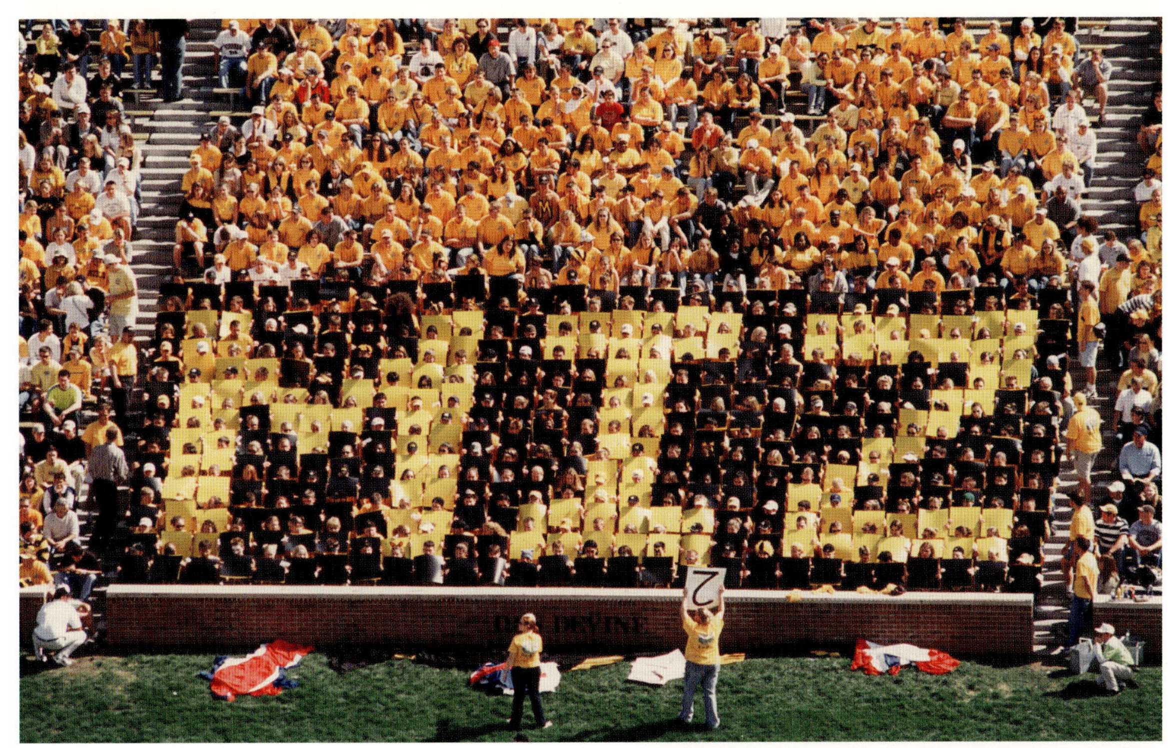

A Faurot Field favorite cheer starts with M-I-Z . . .

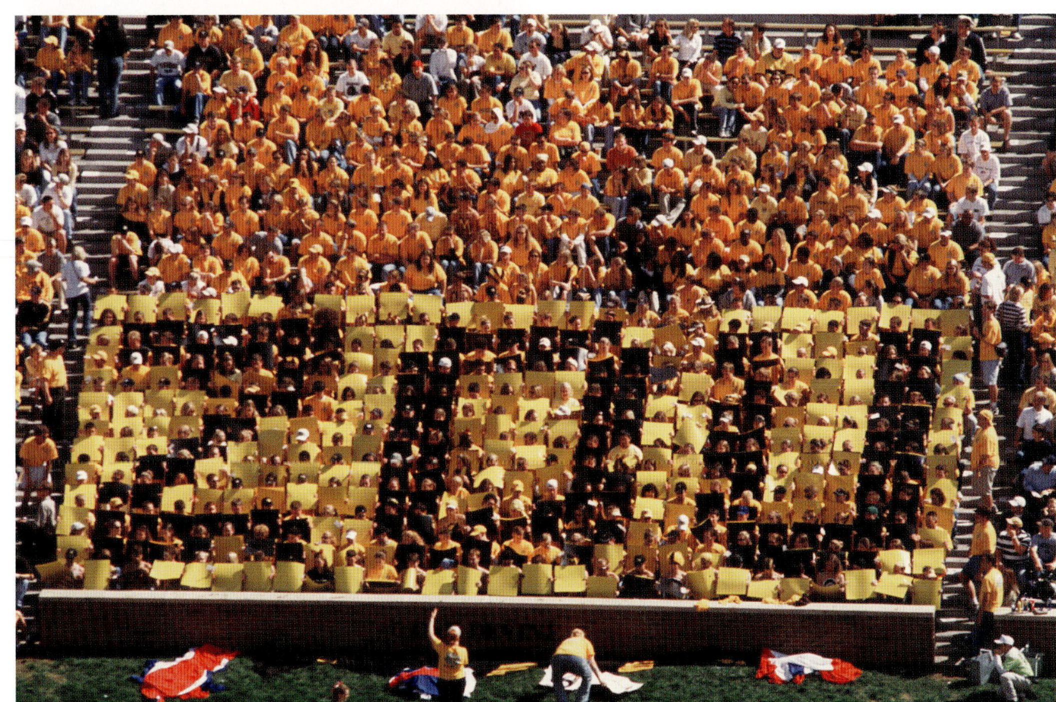

. . . then Z-O-U. Repeat.

Flag corps members proudly wave the black and gold.

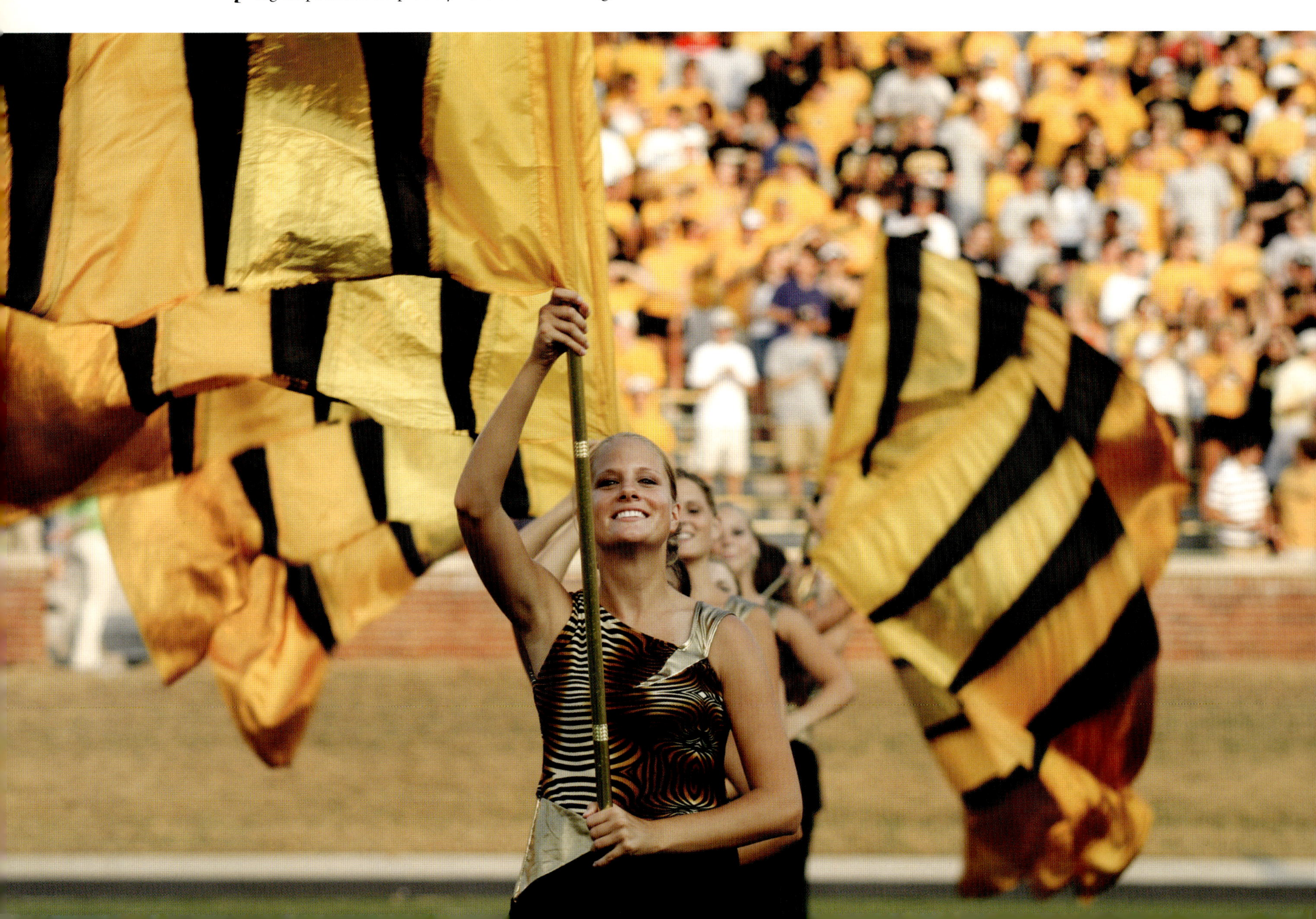

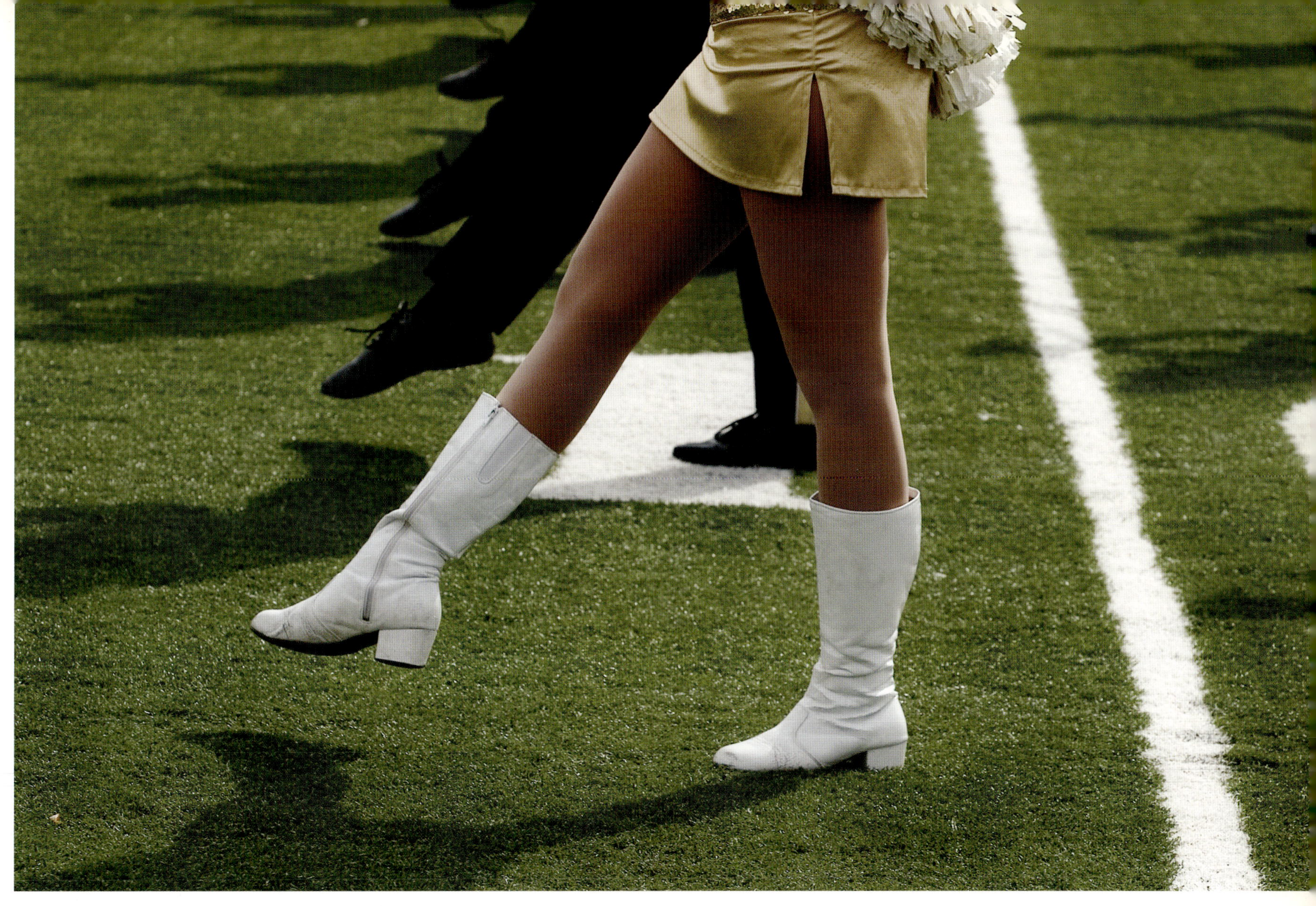

White go-go boots have been part of the dance squad uniforms of the Golden Girls for decades.

*M*arching Mizzou members line up in preparation for their performance on the field.

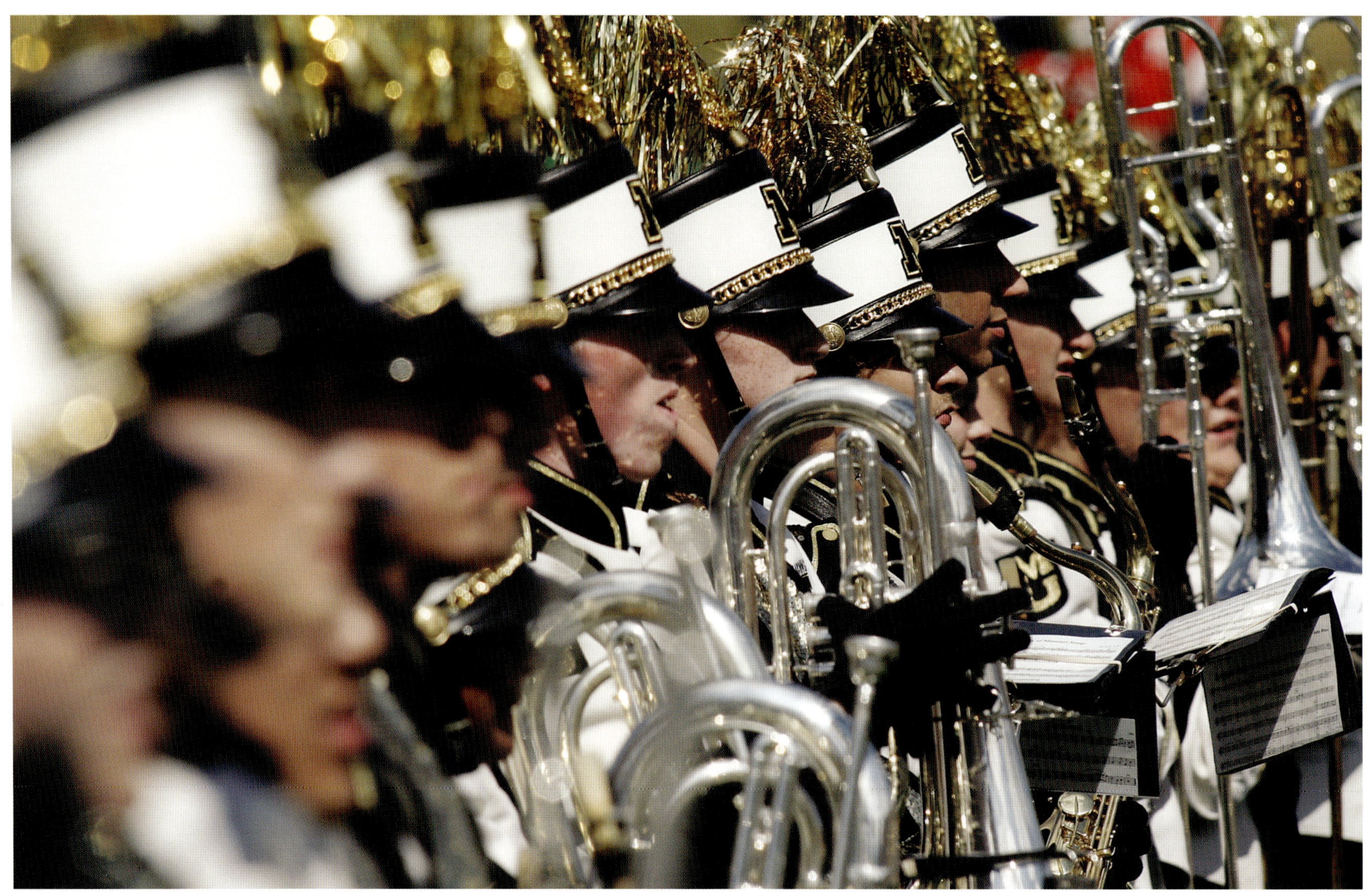

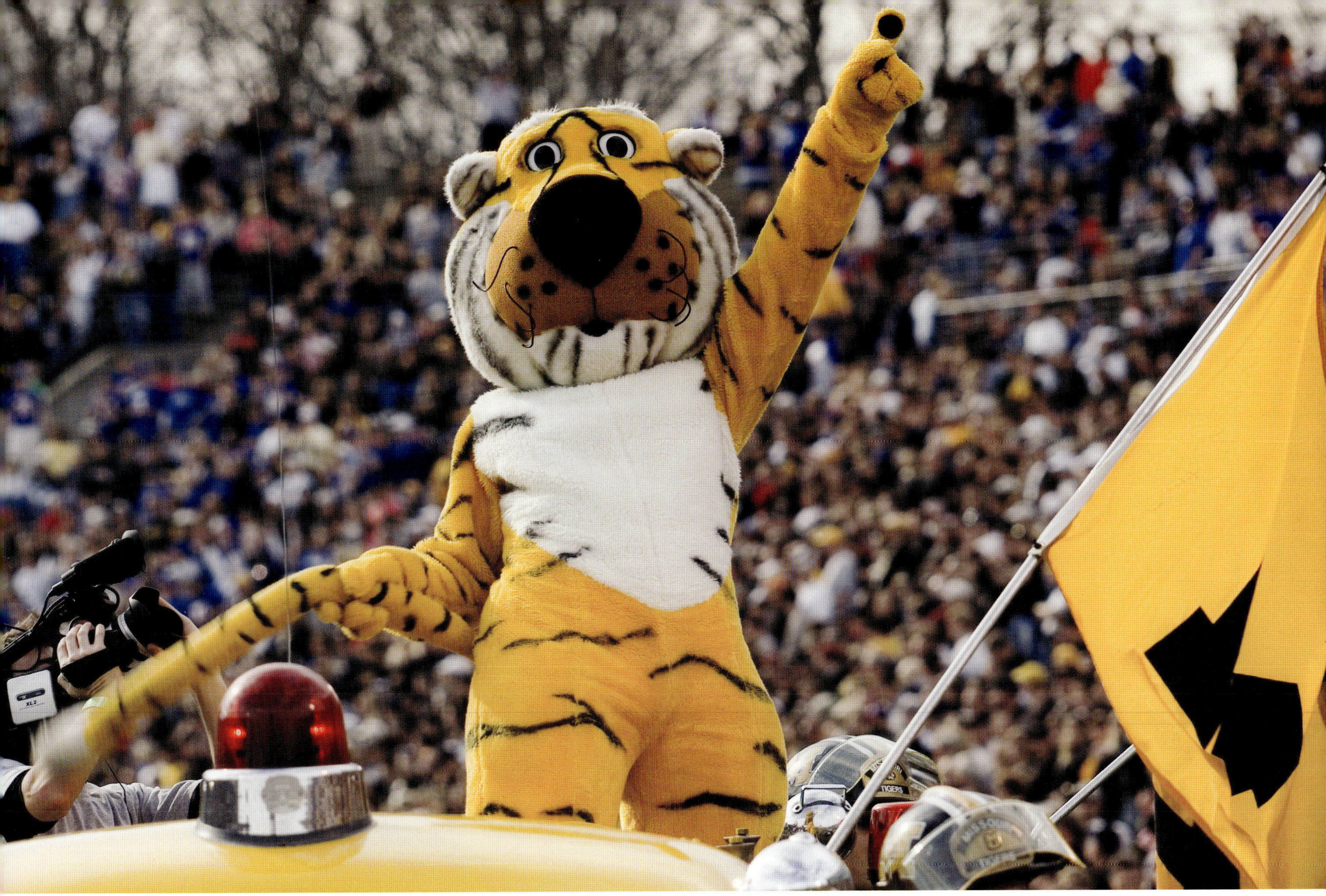

Truman twirls his tail to the sound of the siren on the old fire truck. It is all part of the hoopla of game day on Faurot Field.

Not to be outdone, female fans get into the (almost) chest-baring business to cheer on the Tigers.

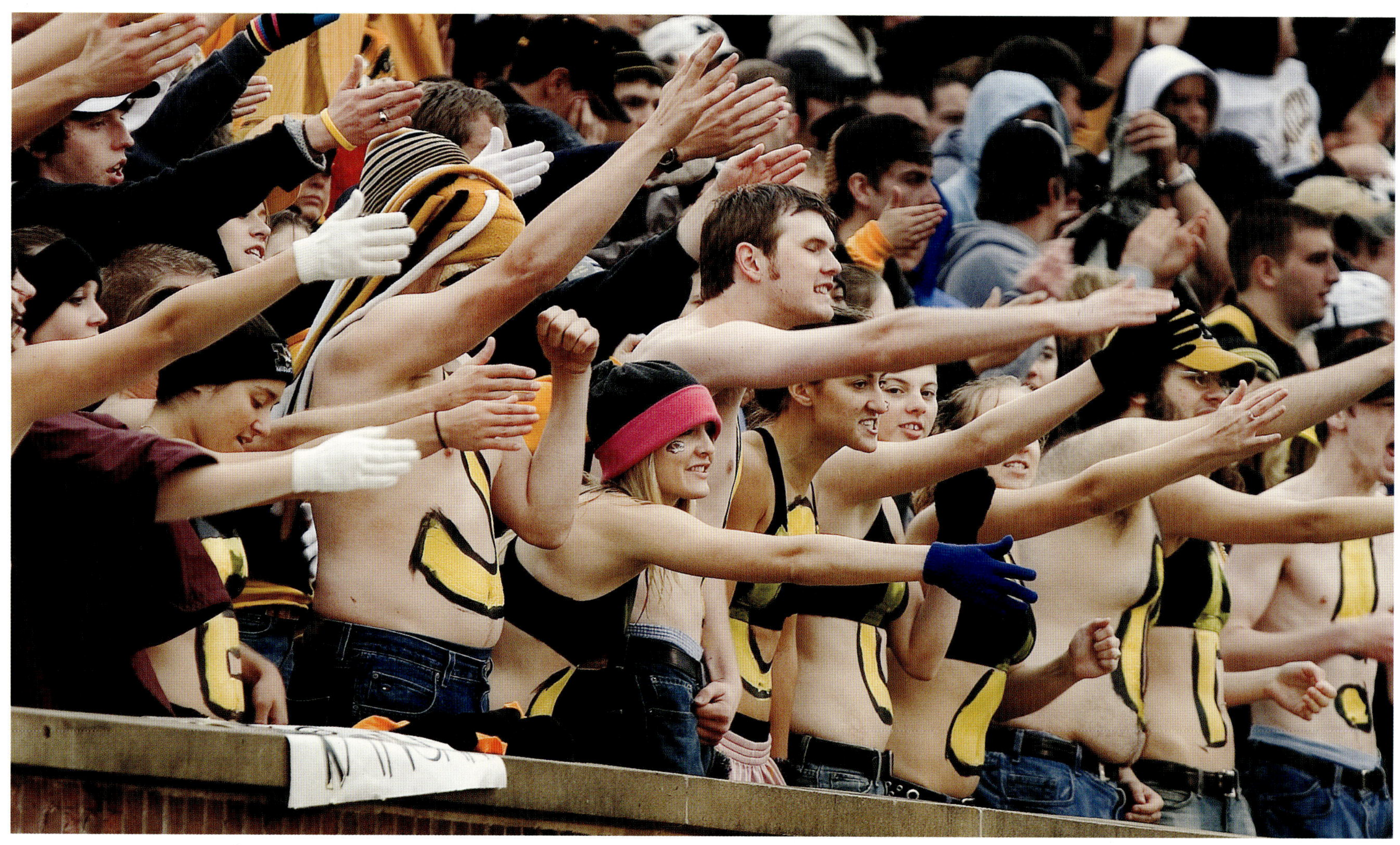

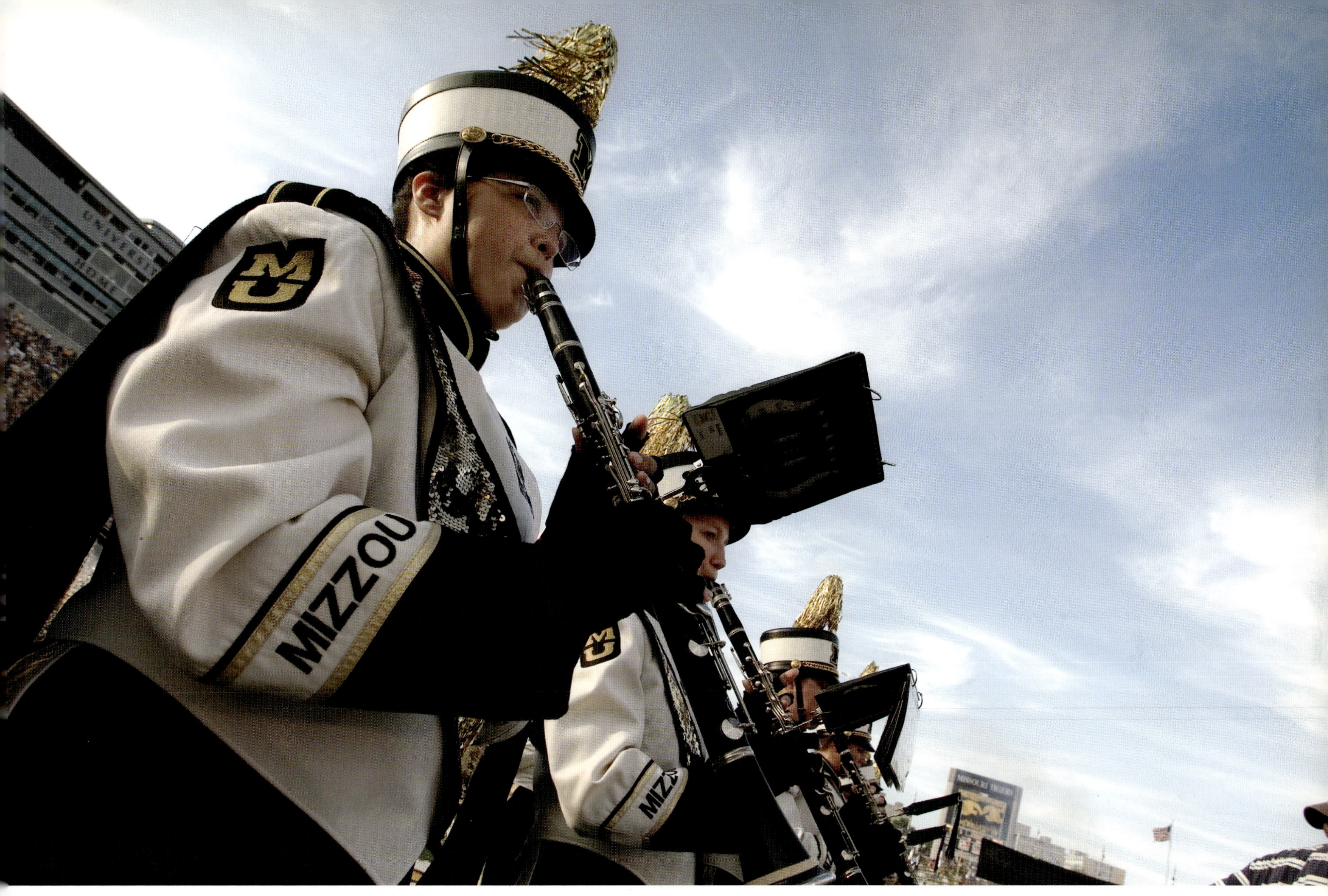

*C*larinets add to the music on game day in Memorial Stadium.

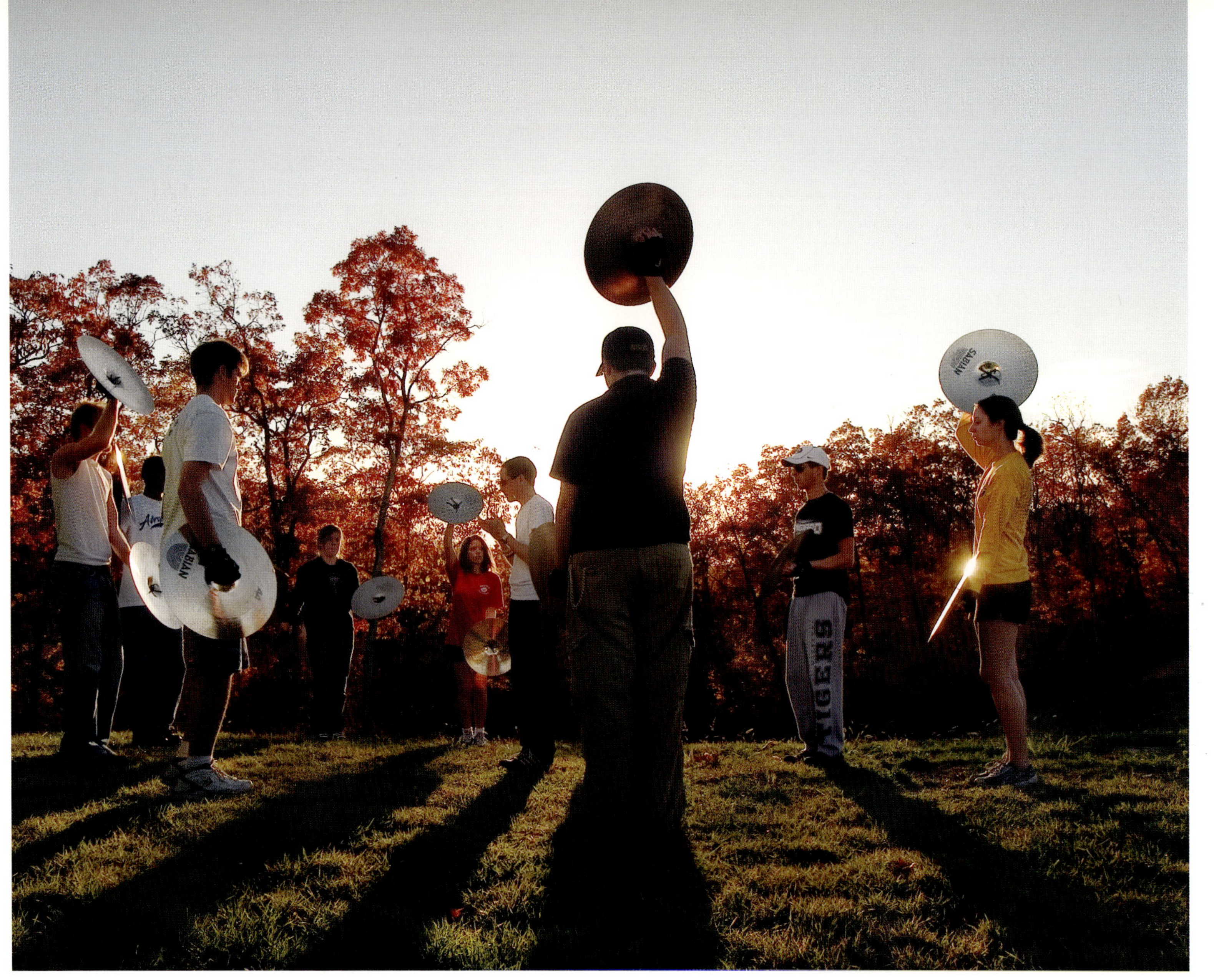

Practice makes perfect for Marching Mizzou members late one fall afternoon south of the Hearnes Center.

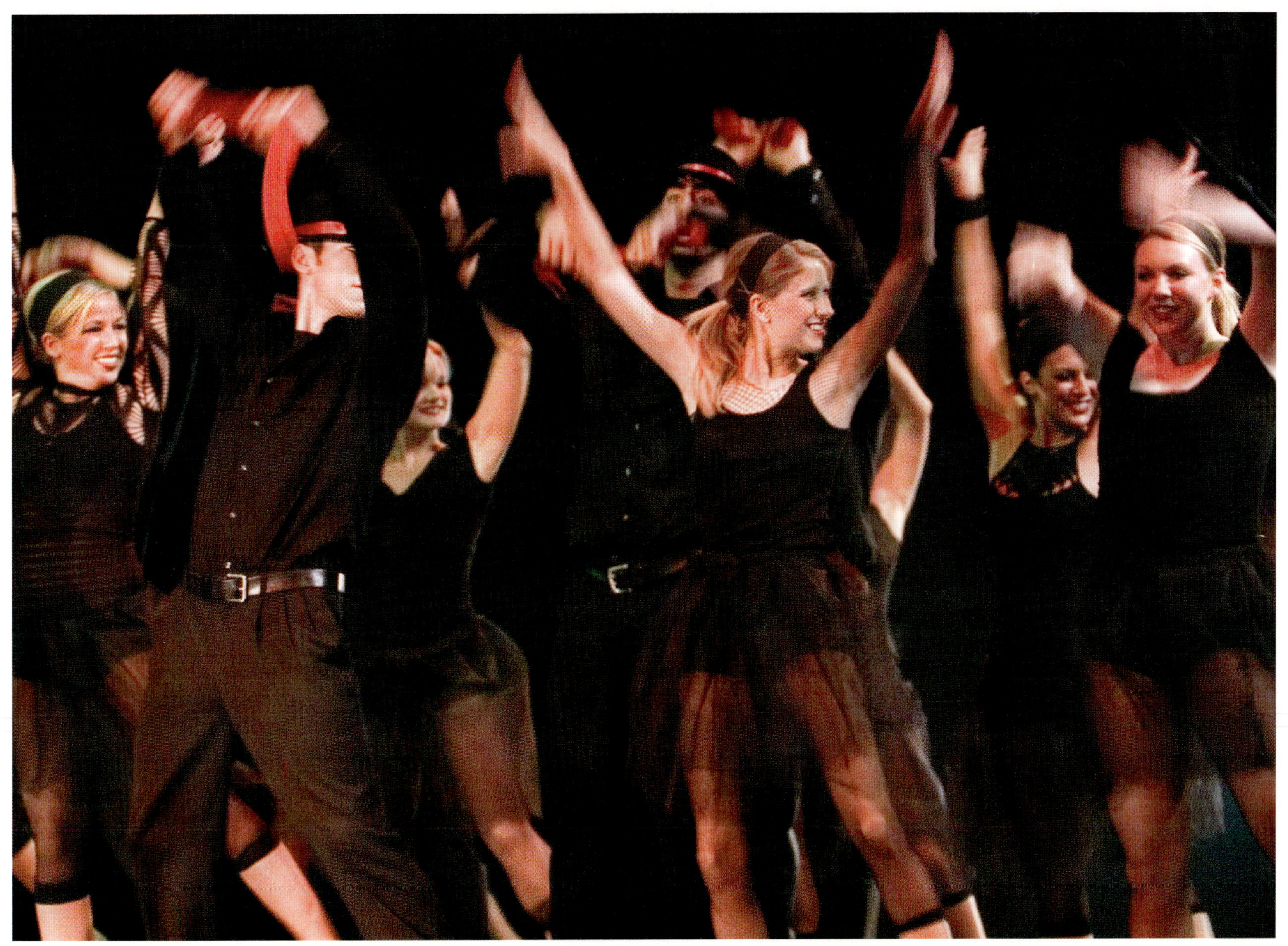

Students dance to the music during Homecoming talent show finals in Jesse Auditorium.

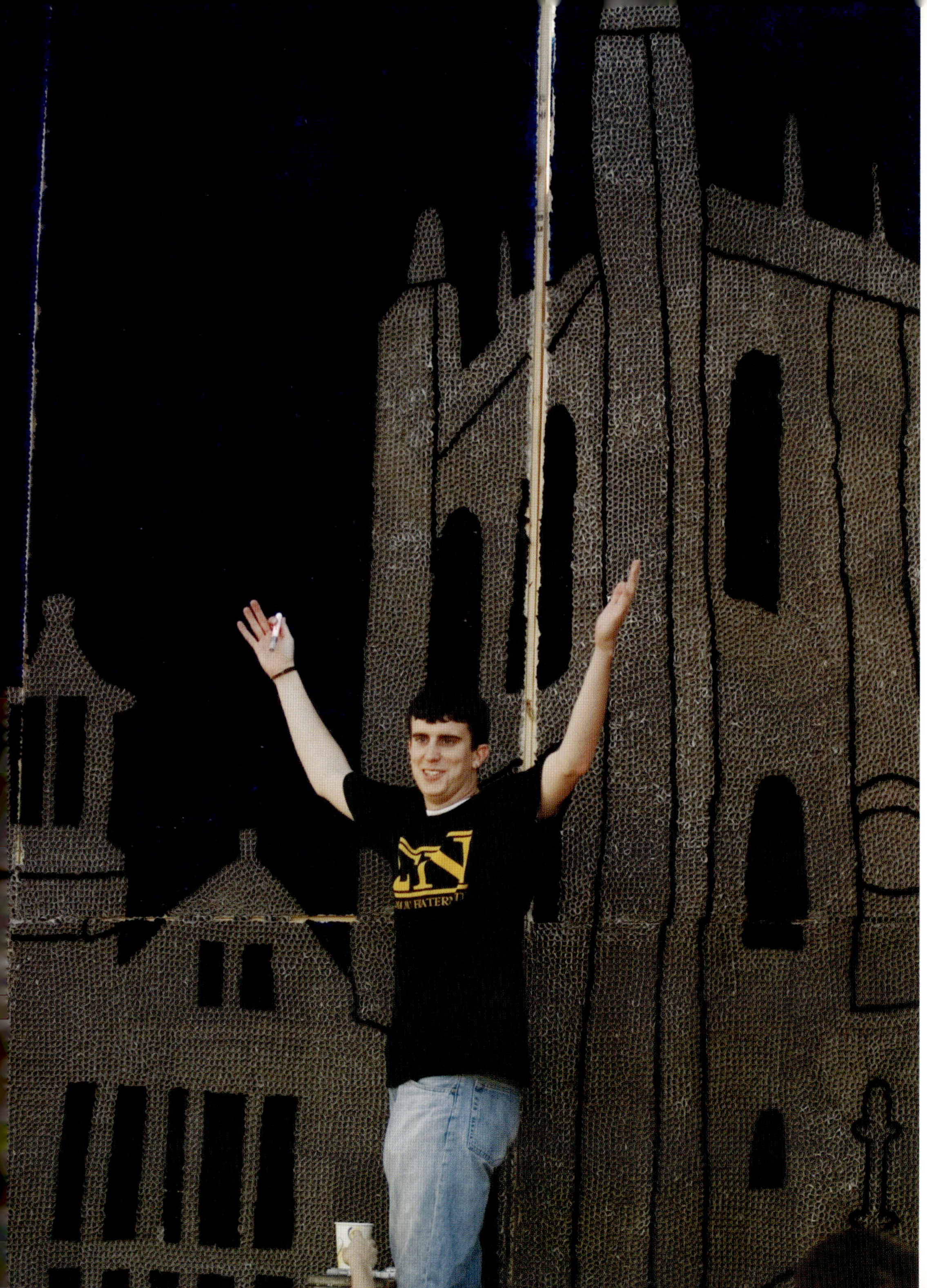

On a sunny day, Craig Kunze constructs a likeness of Memorial Union with colored tissue paper for house decorations in Greektown.

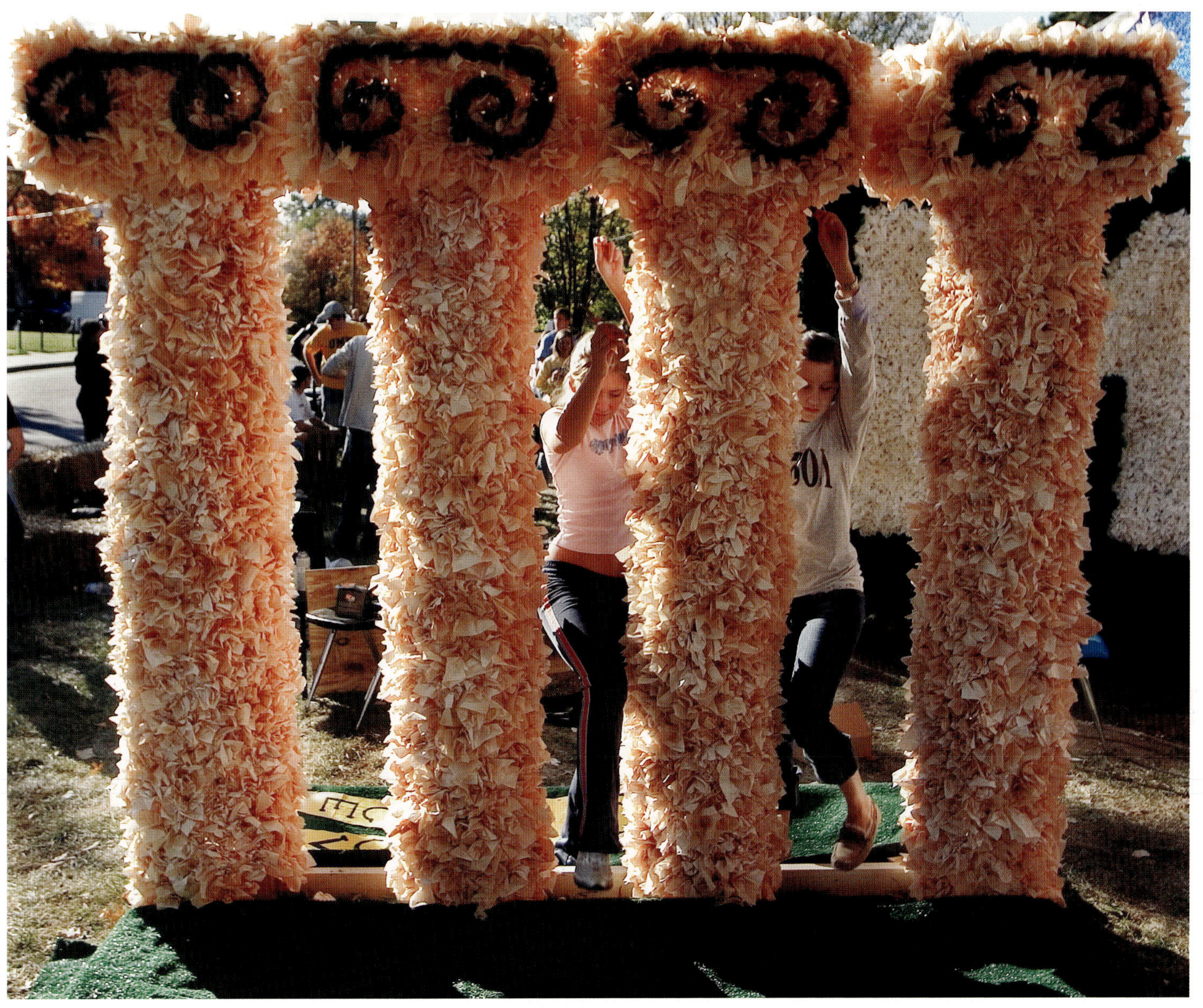

Alisha Koestner (*left*) and Claire Gude put finishing touches on replicas of the Columns for house decorations at Delta Upsilon fraternity.

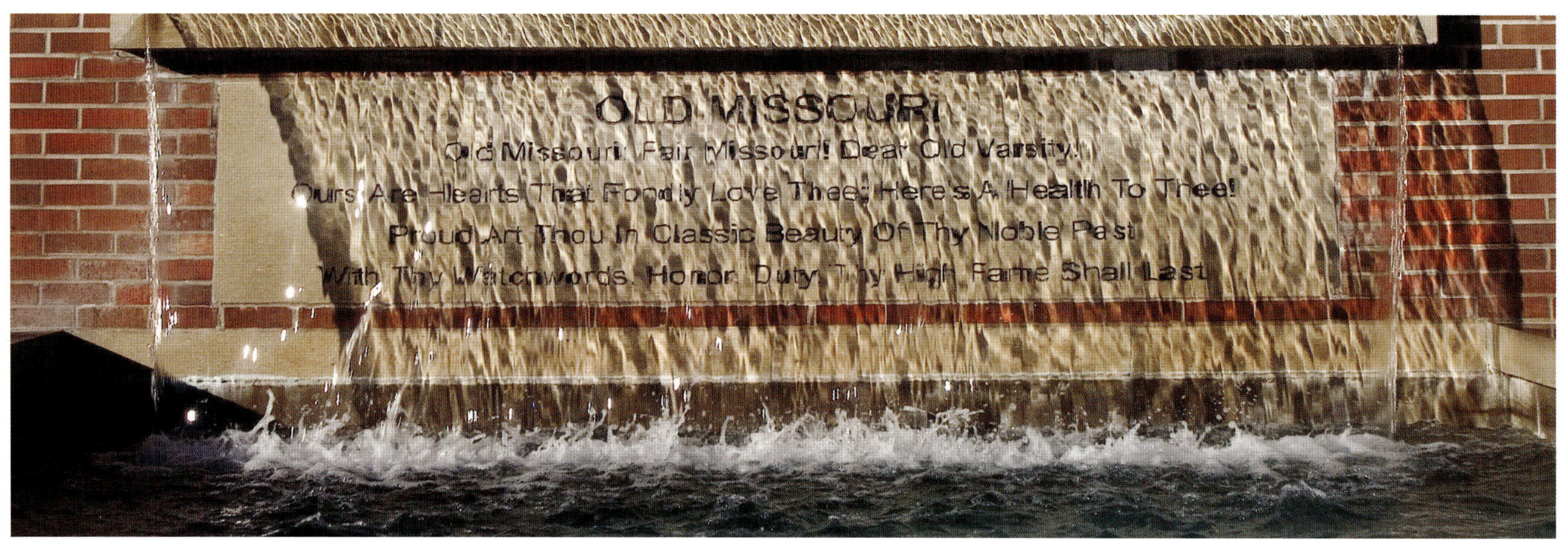

The chorus to the alma mater, "Old Missouri," is engraved behind a waterfall of Tiger Plaza, dedicated by the Mizzou Alumni Association on October 25, 2002, with gifts from more than 2,100 alumni and friends. The plaza, anchoring Carnahan Quadrangle along Rollins Road, includes a bronze Bengal tiger statue created by sculptor Forest Hart.

Appendix Dates and Events

Significant Dates in Mizzou's History

1839 Through the Geyer Act, the legislature establishes the University of Missouri. Thanks primarily to the efforts and contributions of nine hundred Boone County citizens, the University is to be located in Columbia. It is the first public higher-education institution west of the Mississippi River and the first in Thomas Jefferson's Louisiana Purchase territory.

1840 John Hiram Lathrop is hired by the Board of Curators as the first president, and the University starts operations in Academic Hall.

1843 The University holds its first commencement for two graduates. In a three-hour ceremony, cousins Robert L. Todd and Robert B. Todd receive diplomas.

1853 The Alumni Society (later the University of Missouri Alumni Association and, after January 1, 2007, the Mizzou Alumni Association) is established.

1862 The University is closed from spring to fall because federal troops engaged in the Civil War are quartered in Academic Hall.

1867 The state allocates its first appropriation to the University—$10,000 to rebuild the president's home, which had burned, and to repair war-ravaged Academic Hall.

1867 Women are admitted to the University for the first time, but their enrollment is limited to the Normal College for the preparation of teachers.

1870 Under the federal Morrill Act, the University is given land-grant status, and the Curators establish the College of Agriculture in Columbia and the School of Mines and Metallurgy in Rolla.

1875 The citizens of Missouri give the University and its governing body, the Board of Curators, constitutional status and call on the General Assembly to adequately maintain the "state university."

1888 Under the federal Hatch Act, the Agricultural Experiment Station is established and operates first on Sanborn Field in Columbia.

1890 The first residence hall is built to house twenty-five to thirty men.

1892 Academic Hall burns. Alumni and citizens of Boone County prevent the Columns from being torn down.

1895 Jesse Hall opens to replace Academic Hall.

1899 The first Doctor of Philosophy degree is awarded.

1903 Read Hall, a dormitory for women, is built.

1908 With the advent of the School of Journalism, Dean Walter Williams also establishes the *University Missourian* to provide practical training for journalism students. The newspaper is published by a corporation separate from the University, and it continues to operate in this independent mode today as the *Columbia Missourian.*

1908	The University of Missouri is invited to become a member of the Association of American Universities (AAU), the organization that continues to represent the most prestigious public and private research universities in the United States and Canada.
1911	MU hosts the first university Homecoming celebration in the nation.
1941–1947	World War II reduces enrollment from 5,000 to 1,938. The return of veterans and the GI bill push enrollment to 11,452 in 1947, and temporary dormitories (TDs) house these new students. The last of these TDs was not demolished until 1983, when then Chancellor Barbara Uehling drove a bulldozer into TD3.
1950–1951	The first black students are admitted. In 1951, Dr. Gus T. Ridgel (MA '51) becomes MU's first black graduate. In 1998, Ridgel retired as vice president of finance and administration at Kentucky State University.
1953	The first class of four-year medical students is enrolled.
1953	KOMU-TV goes on the air as a lab for students majoring in broadcast journalism.
1956	University Hospital opens.
1959	The Missouri Students Association (MSA) is created, significantly increasing the voice of students in University affairs.
1963	The University of Missouri System is created with the addition of campuses in Kansas City and St. Louis.
1964	The nation's first automated library circulation system is installed in Ellis Library.
1969	Arvarh Strickland is appointed professor of history, becoming MU's first black faculty member.

1988	In anticipation of MU's 150th birthday, the Jesse Hall dome is lit at night for the first time in history. It glows gold on major University occasions.
1988	The Shack is destroyed by fire on Halloween night.
1989	MU celebrates its sesquicentennial.
1990	Ellis Fischel Cancer Center becomes a partner with the University of Missouri Health Sciences Center.
1992	A life-size sculpture of comic-strip star Beetle Bailey is unveiled on campus. It is moved to its current location in front of the Reynolds Alumni Center in 1999.
1997	MU's general education program receives the Theodore M. Hesburgh Award for excellence in undergraduate teaching.
1997	The National Science Foundation recognizes Mizzou for offering one of the ten best programs in the nation for involving undergraduates in research.
1999	Norm Stewart ends a thirty-two-year career as head coach of Mizzou's basketball team.
2002	MU dedicates the Lloyd L. Gaines / Marian O'Fallon Oldham Black Culture Center.
2003	MU announces the For All We Call Mizzou campaign with a $600 million goal.
2005	The $600 million campaign goal is met ahead of schedule, and Mizzou joins only twenty-three public universities in launching a $1 billion campaign.
2006	The Mizzou Alumni Association celebrates its sesquicentennial.

Research and Creativity Milestones

1873 MU lecturer and state entomologist Charles Riley helps save the French wine industry by grafting aphid-resistant Missouri rootstock to French vines.

1893 MU entomologists determine that the cattle tick causes a deadly fever and also discover how to eradicate it.

1911 Psychology Professor Max Meyer publishes the first text to link psychology and physiology.

1914 Dean Walter Williams writes the Journalist's Creed, which continues today to provide global standards for practicing journalists.

1917 Faculty scientists conduct soil-erosion research that provides the impetus for Congress to create field stations nationwide to focus on the problems of erosion and drought.

1927 Geneticist Lewis Stadler discovers that radiation increases mutations in plants, research that leads to faster development of new varieties of plants.

1936 Barbara McClintock begins a five-year stint at MU and later wins a Nobel Prize for her discovery of mobile genetic elements.

1938 Engineer Donald Waidelich initiates a three-decade study of repeating electronic patterns that provides the key to interpreting radar and sonar signals.

1942–1944 Research by Leonard Haseman and L. F. Childers leads to the elimination of a disease that threatens to wipe out the nation's bee colonies.

1945 Professor William Albrecht collects a soil sample from Sanborn Field that provides the golden mold used to make the drug aureomycin.

1946	A. Sterl Artley helps pioneer the Dick and Jane series, which by the 1970s had helped nearly 84 million elementary students learn to read.
1950	Geneticists Ernest and Lotti Sears develop a strain of wheat that is resistant to rust disease and that becomes a worldwide food source.
1957	Plant scientist Gyorgy Redei introduces *Arabidopsis* as a model for the study of the genetics of flowering plants.
1970	Dr. John C. Schuder develops the first automatic and completely implanted defibrillator for the human heart.
1970s	Research at MU results in home dialysis for kidney patients.
1978	The first issue of the *Missouri Review* is published. Today, the *Review,* edited by Speer Morgan, receives more submissions than any other such publication and is nationally recognized as one of the top university literary magazines.
1982	Pediatric cardiologist Zuhdi Lababidi performs the first pediatric angioplasty, which corrects aortic valve stenosis in newborns.
1980s	The interdisciplinary Food for the 21st Century Program is established and, in addition to other accomplishments, eventually produces fifteen soybean varieties and two wheat varieties.
1982	Clyde Ruffin establishes the Black Theatre Workshop (now named the World Theatre Workshop). It is one of only a few university-based theater groups in the nation focused on works by, for, and about African Americans.
1982	Psychology faculty member Donald Kausler publishes the definitive book on the psychology of aging, now in its third edition.

1986 George Smith publishes findings that contribute to the creation of the "phage display," an important tool for advancing scientific understanding of interactions among proteins.

1997 A team of researchers from MU and the Dow Chemical Company receives FDA approval for Quadramet, a radiochemical treatment for bone cancer pain. The drug is one of a series of MU radiopharmaceutical discoveries that have provided important new therapies for cancer patients.

1997 Wife-and-husband team Barbara and Robert Reys found the Show-Me Center, a National Science Foundation–supported information clearinghouse for the development of a standards-based mathematics curriculum for middle-school students.

1998 With Washington University, the Missouri Botanical Garden, and Monsanto, MU is a founding partner of the Donald Danforth Plant Science Center in St. Louis. The center's mission is to find solutions for worldwide hunger, disease, and depletion of the earth's natural resources.

1998 Alumnus James Fergason is inducted into the National Inventors Hall of Fame. Fergason holds patents that provide the technology for the liquid crystal displays used in billions of products, including digital watches, manufactured worldwide.

1999 Chemists Jerry Atwood, Leonard Barbour, and William Orr publish research that paves the way for better electronic devices and "smart" drugs, which deliver treatment to cells that need it.

2000 Giovanni Vignale and his student Irene D'Amico theorize that spinning electrons would be slowed by friction as they move through a semiconductor. The insight will play a key role in the development of quantum computing.

2002 MU's Randall Prather, with Immerge BioTherapeutics, clones the first miniature swine in which a specific gene that causes human rejection is "knocked out" of the DNA. This takes scientists a step closer to the possibility of pig-to-human organ transplantation.

Discover magazine included Prather's research among the top hundred science stories of 2002 and 2006.

2003 A team of MU researchers led by Professor Wynn Volkert wins a $10 million grant from the National Cancer Institute to create a cancer imaging center to foster new methods of cancer detection and treatment.

2004 Professor Emeritus Robert Benfer leads an excavation team, including eleven Mizzou students, that unearths the Temple of the Fox at a site near Buena Vista, Peru. The thirty-three-foot stepped-pyramid temple is a thousand years older than anything of its kind previously found. *Discover* magazine included Benfer's project among the top hundred science stories of 2006.

2005 Biochemist Bruce McClure determines the molecular mechanism by which flowering plants recognize which pollens are appropriate for fertilization.

2005 A team of researchers led by MU's Michael Roberts discovers that culturing embryonic stem cells in a low-oxygen environment significantly slows their rate differentiation.

2005 An artifact analysis at MU's Research Reactor determines that the ancient Olmec people of Central Mexico were the progenitors of Mesoamerica's first cultural flowering. The finding, effectively ending a fifty-year-old debate, was published in the February 18, 2005, issue of *Science* magazine.

Dates of Establishment of MU Colleges and Schools

1867 The College of Normal Instruction for the training of teachers

1870 The College of Agriculture and Mechanic Arts (now the College of Agriculture, Food, and Natural Resources)

1872	The School of Law
1872	The School of Medicine (established as a two-year program; in 1846, the Curators established a relationship with a medical program based in St. Louis; in 1953, the four-year medical program was established)
1877	The College of Engineering (the independent college evolved from engineering courses offered as early as 1849 and a Department of Engineering established within the College of Agriculture and Mechanic Arts in 1871)
1896	The Graduate School
1907	The College of Arts and Science (Arts and Science was an academic department prior to 1907; the arts and sciences had been a core part of the curriculum since the founding of the University in 1839)
1908	The School (now College) of Education replaces the College of Normal Instruction
1908	The School of Journalism—the world's first
1910	The Extension Division
1914	The School of Business and Public Administration (now College of Business)
1920	The School of Nursing (first established in 1901 as the Parker Memorial Hospital Training School for Nurses; became a part of the University in 1920 as the School of Nursing within the School of Medicine; became an autonomous school in 1973; renamed Sinclair School of Nursing in 1994)
1946	The School of Veterinary Science (now College of Veterinary Medicine)
1949	The School of Forestry, Fisheries, and Wildlife (within the College of Agriculture, Food, and Natural Resources and now the School of Natural Resources)

1965 The School of Social and Community Services (renamed the College of Public and Community Services in 1975 and eliminated in 1988 with most of its programs transferred to Agriculture and Human Environmental Sciences)

1966 The School of Library and Informational Science (transferred to the College of Education in 1996 and, in 1997, combined with the School of Information Science and Learning Technologies within the College of Education)

1967 The School of Social Work (moved from the College of Arts and Science to the College of Public and Community Affairs, and then moved again in 1988 to the College of Human Environmental Sciences)

1973 The School of Home Economics (initially established within the College of Agriculture in 1960; became the independent College of Home Economics in 1973; renamed the College of Human Environmental Sciences in 1988)

1975 The School of Accountancy (within the College of Business)

1978 The School of Health Related Professions (within the School of Medicine; in 2000 became an autonomous division as the School of Health Professions)

1986 The School of Fine Arts (now within College of Arts and Science; an earlier School of Fine Arts, created in 1924, was renamed the College of Fine Arts in 1929 and discontinued as a division in 1935)

1999 The Graduate School of Public Affairs (renamed the Harry S Truman School of Public Affairs in 2001)

Gifts of $5 Million or More

Mr. and Mrs. Glen A. Barton contributed $5.4 million to support the Barton Chair in Flexible Pavement Technology, the Barton Professorship in Fluid Power Endowment Fund, and the Glen Barton Gift Fund, all in the College of Engineering. Mr. Barton received a bachelor's of science degree in civil engineering from MU in 1961, attended the Executive Program at Stanford University in 1977, and was awarded an honorary doctor of humane letters degree by MU in 2004.

Harry Cornell Jr. (BS, BA '50) and his wife, Ann, have given $6.9 million for support of the College of Business. This includes a $1.5 million gift for the construction of Cornell Hall, $1.4 million for a new leadership program, and $2.6 million for enhancements to Cornell Hall. Mr. Cornell, chairman emeritus of Leggett & Platt Inc., one of Missouri's Fortune 500 companies, received an honorary doctor of law degree in 2003.

The College of Business received $10 million to support its MBA program from Gordon Crosby Jr. and his wife, Chessie. Mr. Crosby, who died in 2004, attended the College of Business from 1939 to 1941 and was captain of the track team and president of Sigma Chi fraternity. He received an honorary doctor of humane letters degree in 2000.

MU received $7.98 million from the trust of Mrs. Margaret Waters Jordan (BS Ed '31) and her husband, Gerald. For many years, the Jordans owned and operated Waters Furniture in Vandalia, Missouri. They specified that $2.7 million be used for indigent health care provided by the University. The remainder was placed in the Chancellor's Fund for Excellence.

Mr. and Mrs. Thomas H. Lafferre gave $7.5 million for planning and construction of engineering facilities, and Engineering East was renamed Thomas and Nell Lafferre Hall in recognition of their generosity. Mr. Lafferre earned a bachelor's of science in mechanical engineering at MU in 1956, a master's degree at Washington University in 1967, and an advanced management degree from Harvard. Mrs. Lafferre attended MU's College of Education.

In 2001, William J. and Nancy Walton Laurie donated $25 million for a state-of-the-art basketball arena. Mizzou Arena was completed in 2004 and is now the home court for men's and women's Tiger basketball.

A. E. (Al) McQuinn (BS Ag '54) and his wife, Mary Agnes, provided $6.9 million for support of programs in the College of Agriculture, Food, and Natural Resources and the Christopher S. Bond Life Sciences Center.

With its second record-setting gift, the Donald W. Reynolds Foundation gave the School of Journalism $31 million to establish the Donald W. Reynolds Journalism Institute. This gift includes almost $16.7 million for a new building and the renovation of two existing buildings to house the institute. An additional $1.8 million will fund technology and furnishings for the high-tech facility, and the remainder of the gift will fund operations. Donald W. Reynolds, who died in 1993, was a 1927 graduate of the school.

Dr. Russell D. Shelden (BA '42, BS Med '47) has provided support in excess of $5 million, primarily for programs in medicine but also for athletics. Dr. and Mrs. Shelden have funded the Russell D. and Mary B. Shelden Clinical Simulation Center; the Russell D. Shelden, MD, Chair in Anesthesiology; the Russell D. and Mary B. Shelden Missouri Chair in Anesthesiology; and the Shelden Academic Resource Center for student athletes. Dr. Shelden received an honorary doctor of science degree in 2007.

William S. Thompson Jr. and his wife, Nancy, gave $8.5 million to establish the Thompson Center for Autism and Neurodevelopmental Disorders. Mr. Thompson is a 1968 graduate in civil engineering and served on the Board of Curators from 1973 to 1975. Mrs. Thompson also attended MU, majoring in home economics. He received an honorary doctor of humane letters degree in 2005.

Academic Buildings and Athletic Facilities

Building Name	*Year Completed*
Chancellor's Residence	1867
Conley House	1869 (acquired 1980)
Switzler Hall	1871
Pickard Hall	1892
Sociology Building	1892
Thomas and Nell Lafferre Hall	1892
Swallow Hall	1893
Jesse Hall	1895
Parker Hall	1900 (Busch Amphitheater Addition 1901)
Eckles Hall	1901
McAlester Hall	1902
Whitten Hall	1902
Read Hall	1903
Lowry Hall	1904 (acquired 1980)
Waters Hall	1909
Connaway Hall	1910
Schweitzer Hall	1912
Stewart Hall	1912
Lefevre Hall	1913
Ellis Library	1915
Neff Hall	1918
Gwynn Hall	1920
McKee Gymnasium	1922
Mumford Hall	1922
Schlundt Hall	1922
Noyes Hall	1923
Student Success Center	1923 (acquired 1999)

Building Name	*Year Completed*
Professional Building	1924 (acquired 1980)
Tate Hall	1924
Memorial Stadium/Faurot Field	1926
Memorial Union—Tower	1926
Brewer Fieldhouse	1929
Stephens Hall	1936
Townsend Hall	1936
Walter Williams Hall	1936
Crowder Hall	1938
Curtis Hall	1939
Gentry Hall	1939
Heinkel Building	1941 (acquired 1985)
Fine Arts Annex	1945 (acquired 1987)
Psychology Building	1945 (acquired 1990)
Veterinary Science Building	1948
Hill Hall	1952
Memorial Union—North Wing	1952
Jesse Auditorium	1953
Hospital and Clinics	1956
McReynolds Hall	1956
Medical Sciences Building	1956
Agriculture Building	1958
Dutton/Brookfield/McElroy	1958
Engineering Building West	1958
Fine Arts Building	1958
Stanley Hall	1958
A. P. Green Chapel	1959
Middlebush Hall	1959
Veterinary Medicine Building—East	1959
Arts and Science Building	1960

Building Name	*Year Completed*
Brady Commons	1963
Geological Sciences Building	1963
Memorial Union—South Wing	1963 (begun 1930, pre-Depression)
Clark Hall	1964 (acquired 1969)
Laboratory Animal Center	1964
Lewis Hall	1964 (acquired 1969)
Melvin H. Marx Building	1964
Physics Building	1964
University of Missouri Research Reactor	1964
Dalton Cardiovascular Research Center	1967
Tucker Hall	1967
Math Science Building	1968
Trowbridge Livestock Center	1968
Animal Sciences Research Center	1969
General Classroom Building	1969
Chemistry Building	1972
Hearnes Center	1972
Veterinary Diagnostic Lab	1975
Veterinary Medicine Building—West	1975
Nursing School	1979
Gannett Hall	1980
Brady Commons Addition	1986
Taylor Athletic/Academic Resources Center	1986
Agricultural Engineering Building	1987
Ellis Library Addition	1987
Hulston Hall	1988
Student Recreation Center	1989
Reynolds Alumni Center	1992
Clydesdale Hall	1993
Lee Hills Hall	1995

Building Name	*Year Completed*
Anheuser-Busch Natural Resources Building	1996
Brady Bookstore Addition	1996
A. L. Gustin Club House	1997
Audrey J. Walton Field/Stadium (Track and Soccer)	1998
Devine Pavilion	1998
Shelden Academic Resources Center	1998
University Field (Softball Field/Stadium)	1998
Ernie and Lotti Sears Plant Growth Facility	1999
Gaines/Oldham Black Culture Center	1999
Taylor Stadium at Simmons Field	2000
Green Tennis Center at Epple Field	2001
Cornell Hall	2002
Christopher S. Bond Life Sciences Center	2004
Mizzou Arena	2004
Student Recreation Complex Addition	2004
Mizzou Athletics Training Complex	2006
Swine Resource and Research Center	2006

Note: Dates are based on sources available from Space Planning, University Archives, and Intercollegiate Athletics.

University Housing, 2007

Building Name	*Year Completed*
Defoe Hall	1939
Cramer Hall	1947

Building Name	*Year Completed*
Graham Hall	1947
Johnston Hall	1947
Stafford Hall	1947
University Village	1955
McDavid Hall	1956
Jones Hall	1957
Lathrop Hall	1957
Laws Hall	1957
University Heights	1958
Hatch Hall	1962
Schurz Hall	1962
Manor House	1963 (acquired 1997)
Wolpers Hall	1963
Hudson Hall	1964
Gillett Hall	1965
Mark Twain Hall	1965 (acquired 1986)
Tara Apartments	1982 (acquired 2007)
Discovery Residence Hall	2004
Excellence Residence Hall	2004
Respect Residence Hall	2004
Responsibility Residence Hall	2004
Center Hall	2006
College Avenue Residence Hall	2006
North Hall	2006
South Hall	2006

Note: Dates are based on sources available from Residential Life.

Enrollments

Year	*Enrollment*	*Notes*
1842	74	
1850	80	
1860	140	
1862	64	*Civil War*
1870	204	
1880	484	
1890	428	
1892	631	*Academic Hall fire*
1900	1,038	*First year over 1,000*
1915	4,349	*Peak enrollment for next twenty-two years*
1918	2,926	*World War I ends*
1920	3,260	
1930	3,986	
1940	5,670	
1943	1,938	*Lowest enrollment during World War II*
1946	10,593	*With return of veterans, enrollment doubles the prewar level*
1950	8,756	*Korean War begins*
1960	11,216	
1961	12,949	*Vietnam War begins*
1970	21,687	
1980	24,297	
1990	24,972	*Enrollment peak until 2002*
2000	23,280	
2006	28,253	

Sports Milestones

Important Events

1890	Mizzou plays first intercollegiate football game, defeating a handpicked team of opponents by a 22–6 score.
1907–1908	MU joins the Missouri Valley Conference.
1909	Football team wins first conference championship (Missouri Valley) with an overall mark of 7–0–1.
1924	Mizzou plays in first bowl game, losing to USC in the Christmas Festival, 20–7.
1928–1929	MU joins the Big 6 Conference
1935	Football team plays first game with Don Faurot as head football coach, defeating William Jewell, 39–0. Faurot coached nineteen seasons and has more wins than any other MU coach, with 101 victories.
1948–1949	MU joins the Big 7 Conference.
1954	Mizzou's baseball team wins the College World Series, the first-ever team national championship in any sport for the school.
1958–1959	MU joins the Big 8 Conference.
1960	In November, Mizzou is ranked number one in the nation for the first time in football, after a 41–19 win at Oklahoma. The Tigers are upset the next week at home against Kansas (with the game later being forfeited to Mizzou) but go on to win their first-ever

	bowl game (21–14 over Navy in the Orange Bowl) and end the season ranked fifth—MU's highest-ever final ranking.
1965	Mizzou's men's indoor track and field team wins the NCAA Championship.
1969	The football team shares the Big 8 Conference title and plays in the 1970 Orange Bowl against Penn State, losing 10–3.
1996-1997	MU joins the Big 12 Conference.
1997	The softball team wins MU's first-ever Big 12 team championship.

Mizzou National Champions

Team

1954	Baseball
1965	Men's Track (Indoor)

Individuals

1925	Men's Track (Outdoor), Ken Lancaster, pole vault
1925	Men's Track (Outdoor), Tom Bransford, high jump
1940	Men's Track (Outdoor), John Munski, mile run
1943	Men's Track (Outdoor), Elmer Aussieker, shot put
1944	Men's Track (Outdoor), Bill Bangert, discus

1945	Men's Track (Outdoor), Edward Quirk, shot put
1955	Men's Cross-country, Keith Bacon
1958	Men's Track (Outdoor), Bob Davis, pole vault
1959	Men's Track (Outdoor), Dick Cochran, discus
1960	Men's Track (Outdoor), Dick Cochran, discus
1974	Men's Track (Indoor), Charlie McMullen, Dave Rogi, Jim Crawford, Mike Rabuse, distance medley relay
1979	Men's Track (Outdoor), Nat Page, high jump
1984	Men's Track (Outdoor), Albert Lane, 110m hurdles
1985	Women's Track (Outdoor), Sabrina Dornhoefer, 5000m run
1989	Women's Track (Indoor), Natasha Kaiser, 400m dash
1999	Men's Track (Indoor), Derrick Peterson, 800m run
1999	Men's Track (Outdoor), Derrick Peterson, 800m run
2001	Women's Track (Indoor), Ann Marie Brooks, Ashley Wysong, Kerry Hills, Sunny Gilbert, distance medley relay
2006	Wrestling, Ben Askren, 174 pounds
2007	Wrestling, Ben Askren, 174 pounds

Mizzou Conference Championship History

Regular Season Titles by Sport

Football	1909, 1913, 1919, 1924, 1925, 1927, 1939, 1941, 1942, 1945, 1960, 1969
Men's Basketball	1918, 1920, 1921, 1922, 1930, 1939, 1940, 1976, 1980, 1981, 1982, 1983, 1987, 1990, 1994
Women's Basketball	1978, 1984, 1985, 1987, 1990
Men's Cross-country, Indoor and Outdoor Track and Field	1911, 1912, 1913, 1915, 1916, 1917, 1918, 1920, 1925, 1938, 1939, 1943, 1947, 1948, 1949, 1951, 1964, 1965, 1967, 1970, 1974, 1979
Women's Cross-country	1980, 1984
Baseball	1931, 1932, 1937, 1938, 1941, 1942, 1952, 1954, 1958, 1962, 1963, 1964, 1965, 1976, 1980, 1996
Softball	1983, 1991, 1997
Men's Tennis	1975
Men's Golf	1949, 1984
Women's Gymnastics	1992

MU Leadership

1841–1849	John Hiram Lathrop
1850–1856	James Shannon
1856–1859	William W. Hudson
1860–1862	Benjamin B. Minor
1865–1866	John Hiram Lathrop
1866–1876	Daniel Read
1876–1889	Samuel S. Laws
1891–1907	Richard Henry Jesse
1908–1921	A. Ross Hill
1921–1923	John Carleton Jones
1923–1930	Stratton D. Brooks
1931–1935	Walter Williams
1935–1954	Frederick Middlebush
1954–1964	Elmer Ellis
1964–1970	John Schwada
1970–1978	Herbert W. Schooling
1978–1987	Barbara S. Uehling
1987–1992	Haskell M. Monroe
1993–1996	Charles A. Kiesler
1996–2004	Richard L. Wallace
2004–present	Brady J. Deaton